# Embracing Presence

# Embracing Presence

## An Understanding of
## Religion and Spirituality

## Kenneth Collier

Bodhi's Books
SANTA BARBARA, CA

**Bodhi's Books**™
Santa Barbara, California

10 9 8 7 6 5 4 3 2 1
First English Edition 2021

ISBN 13: 978-0-578-99759-9

Library of Congress PCN Number: 2021921707

Cover and book design by Dynamic Book Design
www.DynamicBookDesign.com

# Table of Contents

# Acknowledgments

This book began when I was in graduate school over 50 years ago. Conversations I had with professors and fellow grad students kept me puzzling about knowledge and the different ways we use the language of knowledge. Special mention has to be made of the late Joe Camp, with whom I took many classes, and Nick Rescher, who was my dissertation advisor.

The puzzlement continued in my early career as an Assistant Professor of philosophy at Southern Illinois University at Edwardsville. My colleagues, of course, egged me on, but conversations with John Barker were especially stimulating. And my students kept asking me hard questions as well, questions to which I often did not know the answer. Two of these students in particular deserve special thanks: Kenneth Buckman and Theresa Norman.

After five years as assistant professor, I left academia for the Unitarian Universalist ministry. In 1976, I enrolled at Starr King School for the Ministry, graduating with an MDiv in 1979. The 1970s were a heady time to be in Berkeley, CA. It was here that I began to wonder what would happen if I took religious knowledge and truth claims seriously. What kind of epistemology would be required to accommodate both science and religion as legitimate forms of knowledge? It also occurred to me that if I could find an answer to that question, I could reconcile science and religion without having to deny either the mythology of the Bible or the discoveries of science. This quest is what really gave this book its life. I now feel ready to suggest an answer.

Colleagues in ministry over the ensuing 40+ years have drawn me to ask myself what sort of theology would emerge out of that epistemology. Long conversations at retreats, District Assemblies, General Assemblies, and just over drinks kept the puzzles alive.

More specifically, I owe thanks to several people who helped me in the actual writing of the book. First, Anne Anderson read an early draft and made an enormous contribution to this work in the form of suggestions and criticisms that helped shape my prose into something that is actually readable. In a similar vein, Andi Cumbo-Ford and Meera Collier read a draft and made very important editorial suggestions that helped me to shape the text into a much tighter form. The late Charles McCracken and Ted Tollefson read part or all of an early draft and made valuable comments and suggestions that improved many of the arguments. By the same token my colleague, the Rev. Frederick Wooden read a later draft and made many useful suggestions. And last but far from least, Professor Ann Taves, of the Department of Religious Studies at the University of California at Santa Barbara, read an early draft and suggested that I recast the manuscript in a more personal, memoirish tone. She was right.

I would be remiss were I to fail to acknowledge our little Shih Tzu, Bodhi. He was a never-ending source of delight and refreshment. Through most of the writing he sat at my feet, whether asleep or awake, a presence that kept me at it. Unfortunately, he did not live to see the book's publication, but his gentle presence is all over these pages.

# Acknowledgments

My beloved wife, Anne Anderson, and I have spent hours discussing the ideas I present here. She has supported me in my weakness, believed in me when I doubted myself, put up with me when I went way beyond the pale, and loved me unconditionally. My debt to her in this project, as in life, cannot be reckoned.

As all authors must do, I accept responsibility for all misstatements and errors (which I am certain appear in the text), misconceptions (how could there not be some of these?) and infelicities of language (an inevitability).

For my closest friends:

te norman

Gordon Koizumi

They are family cleverly disguised as friends

# Preface

Though this book begins with a prologue, a few prefatory remarks will be helpful. The issues raised in Parts I and II involve concepts that are, while separate, intimately intertwined. This is, I think, because they point to a larger ideal, that of being human. It is not unlike my two lungs, separate and yet integrated into the larger respiratory system. As a result of this intertwinement, a certain amount of repetition, redundancy, and backward and forward referral is inevitable. I might apologize for that, but since it is unavoidable, all I can say is, there it is.

## TRANSLATION

I quote extensively from three sacred texts, the Bible, the *Tao Te Ching*, and the Dhammapada, none of which were written in English. Each of these are extensively translated, so a word about the translation I use is appropriate. The version of the Bible I use is the Reader's Edition of the Jerusalem Bible. Among all the modern translations I am acquainted with, it is, to my ear, the most eloquent combination of graceful, poetic English and scholarship.

The *Tao Te Ching* I use is my own rendering, based on Jonathan Star's character by character literal translation. Since I do not read

Mandarin, I do not pretend that mine is a translation. Instead, it is what I, reflecting on Star's translations, understand the text to be saying to me.

*The Dhammapada* I use is Thomas Byrom's rendering. I do not know whether Byrom could read Pali, the original language, but I note that he is careful not to call his version a "translation." In fact, it is from him that I have adopted the characterization of my version of the *Tao Te Ching* as a rendering.

It is certainly true that Byrom has taken some liberties with the text, and as a result his version is highly controversial among Buddhist scholars. However, I have elected to use it for several reasons. First, the text is graceful, beautiful English, while translations that are closer to the original text often strike my ear as clumsy and verbose. Having a poet's sensibility, I prefer Byrom's English.

Second, I think there are two ways to treat texts like these. The first is to stick as close to the original as English allows and wrestle recalcitrant passages into English, sometimes seemingly against their will. This is the more scholarly approach, and it is what often produces those clumsy, verbose versions that I object to. The second way is to reflect on the text and speak in English what the text is saying to the reader. This often strays from the original, but it produces a more heartfelt version. This method speaks deeply to some readers and less deeply to others. It is, I think, what Byrom does, and his version speaks to me.

Third, Byrom's version was my introduction to the text. To be sure, I have read many other versions since then, some graceful, and some rather less so. I have found that it is often to the first version one reads that one turns most often. This is certainly true for my relationship with the Dhammapada.

## Privilege

This book is the intellectual memoir of a very privileged person. I am a white, cis-gendered, straight male. I was raised in an upper middle-class family, and I have lived most (but not all) of my life resting comfortably in that upper middle-class milieu. I hold an undergraduate degree and three graduate degrees, including a PhD. As a result of all this privilege, I have had opportunities that many people will never have.

One of those opportunities is the chance to stop occasionally, look at the flow of my life, and change its course several times. This has allowed me to align the living of my life with what I am called to do with my life. I am well aware that not everyone has the opportunity to do this and that not everyone is able to make a living doing what gives them the deepest satisfaction and authenticity.

Another opportunity my privilege has bestowed on me is the leisure in my retirement to look back on my life and see how its currents have shifted. And yet even as those currents shift, they unerringly move me forward into a richness that is a blessing. And that is yet another dimension of my privilege. Not everyone has that leisure. Not everyone has the chance to live into a long and fruitful retirement. Not everyone is as blessed as I.

This book is the fruit of that leisure. I write it and offer it as an act of thanksgiving for the privilege that I have had in my life. I do not know whether it will help to close the gap between those who have this kind of privilege and those who do not. But understanding another person's life cannot help but illuminate the possibilities within one's own life. With trust that this is the case, I offer the book to the world.

"There can be no doubt that

all our knowledge begins with experience."

—IMMANUEL KANT

# PROLOGUE I:

# Childhood

In 1955, my mother's father started spending the months from about Memorial Day to about Labor Day with us. I was ten; he was seventy-three. I was a child; he was, at least in my eyes, an old man. As I began writing this book, I was seventy-three years old. While I didn't believe I was an old man, I did believe that I was standing on the threshold of old age. It has been a liminal time for me, a time when my life was starting its inevitable shift toward its ending. And so, it seemed to me to be appropriate, standing there in that doorway, to reflect on my life and some of what I have come to think and believe.

It does seem that some people love to write about themselves, and, surprisingly enough, other people seem to love reading what they write. When asked why she wrote so much autobiography, Maya Angelou once responded, with a smile and twinkle in her eye, "Because I love writing in the first person and meaning the second."[1] On the other hand, Elie Wiesel once remarked that he wrote not so much to be understood as to understand.

I find myself somewhere between Angelou and Wiesel. My initial impetus in writing was closer to Wiesel; I wrote in order to examine and understand the flow of my own life. But as I wrote, I

---

[1] I heard this in an interview years ago, but try as I might, I am unable to find the original citation.

began to see that some of the things that I have come to understand and believe might actually be helpful to others as they struggle with their own lives. And so, I moved toward Angelou.

All good writing, as indeed all good art, has structure. That structure is sometimes so well hidden that it is not immediately obvious, as in Jackson Pollock's paintings, but it is there. Memoir writing is no exception. The structure of a memoir should mirror the structure the author's life.

The structure of these reflections is provided by three rivers that seem to have been flowing through my life nearly from its beginning. The first river is the River of Art, especially music and poetry. Second is the River of Science. And the third is the River of Religion. The springs from which these three rivers arose all lie in my family of origin.

And so, to begin with a few basics. My father was a chemical engineer, and, with the exception of a few years immediately after he graduated from college, his entire career was spent working for the DuPont Company. During World War II he made gunpowder, first near Memphis, TN, where my brother was born in 1942, then near Tulsa, OK, where I was born on March 26, 1945. World War II was soon over, and he was transferred to a pigment plant in New Jersey. I was about six months old when we moved, and a little more than three years later, he was transferred to Wilmington, Delaware. My mother, brother, and I followed soon after.

While I do have a few scattered and dim memories of New Jersey, my first truly dateable memory is of the move to Wilmington. I was very impressed with the staying a night in a real hotel, The Hotel DuPont. We went to a restaurant for dinner where I had my first taste of steak not ground into a hamburger, and I felt very grown up indeed. The next day we moved into our new house, 104 Kenwood Lane. I insisted that it was actually 104 Kennywood Lane! Clearly named for me.

## CHILDHOOD

### Music

A little later but still one of my earliest memories is of music. My father was a great fan of classical music, and as soon as he was able, a year or two after the move, he bought a combination radio and record player. (This was about 1950, and we did not yet have a television. We got our first TV in 1952.) Among the first records he bought was the Toscanini recording of Beethoven's Pastoral Symphony. After putting my brother and me to bed, he would often play this record. My memory is of being deeply moved by the music. I lay there in my bed, listening and struggling to stay awake to hear more. I tried not to move, tried to keep my eyes open, fighting sleep. But it was ultimately futile. I was too young to get beyond the second movement, Scene by the Brook. At this age, of course, I had no notion whatever of program music. Nevertheless, in my mind I saw the brook flowing through the music, water running over rocks down a ravine in the woods. Thus, was my love of music, especially classical music, ignited.

My father also loved opera, though my mother did not. He bought recordings of several operas. On Saturdays when my mother happened not to be at home, he would often play one of them. Sometimes instead playing one of his recordings, he listened to the

Met broadcasts. I loved that music, and I wondered how sound could do that. However it was that music did it, I wanted to learn how to do it too.

## An "Opera"

All kids get in trouble from time to time, and I was certainly no exception. My brother hated being sent to his room as a punishment. I think he would almost have preferred being spanked to being sent to his room. So, my parents began using the same punishment for me. Didn't work, though, because I loved to make up stories. Being a budding introvert, I often made up stories and adventures alone in my room. Sometimes the stories were entirely in my head, and sometimes I told them out loud to myself. Years later, my mother told me that she would sometimes hide outside the door and listen to my stories. So, I was used to being alone in my room.

My storytelling and my love of music came together one Sunday afternoon at church. I think I was about six, certainly no older than seven. My parents had some sort of meeting, and I was more or less left to fend for myself. I wandered through the Sunday school rooms and noticed a piano in one of them. I sat down at it, thought a minute or two, and a story began to take shape, a story about a cat stalking some mice.

Before long, my left hand landed on the bass side of the keyboard and took on the character of the cat, and my right hand landed on the treble side and took on the character of the mice. Thinking of this as my opera, I was suddenly so totally lost in the music unfolding through my hands and the story unfolding in my head, that I was unaware of anyone or anything around me—until I happened to look up. And there was a woman watching me with one of those humiliatingly smarmy smiles on her face that said, "Oh isn't he cute!" in that condescending way some adults have. I was embarrassed and felt dismissed and belittled. This was the beginning of a very complicated relationship to music; both loving it and being embarrassed by my own attempts to create it on my own.

## The River Is Dammed

Time went on, and I continued to love music and wanted desperately to be able to make music. I practically begged my parents for a piano and music lessons, but there was always some excuse.

"A piano is too expensive and besides there is no room in our little house for one."

"OK, how about clarinet or flute? Or even better yet, singing?"

"Well. We'll think about it."

And so it went. And went. And went. And it never happened.

I think now, looking back over all of this, that even though both of my parents, especially my father, loved music, they did not understand how deep my need for music was. Nor did they think of music as an option for a boy growing up in Northern Delaware in the 1950s. My parents had no experience with music as more than something to listen to and be moved by. It simply did not occur to them that I might have longed to create music. I think they dismissed my requests for lessons as something with a very low priority.

I have memories of my father needing to stop whatever he was doing and just listen when something particularly beautiful was playing. Nevertheless, he never realized that this beauty was something I, his son, could create. The world of music was a place to visit as a tourist, not a place to live as a citizen.

The elementary schools I attended did not have much in the way of music education. It pretty much depended on the teacher you had, and I never had a teacher who took much interest in teaching music. Some people understand the basics of singing intuitively.[2] Unfortunately, I am not one of them. Since no one ever took the time to teach me to sing at an appropriate age, I never learned.

Every other summer we would spend time in the little town in South Florida where my parents grew up and where my grandparents, aunts, uncles, and cousins still lived. My mother, brother and I went down for most of the summer, and my father joined us when he could take his vacation. On one of these visits, when I was about 6 years old, we kids were sent to the Vacation Bible School at the small community church there. I loved it, and at the end we had a kind of ceremony. I was chosen to sing "This Little Light of Mine."

I was excited beyond the telling. I insisted that my mother come to the ceremony but would not tell her why. (My father had not yet

---

[2] For example, Joan Baez said in an interview that she knew how to sing from earliest childhood. Again, I am unable to find the source of this. I seem to remember, though, that it was a Terry Gross interview.

joined us.) The church filled with parents and relatives. I waited nervously for my time to sing. And then, I was on! I sang at the very top of my lungs, so loud, I am told that people across the street heard me. But since I was not born with an intuitive sense of how to sing, I sang poorly. My singing that day became the occasion for laughter, and I was crushed. After this, I was labeled as the kid who could not sing. Since adults told this to me, I believed it, even while wanting desperately to sing.

I did sing every chance I got, by myself, in church singing hymns, occasionally at school. Of course, I sang poorly, off key, out of tune, and with little voice quality. And this added to the perception that I could not sing. I did not know any better, but no one bothered to take me in hand and teaching me to sing properly. Adults criticized me ("Ken, you can't sing, so just move your lips, or, better yet, hand out the programs.") and other kids teased me. Of course, this just made me even more self-conscious and embarrassed. It became a vicious cycle. As a result, the neural connections that should have been made and may have created the proper instincts never happened. And the muscles in my throat that are needed to sing properly began to atrophy.

## Learning to Read Music

One day the summer I was about thirteen or fourteen, I found myself at loose ends. I wandered over to my father's record collection and purely by chance pulled out his recording of Beethoven's Middle Quartets. As luck would have it, this album happened to come with the complete scores of the quartets. I don't know whether my father could read music, and I am sure he did not buy this recording because of the scores. But there they were.

I certainly could not read music, but nevertheless it occurred to me to wonder whether I could follow the score. I mean, how hard could it be? So, I put one of the records on and tried. Of course, I got lost more often than not, but I was intrigued. That summer I gave myself the task of figuring it out. I played those records over and over (which must have driven my mother nuts), poring over the scores and figuring out what all those little marks meant. By the end of the summer, I had taught myself the rudiments of reading music. This was the first real crack in the dam of embarrassment across the River of Music.

## Story Telling and Poetry

From the time I was very little, I would lie in my bed for hours spinning out adventures in my head, and when my parents read to me, I saw the characters in my mind. Sometimes I would close my eyes and the story would become like a movie playing just for me. When I learned to read, the same thing happened with the books that I read. The characters were alive to me, real—though not real in the same way flesh and blood people are real. When my mother read the first chapter of *Lassie Come Home* to me one night, I could see her leaving home and felt the sorrow her family felt. I cried bitterly and uncontrollably.

We had a set of books of literature for young children. One volume had mostly poetry, and before I could read, I asked my mother to read from it so often that I memorized some of my favorites.

# Prologue I: Childhood

One poem I still remember is this:

> A race, a race to Moscow,
> Before the close of day!
> A race, a race to Moscow,
> A long, long way!
> First comes a butterfly a-riding on a frog.
> Next comes a water rat a-floating on a log.
> A caterpillar on the fence, a hopper in the hay—
> Who'll get to Moscow before the close of day?[3]

I could see that butterfly and that water rat! They were real to me.

It didn't take long before my friends began to turn to me to make up the story when we would play games like Cops-and-Robbers or Cowboys-and-Indians or whatever else adventure-like games we played. The stories seemed to flow out of my head with my breathing. As I got older, these stories got more and more complex and the plots for our games got more and more complicated. I created plots and sub-plots, and continuing dramas that took several days to finish. I found myself having to direct the action occasionally. Eventually I realized that I had to tone things down a bit because my friends could not keep the complexity in mind as they acted out their parts.

This ability to make stories real in my mind is something that I have never lost. To this day, I create faces and voices and scenery in the novels I read, and as I write I see the world I am writing about. Writing sometimes becomes little more than describing what I see

---

[3] Attributed to Leroy F. Jackson (1881-1958) in Karen Michelle Barad, *Meeting the Universe Halfway*.

in my mind. This is especially true when I am writing poetry, but it is also true when I write prose. I see whatever it is that I am writing about, and it is so real to me that I am convinced that there is a sense in which these worlds *are* real.

I think there is an indelible link between the reality of the world of a story and the truth that it tells. It is a commonplace that the novelist writes about events that never happened, to people who never lived, in a world that never existed, and through this pack of lies, manages to tell us the truth. But I object, those people do live, and that world does exist, even though they do not exist in the way that sealing wax, cabbages and kings exist.

After I got a bit too old for the poetry in those books I loved when I was little, I did not read much poetry. At least in those days, there was not a lot of poetry available for kids from, say, six or seven to early adolescence. But when I started middle school (then called junior high school) and then high school, I began to discover the world of great poetry, especially the English Romantics, and it enthralled me. It was like music to me. I didn't know it then, but as it turns out, my Celtic ancestors thought of poetry as a form of music, a notion that makes perfect sense to me to this day.

## Science

My relationship to music was inherent in my soul, but my relationship to science was a rather more checkered one. I grew up in an insular and isolated world, the world of middle and upper middle-class Northern Delaware in the 1950s and early 1960s. This was a world dominated by the DuPont Company and its commitment to business and technology. Most of my parents' friends were either employed by DuPont, primarily as engineers or chemists, or were married to an engineer or chemist. As an inquisitive and curious child, I could not have grown up in this milieu and not have absorbed an interest in science.

Though I have a lot of early memories that related to science, my first truly deep interest was in the world of nature. The move from New Jersey was to a house in a near suburb of Wilmington. The nearest woods were too far for me to get to comfortably. But when I was about eight years old, I went to a weeklong YMCA camp on the Eastern Shore of the Chesapeake Bay. This camp was located in the woods, and it felt like a new and fascinating world, a world in which I could lose myself. I spent two weeks at that camp each of the next four years, and I began reading everything I could about nature and what I would now call field biology.

Entomology became a particular interest, and I read several books about insects. One of these books contained the story of an experiment by the early naturalist, Louis Agassiz. There is a species of caterpillars that march along in single file, head to tail, laying down a trail of silk threads as they go. Agassiz wondered whether their instinct to overcome hunger was stronger than their instinct to follow one another, so he rigged up an experiment to find out.

He got a bowl that was shallow enough for them to be able to climb into and out of if they chose and placed some leaves, he knew they would eat near it. Then he placed enough caterpillars along the rim that they covered it completely and watched what happened. The caterpillars never wavered from their march along the rim. As I read the description of the experiment, I saw the bowl, the leaves and the caterpillars in my mind. And the whole set up fascinated me. I wanted to duplicate it, but I did not have access to the caterpillars. Looking back on this and my fascination with it, I think I saw it not as an introduction to scientific method, but as another story. I was using it, not to feed my I interest in entomology, but to feed my love of story.

In 1955, we moved again, this time to what was then a very rural new housing development located more or less between Wilmington and Newark, at that time the second largest town in Delaware and the home of the University of Delaware.[4] This was heaven for me. I spent hours and hours alone in the woods and fields around our new home.

It was during these wanderings that I began to realize something that has turned out to be very important in my life. My interest in nature had less to do with biology than it had to do with religion. It was here, in these woods and fields that I would sometimes feel the walls that separated me from the rest of the world to weaken and threaten to dissolve. At the time, I found this both fascinating and scary. Now I understand it to have been the beginning of my mystical life.

Within a few years, my interest in biology was replaced by an interest in physics. I no longer remember what sparked that interest, but it became an absorption. My father had a subscription to *Scientific American*, and I found myself reading it, especially any articles relating to physics. The night sky was especially dark and beautiful around our house, and so my interest in physics led me pretty quickly to astronomy. I even tried to build my own telescope out of a kit. (That turned out to be a bad idea, though, because the

---

[4] It may have been the second largest town, but its population then was only about 20,000.

blank that had to be ground into a mirror was made of very hard Pyrex. At about twelve years old, I was not strong enough to grind it, and I abandoned the project.)

## Early Thoughts of a Career

In the 1950s and 60s in my corner of Northern Delaware there was a clear hierarchy of professions available to young men. At the highest level were engineering and science, business, law, and medicine. Distinctly second to that were teaching, journalism, and ministry. Within teaching there was another hierarchy: university, high school, junior high school, and elementary school (and there were very few men teaching elementary school). And then there was everything else, which included the arts (unless you happened to be world-class, in which case you moved up to the second level.)

Most of the men I knew were, like my father, employed at the top level of this hierarchy, and so I just assumed that I would be as well. Business and law did not interest me in the slightest. Had life turned out a little differently, medicine may have been a possibility, but between becoming more interested in physics than biology and having an ineffective biology class in high school, medicine did not appear to me to be a genuine option.

And so it was that I assumed that I would find a career in some sort of technical or scientific profession. Since everyone—including me—knew that since my mind did not run to the practical, I would be a miserable engineer, it seemed that I would be headed for a career as a physicist, most likely at a university. I entered college as a physics major.

## And Yet

It is the "and yets" that mar the easy landscapes. At a place in my heart that was deep and almost inaccessible, I knew that this was a mistake. From the age of about eleven or so, I realized that there was a significant disconnect between me and the rest of my family. I certainly did not feel unloved or rejected, but I did feel misunderstood and out of place. I was beginning to see that many of the things that were natural, intuitive, and fascinating to them left me cold and vice versa.

My father was an engineer, and my mother was a registered nurse, which is a kind of medical engineer. My brother was destined to be an engineer as well. When he was little, my parents gave him a Tinker Toy set. He loved it, wore out the first set, and was given another. Before long, when he began to wear that one out as well, they bought him an Erector Set. He thought he'd died and gone to heaven.

So, when I was the appropriate age, they gave me a Tinker Toy set, expecting me to do the same. My reaction was, "OK. You follow the directions, doing just what they tell you to do, and pretty soon you get just what they told you you'd get. So? Where's the fun in that?" My reaction to an Erector Set was pretty much the same. And later when they gave me a chemistry set my response was the same. The instructions said, mix this stuff with that stuff and it'll make a red precipitate. And sure enough, they were right. That's exactly what happened. I didn't play with any of these very much, and my parents were flummoxed and probably a bit hurt.

One day they sat me down and wanted to talk about it. I don't remember how old I was, though I imagine I was probably around seven or eight years old. And I don't remember whether we were talking about the Tinker Toy set or the Erector Set. What I do remember is their calling me into the living room one Saturday morning and sitting me down in the sofa. My father said that my brother had loved his Tinker toy, but I rarely played with mine. And then he asked why.

I kind of shrank into my body, looked at the floor, and shrugged my shoulders. I did not know then how to explain it, but the reality is that I found the Tinker Toy boring. There was no creativity in it. So what if you built exactly what the instructions said you would? I could not tell my parents "So what?" Even if I could articulate it, I knew they would not understand.

They never said anything like "What's wrong with you?" but the comparison to my brother felt like that. I felt that I had disappointed them and not lived up to their expectations. I felt that I had somehow failed them. Just as importantly, I had no idea how to get them to understand that my interest was in the world of my imagination rather than the world of my hands.

And so, by the time I was ready for college, I knew that all this clamoring about physics was a substitute for the life I really wanted to live. I did not let myself look at that very carefully yet, but when I was being honest with myself, I knew it perfectly well. Something was wrong. My life was out of harmony with my soul.

## Religion

I can hardly remember a time when religion was not important to me. My parents, especially my mother, were committedly religious, and we attended a Presbyterian church. Even as a very young child, I enjoyed going to Sunday school, and I enjoyed memorizing Bible verses.

Sunday School classes were during the hour before the service, and we kids were expected to attend both. By the time I was about 9 years old, I began to pay attention during the service, and I was often moved by the service, a few times even to tears. This last was something my family did not understand, and I was powerless to explain. My parents' religion as not a matter of the heart as much as it was a matter of the mind. And so my emotional reaction to church was a mystery to them. In early adolescence, when I asked my parents to take me to Wednesday evening prayer meetings, they did. But I could tell they were humoring me, and it did not last.

In those days, children could become members of a Presbyterian church when they became twelve years old, after they attended a class that met over the course of several Sunday afternoons. In our church, these classes were offered just before Easter, and the graduates would become members as part of the Holy Thursday evening communion service. In 1957, Easter was late April.

I had turned twelve in March, and so I joined that year, the first year I was able. The ceremony was a solemn one, and as I knelt at the front of the church and felt the minister's hands on my head, my heart opened. This was before I had begun to feel those moments in the woods and fields, but as I look back on it, I realize that it was very similar. In time, it would ripen into the world of mystical spirituality and religion.

## Dissolving into Green

This opening of my heart was something that continued in apparently random places and times, working in the yard, or listening to music, or reading a book. At first, I understood this in the Christian terms that I had been taught. I told myself, "Surely the Holy Spirit has entered my heart." But then as I began to experience the dissolving of walls of separation, it began to be harder and harder for me to fit it all into that way of thinking.

Being essentially an introvert and feeling vaguely strange and something of a misfit both in my family and among my friends, I spent a lot of time alone. About the time I reached puberty (about eleven years old), these times alone were spent increasingly in the woods and farm fields that surrounded our little community. I especially loved the woods and would spend hours there. In the summer I would go out right after breakfast, come home in time for lunch, return to the woods, come home in time for dinner, and often go back out again in the evening.

There were a few special places that I favored. In one, I would sit on a fallen log and watch the water flowing past in a tiny little stream beside me. There were times that I was still enough that birds would fly down beside me, and on a very few occasions small animals would come to check me out. These were elevated times.

It was the summer I was thirteen that those very early mystical experience began happening. They did not happen often, but they were often enough to get my attention. It is difficult to describe. I would be sitting on my log, watching the woods around me, and it seemed as if the edges between the woods and me were beginning to melt or disappear. The way I once put it was that it was as if the woods were dissolving into green.

These experiences were exciting because they touched my soul and opened new possibilities of understanding my life. But they were also frightening because I seemed to be about to disappear into them. If the world and everything in it was an undifferentiated unity, where was there room for an individual? Where was there room for me? I also could not fit them into any Christian thinking that I knew anything about. And that bothered me. How could I accept these experiences as truth when they did not fit what I was being taught at church?

This struggle came to a head the spring I was 16. Among other natural phenomena, I dearly loved thunderstorms. As most people were running inside when the storm hit, I would do whatever I had to do to watch the incoming storm, even to the point of standing out in the rain and wind as long as I could. That used to drive my mother, who was afraid of thunderstorms, nuts. But I persisted.

That spring, a thunderstorm came up late one afternoon. As usual I wanted to watch it as long as I could, but dinner intervened. I ate as quickly as I could, and by the time I finished, the storm had mostly passed by. But the remnants remained, and I walked out into them. It was these remnants that changed my life forever.

There were dark storm clouds off to the east, but to the west, the clouds were bright and shining. The usual chorus of evening birds was sounding as the sun was setting. In the western sky, though, there were some rapidly rising clouds that reflected the setting sunlight. The clouds were in just the right place and rising at just the right rate to reflect the sunlight even after the sun had set. I noticed that all around me a beautiful golden light had fallen onto the world I was walking in. This wonderful light seemed almost to be rising from within the earth. To borrow an image from Annie Dillard[5], it was as if the world were a bell that the light had struck, and the clear sound of the bell was resounding throughout my world.

This beautiful and unusual light prolonged the evening bird chorus, but eventually the clouds could rise no higher and the light was extinguished. Night fell suddenly and completely. The birds hushed their chorus, but the crickets, katydids and evening frogs took up the anthem so subtly that the level of sound never changed. All that changed was the nature of the sound.

As I walked through all of this, I felt that melting of edges begin again, and allowed myself, for the first time, to be fully embraced by it. I was lifted from the world of things into a different world, a world where there is neither this nor that, neither here nor there, neither now nor then. There was only this, here, now, only this instant, eternal and blessed.

I returned home again exhilarated and exalted, and I knew that I had been changed, though I did not know how. I tried to explain it to a few people and found that I couldn't. I tried to fit it into a Christian context and theology, but the more I tried, the more impossible it became.

## Early Reflection

The real difficulty was that the Calvinist Christianity I had been taught, put its emphasis on the innate depravity of humanity, but in

---

[5] Annie Dillard, *Pilgrim at Tinker Creek*, p. 35.

that thunderstorm I had experienced a radical acceptance and love, and I knew that I would feel that acceptance and love over and over for the rest of my life. I felt embraced by a deep compassion that assured me that no matter what my life brought, be it pain or joy, I was loved with a deeper love than any I had ever known or would ever know. In the light of this, how could I understand innate depravity? It made no sense. The dilemma was this: should I accept what I was taught and discard what I had experienced, or should I accept the experience and discard the teaching? This became the context of my early life-struggle, though I did not realize it until rather later as I reflected on the flow of my life.

By this time, I was feeling especially deeply the struggle between what I thought I wanted and what I knew I wanted. I experienced this struggle as being torn between thinking I wanted a career as an academic physicist—what I thought I wanted—and feeling a call to ministry—what I *knew* I wanted.

My senior year in high school, there was a young woman, a year younger than I, who was somewhere between my friend and my girlfriend. I spoke with her about this struggle rather often. She was clear that she felt a call to ministry. When I talked about earning a PhD in physics and then entering the ministry, she discouraged me, saying that I should choose one or the other, not both. It was a choice I was not yet able to make.

# PART I:
# How Do You Know That?

## Toward a New
## Epistemology of Religion

"There are more things in Heaven and earth,
Horatio, than are dreamt of in your philosophy."
—William Shakespeare

# PROLOGUE II:
# From Science to Philosophy

1963 was a year that changed everything.[1] In the fall, I entered Carnegie Institute of Technology (CIT)[2] as a budding physicist. All science and engineering students were required to take the same curriculum: Calculus, Physics, Chemistry, English, and World History (which really meant Euro-American History, but that's another conversation).

My chemistry lab happened to be Friday afternoons. One Friday in late November, we had just begun our lab when the teaching assistant came on the PA to announce first that President Kennedy had been shot and then that he had died. At first, no one quite believed him, but I happened to look out the window to see the flag being lowered to half-mast. It was true. President Kennedy had been assassinated. I was stunned. A Presidential assassination was unimaginable, and yet it had happened. I had been insulated from political violence my whole life, and here it was, in full force.

In those days, the Republican Party in Delaware was the liberal party and the Democrats were the conservatives. This was a leftover of the old Post Civil War days when this was the pattern throughout

---

[1] I would argue that "the 60s" actually began that year and ended with Nixon's resignation in 1974.

[2] This was before the merger with the Mellon Institute. When I was there, it was still CIT.

the South. Since my parents, though Southern, were more liberal than conservative and could not stomach the blatant racism that the Southern Democratic Party embraced, they were Republicans.

As a result, I had not been much of a fan of Kennedy. I was even young and politically naïve enough to have supported Richard Nixon in the 1960 election. So, I was surprised at how upsetting the assassination was to me. It took the wind right out of my sails. The country was in deep mourning, and party affiliation did not matter.

## ON TO PHILOSOPHY

All during that year at CIT, I was struggling with my technical classes. One spring afternoon, I was walking back to the dorm feeling rather despondent, knowing I had done poorly in a calculus test. As I crossed the mall, I had a conversation with myself. "Ken," I said, "you are working hard on these technical subjects, and you are neither enjoying them, nor doing very well in them. But you are enjoying the English and the History classes. They are fun, challenging, and you are getting good grades in them. You are working at the technical subjects and almost playing at the others. So why are you bound and determined to spend the rest of your life working when you could be playing?"

When I realized that I had no good answer to that question, I realized that I had to get out of physics in particular and science in general. The question was to what I should go into instead. The history class was not about dates and events so much as the ideas that led to the events. It was those ideas and how they played out that I found fascinating. I also remembered reading Will Durant's

*The Story of Philosophy*[3] in high school and being enthralled by it, even though there was a lot that I did not understand. Durant explains how the philosophical ideas that lie behind the development of Western civilization evolved. It was this that grabbed my attention, and that I remembered. Philosophers grappled with the very thing that I found so interesting in my history class. So that was it. I decided to leave physics and major in philosophy. I would still be an academic but an academic of a different sort.

Since CIT had no philosophy major, I had to transfer to another university. My overall grades were not good enough to transfer anywhere but the University of Delaware. I was admitted there, not because their standards were low, but because I was still a Delaware resident. After graduating with a BA in philosophy, I earned a PhD in philosophy at the University of Pittsburgh. In 1971, I began teaching at Southern Illinois University at Edwardsville (SIUE).

I was hired largely because of my expertise in logic, becoming sort of the department's resident logician. In that capacity, I taught several logic classes, from the most basic introductory level to graduate-level seminars. A colleague and I even organized an international conference on a rather esoteric topic that my mentors at Pitt were heavily involved in. But as time went on, my interests began to drift away from logic toward the philosophy of religion and aesthetics. One of the classes that I enjoyed teaching the most was an undergraduate introduction to the philosophy of religion.

As my professional interests drifted, my satisfaction with academia diminished. There are three dimensions to academia: teaching, university politics, and research. I did enjoy teaching, es-

---

[3] The book is really the story of Western philosophy, totally ignoring Islamic, Indian and Chinese philosophy, but I didn't notice this shortcoming at the time.

pecially the younger students. But. I found the politics of academia truly disturbing. For example, a woman in our department who was hired the same time I was wanted to teach courses in Feminist thought. Another colleague argued long and strenuously against this proposal, claiming that there is nothing philosophically respectable in Feminism. Rather than trusting a colleague, this man belittled her and fought against her expertise, revealing his own sexism and inability to comprehend that the net of philosophy is cast wide and covers the real world where real people live, struggle, and hurt one another. But since he was a male full professor and she was but a woman assistant professor, his voice was heard first. The courses were eventually accepted, but that approval came only after a long and sometimes very acrimonious and bitter struggle.

I also became increasingly unhappy with what I think of as academic discipline. For example, I was becoming more and more intrigued with Chinese thought in general and Taoism in particular. A genuine academic finding themselves in that situation would have set out to learn to read Mandarin. But I just could not muster the discipline to do that.

By 1974 this dissatisfaction had risen to a critical level. It was the culmination of the same troubling realization that drove me from physics to philosophy in 1963: I was trying to be someone I was not. I was due for a sabbatical in 1976, and I wanted to use the time to explore the aesthetics of still photography in some depth, but my department chair would not approve that project. "After all," she said, "you were hired as a logician." I doubt that she meant that as handwriting on the wall, but it felt that way to me. I knew that I had to get out of academia. I am simply not an academic, and by then I knew it. What I didn't know was where to go from there.

A series of events that I will describe in more detail in Prologue III provided the answer. In short, I began to think that that I needed to leave academia for the Unitarian Universalist ministry. The final push came in the very early spring of 1976. I stopped by a colleague's office just to chat, but she needed someone to listen to her talk about the unhappiness in her life. I spent the next hour or more listening and comforting her. I left the office and knew that the time had come. I had to leave now or spend the rest of my career in a profession that I knew was not my profession. The summer of 1976 I packed up my little family, moved to Berkeley, CA, and enrolled in Starr King School for the Ministry.

Though I eventually left professional philosophy and abandoned a career in academia, I have never regretted the time I spent as a philosopher. It taught me a way of thinking about the world that served both my ministry and my life. A philosopher will look at the world and ask, "What is going on here?" though this "what" is not the "what" of science. The scientific version of this question opens a search for a deeper and more finely tuned description of the empirical world. The philosophical version opens a search for a deeper understanding of the mental and spiritual world.

I was trained in what is called analytic philosophy. The analytic philosopher will ask questions like, "What do we mean when we say that one event causes another, and how do we know that the first causes the second?" Or, "What does it mean to say that one action morally preferable to another?" Or, "What do we mean when we say that something is a work of art?" These kinds of questions have lingered in my mind and still fascinate me. In fact, it just this kind of thinking that has occasioned this book.

## ADULTHOOD

While in graduate school, I didn't really get all that far from science. I concentrated mostly on epistemology, logic, and philosophy of science. My PhD dissertation was on a very esoteric topic at the border between epistemology and formal logic. There was something about the very nature of the philosophy that I was taught that puzzled me, though.

Logic is a good illustration. A great deal of the logic that I studied turned to be the construction of strictly formal logical systems[4]. It is certainly possible to churn out formal system like these by the dozens, and people did just that. I had to ask myself why. What do these arcane formal systems have to do to anything in the real world? In short, so what?

Just out of pure curiosity, a logician or mathematician will sometimes turn out a formal system that surprisingly enough turns out to have an application to the observable world. (Suppose there are no lines, or an infinite number of lines, through a given point parallel to a given line. What would such a geometry look like?) But that is not typical. More often, like the increasingly esoteric systems of modal logics, they turn out not to have any application to the real world at all[5]. And when that happens, the whole enterprise began to look to me like a game—fascinating and fun, perhaps—but having nothing to do with philosophy, the love of wisdom. So, other than wanting to have a little fun, why do we do it?

---

[4] A formal logical system is one that is built solely on valid inferences, usually—though not always—beginning with a set of axioms. Euclid's geometry is a good example of a formal logical system.

[5] Modal logic is the logic of necessity and possibility.

The problem I was having was that I saw a divide between what we were doing as philosophers and the world around us where real people lived their real lives. The result was that people were missing the connections that hold the various aspects of human life together. And that bothered me. What appears to be a conflict between science and religion is one of the most obvious examples of this divide. Neither side is willing to imagine a world in both can be true, because neither side can imagine any sense at all in which the other's claims can be true.

I never said much about this, either in grad school or while I was teaching philosophy at SIUE. Instead, it lay like a shadow across the back of my mind, a niggling internal itch that never quite got scratched. The longer I stayed in academia, the more it itched and the less comfortable I was as an academic.

I did not know it at the time, but these two events—the Kennedy assassination and changing my major from physics to philosophy—marked the beginning of a convergence of two of the three rivers. Eventually the River of Science would diminish to a much smaller stream, and the River of Religion would flow in spate. But they were beginning to assume dimensions more appropriate for my life.

PREFACE:

# A Short Primer on My Epistemology

Epistemology (from the Greek "episteme" which means "knowledge" plus "logos" which means "a rational account of") is the branch of philosophy that examines the idea of knowledge. It considers such questions as what is knowledge, when can we claim to know something, and what can we know? It is generally accepted that truth and belief are two of the central concepts underlying knowledge. Indeed, a classic, though inadequate, definition of knowledge is that it is justified true belief.[1] Now, consider statements such as these

1. We know that space is absolute.
2. We know that nothing can travel faster than light.
3. The task of the artist is to express aesthetic truth.
4. I know that my Redeemer liveth.

All are claims about knowledge. The first is false; the second is true; the third and fourth are open to further conversation.

When I reflect on these kinds of statements, I cannot help but ask myself "How does someone know that?" How do we know that the thing that destroys our ability to become human is violence? How do we know that The Divine is both transcendent and im-

---

[1] For an explanation of why this is an inadequate definition of knowledge, see Gettier, "Is Justified True Belief knowledge?" *Analysis*, 23 (1963), pp 121-123.

manent, depending on how we think about it at a given moment? How do we know anything theologically or religiously? In spite of the fact that people ask themselves—and each other—"how do you know" all the time, rarely do people stop to notice how there is an ambiguity hidden within the question. "How do you know that?" can be understood in two very different senses:

A: What is your evidence for that?

B: In what manner do you know that?

One rarely hears B being paid attention to because, at least since the Enlightenment, it has been assumed in Western philosophy that the only ways of knowing are the ways of science and mathematics.

This has led to some rather unfortunate consequences. If all knowledge is scientific knowledge, and if, as classical Christian philosophy and theology has asserted, faith is also a source of knowledge, then it is possible (perhaps even inevitable) for there to be a conflict between faith and science. Medieval philosophers and theologians argued at some length about whether faith or reason should take precedence were there to be such a conflict, most coming down in the side of faith. Unfortunately, however, history is replete with such conflicts at least since Copernicus suggested that the earth is not at the center of the universe. Over time, faith has lost its privileged place, at least in most philosophical circles. Yet the conflict continues.

Like the conflict between evolution and creationism, these conflicts have often become the turning points of Western Culture. There seems to be only three ways to resolve them:

1. One can reject one of science or faith when they are in conflict.

2. One can attempt to find a way to reconcile the discoveries of science with the revelations of faith such that both create a consistent and single body of knowledge.

3. One can deny that all knowledge must follow the model of science, thus making space for different senses of knowledge, one generated by science and one generated by religion.

The first option has been the preferred option over the last several hundred years, and it is still the favorite. For an example, one has only to consider the 150-year-old conflict over Evolution, a conflict that continues to plague us. This option tends to generate two extremes. I think of one as the militant atheists, who claim that religion is, at best, nothing more than bad science, and, at worst, a pernicious attack on intellectual honesty. The other I think of as equally militant theists who insist that science is, at best, a distraction from the True Faith that alone can save humanity and, at worst, a deliberate attempt to undermine revealed Truth.

## JOHN HICK'S ATTEMPT

The second option usually takes the form of demonstrating that religious knowledge in fact does conform to the cannons of science. John Hick provides an example of this. In his book, *Faith and Knowledge*, he writes:

> "There is…[a] fundamental ground on which someone might disallow the religious man's [sic] knowledge claim. He [sic] might hold that such a claim has no content since

the religious concept of God is so formed that there can be no possible verification or falsification of belief in divine existence. This is a relevant and weighty argument, which can be met only by withdrawing the factual element in the religious knowledge claim or by showing that this claim is, after all, open to eventual verification or falsification within human experience.[2]

Hick opts to embrace is the second horn of this dilemma.

He does this by invoking what he calls an eschatological argument that boils down to the claim that while we cannot verify or falsify Christian knowledge claims in the lived-world, in the world-to-come, after death, we will be able to verify these knowledge claims. At that point, we will see that either the Christian claims are true, or they are not. (Presumably we might also discover that the eschatological claims of some other religion that posits post-death existence are true but those of Christianity are not, or even, paradoxically, that both are true.)

This, it seems to me, is a weak argument. The main problem is that it makes two assumptions. First, it assumes that there is a world-to-come. Second, it assumes that this world-to-come is sufficiently like the lived-world that whatever may be true the next world has bearing on what is true in this world. At the very least, Hick has not shown that either assumption is true, and it seems to me that the second assumption begs the question. The point of the verificationist criterion of truth is that it must be possible to specify a test for the truth of a proposition that could, at least in principle,

---

[2] John Hick, *Faith and Knowledge*, p. 211.

be carried out in *this* world. Whatever may or may not be the case in any other world (in particular the world-to-come if such there be) need not bear on the lived-world. The most Hick's argument can show is that the religious knowledge claim has a factual basis in the world-to-come, but from that it does not follow that it has a factual basis in the lived-world. Thus, for example, God may exist in the world-to-come and not in this world. Scientific knowledge, after all, is about this world, and Hick grants that scientific knowledge is the only species of knowledge there is.

## My Speculation

The opening sentence to the second edition of Immanuel Kant's *Critique of Pure Reason* is this: "There can be no doubt that all knowledge begins in experience."[3] By Kant's time it had come to be assumed by most philosophers that "experience" means the kind of intersubjective experience that is epitomized by science. Kant's project was to understand how we construct knowledge out of that experience in such a way that knowledge is also intersubjective. The whole idea of private or privileged experience accessible to one and only one person seemed an oxymoron. One of the implications of this is that knowledge was thought to be univocal in the sense that there is one and only one form of knowledge, specifically the knowledge epitomized by science. Knowledge is that informed (Kant's term for "justified") and true belief that arises intersubjectively out of our experience. Anything else is mere belief or poetry

---

[3] Immanuel Kant. *The Critique of Pure Reason*, Norman Kemp Smith, trans., p. 41.

or nonsense, depending on the specifics of the case.

Of course, mathematics and later formal logic, presented a difficulty for this epistemology. After all, it is not clear how it is that, for example, the theory of infinite sets and infinitely large (transfinite) numbers arises out of experience. After the advent of non-Euclidean geometries, it was not even clear just how human experience and formal systems are related, or even if they are related at all. One suggestion is that formal systems are not in fact grounded in experience but are simply reflections on—or perhaps generalizations from—the world as we experience it with our senses. But then what are we to say about formal systems that have no correlate in sense experience—like transfinite numbers? One would surely not want to say that we have no knowledge of transfinite numbers.

Another suggestion is that formal systems are grounded not in sensory experience but in intellectual experience[4], an experience that arises solely within a person's mind. But what is the sense in which intellectual experience is intersubjective? Intersubjectivity is typically thought to point to a "real world" outside of the mind. The reason why empirical knowledge is intersubjective is exactly that it is knowledge of something external to our minds that can be experienced by minds other than our own. But how does this extend to an intellectual experience? To what reality outside of the mind could it point? When a logician says that transfinite numbers exist, do they mean something that is in any way comparable to what a physicist means when they assert the existence of quarks?

---

[4] Experienced in the mind only and not through the senses.

If so, how might we explicate that comparability? If not, just what does the logician mean?

As puzzling (and fascinating) as these philosophical issues might be, for the last several hundred years there has been general agreement in Western philosophy that knowledge does not apply outside of science and mathematics (and formal logic). One typically does not say, for example, of artists that they contribute to human knowledge. This is not to say that the arts are not important. It is simply to say that they do not generate knowledge. They generate something else. (But what that "something else" is turns out to be a very difficult question to answer.) The same might be said of religion. One does not, strictly speaking, know God, because God is notoriously not the object of intersubjective experience. It is simply not true, for example, that if you pray hard enough you will experience God in the same way that, say, the Pope experiences God. There are just too many apparently incompatible experiences of God.

I think the difficulty with Hicks' attempt revolves around his assumption that science (empiricism) exhausts factuality and knowledge. If there are senses of knowledge that do not involve the empirical world—the world as perceived—and if religion is one of these, then religious knowledge claims need not be verifiable/falsifiable in the sense that empirical knowledge claims must be. Suppose religious knowledge claims may be of a different nature entirely. It would follow that the fact that these knowledge claims cannot be given empirical content is irrelevant. In the same vein, the fact that knowledge claims about transfinite numbers (infinitely large numbers) or complex numbers, like the square root of -1, cannot be given empirical content is irrelevant to their correctness.

This would be to embrace the other horn of Hick's dilemma, and it is what I try to do in the first section of this book.

In short, I opt for the third alternative above, which requires a rather different view of epistemology. We certainly talk about aesthetic and religious truth, and equally certainly truth is an epistemic category. Indeed, if there be truth, can knowledge be far behind? I think not. And so, if it makes sense to talk about aesthetic truth or religious truth, then it must also make sense to talk about aesthetic and religious knowledge[5]. Suppose we expand our understanding of human experience. Suppose that in addition to an empirical dimension, we grant that human experience also has an aesthetic and a religious/spiritual dimension. Then, following Kant, we could also talk about knowledge arising out of those dimensions of experience.

If I am correct that both militant atheism and militant theism are founded on the same incorrect assumption—namely that all knowledge must be like science—then the problem evaporates. It is not true that religion is bad science for the very good reason that it is not any kind of science at all. If religion is a completely different way of knowing the world, then it is no more an attack on science and intellectual honesty than is poetry. By the same token, if the truths of religion and the truths of science are different in kind, then science could be no more of a threat to religious truth than arithmetic. I suggest, the whole argument could be seen to be

---

[5] In the next few chapters I develop the idea that Knowledge is that which moves us forward in becoming human and suggests that there are at least four species of Knowledge. Science does this by developing our understanding of the empirical world; logic (and mathematics) does this by developing our understanding of rationality; art does this by expressing our emotional responses to our lives; and religion does this by healing the brokenness of our lives.

based on a category mistake.[6] Religion and science could be seen as compatible as science and poetry or religion and arithmetic.

Such an epistemology would require multiple senses of knowledge. I suggest that we seek for both a genus and some species of knowledge, the species being distinguished by different senses of truth and belief. In fact, we are already quite comfortable with multiple and irreducible senses knowledge. Since mathematical truth is different than empirical truth, must it not follow that mathematical knowledge is different than scientific knowledge? Exploring the genus Knowledge and various of its species is the subject of the next chapter.

---

[6] A category mistake is the conflation of incomparable things, of things in different categories. This can work in poetic imagery but rarely works in philosophy.

# CHAPTER 1:

# Knowledge and the Human Project

Being trained in analytic philosophy, I asked myself what we might mean when we say that we know something. There are three competing answers that are often considered by philosophers: the pragmatic theory, the correspondence theory, and the coherence theory.

The twentieth century philosopher, John Dewey, championed the pragmatic theory of knowledge. Dewey argued that knowledge claims are the assertion that we have sufficient evidence that further investigation is unnecessary. Thus, I know that Force equals mass times acceleration ($F = MA$), because the equation has been tested sufficiently that it need not be tested again. Further investigation is not necessary.

According to the correspondence theory, we know propositions that correspond to the way the world is put together. Thus, I know that $F = MA$ because when I measure the force necessary to accelerate a given mass a given amount, that force is (and corresponds to) what the equation predicts it will be.

According to the coherence theory, we know propositions that follow from a consistent body of theory. Thus, I know that $F = MA$ because it follows from Newton's Laws of Motion.

There are problems with each of these. Pragmatism is all well and good, but it would seem to open the door to prematurely shutting down investigation. It is a commonplace in science that further investigation reveals that what had seemed to be well-established turns out not to be true after all. Some rebel scientist looked more carefully and noticed something that the others had missed. Evolution is a good example. Prior to Darwin, people thought that was obvious that species are fixed. Darwin looked more carefully and noticed that species are not fixed but evolve.

The problem with the Correspondence Theory turns in the finitude of sense observation. Ultimately the only statements that can correspond to the observable world are statements about what we can sense, and we can sense only a finite number of things. Yet there are an infinite number of possible theories that could predict that finite set of observations. So how can we tell which of the infinite number of possible theories is the one that in some sense corresponds to the real world? Again, there must be more to knowledge than just correspondence.

The Coherence Theory seems to make sense in mathematics and logic—but when applied to science, the same problem appears. We never have more than a finite number of real-world observations. These observations become data points. But a theorem of geometry is that there are an infinite number of curves that can be drawn through any finite set of points. Each of those curves can be seen to follow from a different set of axioms (a theory, if you will). So how does one choose which theory is the known one? There must be more to knowledge than consistency.

And yet even though each of these theories of knowledge (epistemologies) has difficulties, each also seems to have a certain plausibility. There does seem to be a lot more urgency to investigating newly proposed theories than well-established ones. If the observation statements that follow from a proposed theory turn out to be false, the theory really should be at least modified, if not abandoned. And certainly, if it can be shown that a proposed theoretical statement does not follow from a set of laws, the proposed statement needs to be either abandoned or modified.

What is a philosopher to do in the light of all this difficulty? Not surprisingly, advocates of each of these theories of knowledge have worked to explain within their epistemology what else needs to be added to create knowledge. I have come to think something rather more radical. I believe that the essential difficulty is that we have come to think that there is only one sort of knowledge, the exquisite model for which is science. Suppose, I asked myself, there are more sorts of knowledge than science. Suppose knowledge is more like a genus than a species and different sorts of knowledge are species within that genus. Then what?

Then we would have room for different ways of knowing that do not conflict with one another. This is the sort of epistemology I was looking for and that I outline in this section of the book. For clarity, I shall refer to the genus as "Knowledge" and the several species either with a designation, such as "scientific knowledge," or, when the species is clear from context, simply as "knowledge." To begin with the genus, then, let us consider Knowledge.

## HUMAN AND HOMO SAPIENS

I find I have to start way out in left field, near the bleachers. It is important to distinguish between our being as biological creatures and our being as moral and spiritual agents. The latter I think of as our humanity and the former as our biology. As biological creatures, we are only one among thousands of other biological creatures, all of which fit into a complex and constantly evolving taxonomic system. We share our essential biology with lots of other creatures and are properly studied along with the rest. There is more to us, though, than our biology. It is as human beings that we are something more. It is as human beings that we Know the world. It is this Knowing that creates our humanity and transfers these rather interesting biological units into human creatures.

Without Knowledge, we are but very sophisticated termites, moving around in the world, satisfying our biological needs with little or no understanding of personal relationships, interconnection, responsibility, or accountability. It is these latter that define us as moral and spiritual agents, as humans, and it is Knowledge that creates or reveals them. Therefore, I think of Knowledge as a kind of moving boundary between our mere biology and our evolving humanity, between our existence as things and our existence as moral and spiritual agents. It is the possession—or, perhaps, the acquisition—of Knowledge that transforms Homo sapiens into humans.

My choice of words suggested an interesting question: Is our biology a necessary condition for our humanity? Somewhat unconventionally, I don't think so. For convenience I shall refer to all moral and spiritual agents as persons. I don't think that the term "human person" is redundant. On the other hand, whether or not there actually are non-human persons is not a question that can be answered by philosophy.

For example, we might discover that we are not alone in the universe. Suppose there are other intelligent beings elsewhere than Earth, and we discover them. Among other things, we might discover that they are moral and spiritual agents and so want to include them in the category of persons. For another example, we might come to realize that even here on earth there are other animals (dolphins, elephants, or chimpanzees, for example) that are sufficiently intelligent and morally and spiritually compassionate that we would want to include them as persons.

For a final example, there may someday be computers that we would want to include as well, computers that had become moral and spiritual agents, responsible and accountable for their actions and thus are persons. As a matter of fact, as Artificial Intelligence becomes increasingly sophisticated, there are computer scientists, among other people, right now who are contemplating this very possibility.[1]

None of these examples is a prediction. They are only possibilities that illustrate that even though it might be incorrect, it is neither absurd nor contradictory to suggest that the category human and the category person are not logically equivalent. The two categories need not be coextensive, though they might be. Homo sapiens is defined biologically, based ultimately on the sharing of a gene pool. "Personhood" is defined philosophically, based ultimately on what I think of as existential, moral, and spiritual considerations. To say that something is a person is to say that it is a moral and spiritual agent, responsible and accountable for its actions and cognizant of its place in the universe.

The question whether or not the categories human and person are coextensive, then, is an open one. It could turn out to be the

---

[1] I hasten to point out, though, that this is not an empirical problem, but a philosophical one.

case that they are, but that is an empirical question, not a philo-sophical one. It is also an open question whether or not there are degrees of being a person. This could be the basis of the claim that we owe moral obligations to non-human animals, though we do not normally hold them morally accountable for their behavior.

At this point, though, I want to leave these questions open since there is no consensus. In what follows, the only persons I shall con-sider are humans. Whether or not there are degrees of personhood outside of humanity, it is clear that there is a continuum of being human between an infant and an adult. Since personhood as I am using the term is created by moral and spiritual agency, one ear-mark of personhood is accountability. We do not hold a newborn accountable in anything like the way we hold adults accountable precisely because the humanity of an infant is mostly—but certain-ly not entirely—potential. For example, we do not hold an infant accountable for keeping its parents awake at night with its crying, though we do hold the adult neighbors next door accountable for keeping us awake with their drunken party.

The biology of the infant, on the other hand, is fully actual, even though the expression of the infant's biology changes over time. At least at the genetic level, a newborn is the same Homo sapiens as the adult it will grow up to be. Its potential humanity is transformed into actual humanity as the infant moves along into childhood, adolescence, and finally adulthood. This transition is the true aim and function of education.

It is tempting to think that adulthood completes the transition, but this would be an error. The transition is never completed, and so the concept of being fully human is really what the ancient Greeks would have called a *telos*, a goal or ideal that draws us onward.

It is an ideal that is never fully achieved, but always reached for, constantly beckoning us to move beyond the complacency of being content with the achievement of the moment, satisfied with the "not quite." "The Human Project" is what I shall call the project of a constantly evolving humanity, the project of continually becoming human, driven by the urge to Know.

## PRESENCE

Knowledge as a genus is a basic drive of human beings. It involves more than sense experience, reason, and satisfaction. It also involves a sense of mystery, the apprehension of which excites awe and moves us to compassion. I call this awe-inspiring mystery[2] "Presence." What is it that transforms the potentially human infant into a more fully realized human being? I think that our humanity is a manifestation of Presence. As we move from potentiality into actuality, it is toward Presence that we move. I have had many religious/mystical[3] experiences in addition to the one I wrote about in the first Prologue. People sometimes ask me whether I believe it is God that I experience in these sacred times. The brief answer is that I what experience is simply a Presence that is never absent from my life. This Presence is summed up in a dream I had several years ago. It consisted entirely of a voice telling me "Go thou peaceful in the

---

[2] I use the word "mystery" to indicate that which excites awe, not something that is as yet unknown or as a cop-out word for something I don't understand. This should become clear as the book progresses.

[3] I think that the difference between a religious and a mystical experience is one of interpretation. Phenomenologically they are the same.

world, for I am with thee." I am with thee. Presence. I am not at all concerned with whether or not someone else thinks of and talks of this as God. For me the best word is "Presence." The rest is verbiage.

To be fully human would be to a full manifestation of Presence and thus to be fully present in the universe. What would it mean to be fully present in the universe? It would to be fully aware, fully able, and fully responsible. When one is present, one fits, as it were; one is in place and "know[s] the place for the first time" (T. S. Eliot)[4]. This requires full awareness of and comfort with one's place among the "ten thousand things" (to use a Chinese idiom meaning "everything that exists") and an understanding of how these things create a whole. It requires the ability to reason fully and being fully open to an equally valid intuitive understanding. At the same time, it requires that one grasp the limitations of both reason and intuition and how they complement and complete one another. It requires one to be able to speak fully from the depths of one's heart and soul. It requires one to be fully awake, as The Buddha was awake. In short, it requires one to be in the world and to Know it fully.

To be fully human, then, would be to have turned the potentiality of infancy completely into actuality. There would be nothing left to become. No one, I assert, ever *is* fully human. We are always *becoming* human. The Human Project is never complete, only engaged. Not even The Buddha was fully human.

Nevertheless, we do have glimpses, intimations of a deeper and more complete humanity:

---

[4] See the "Little Gidding" section of "Four Quartets."

- When "we see into the life of things"[5]
- When we understand with our minds, our hearts, and our souls
- When we feel as well as think
- When we stand under the truth that all things are exactly what they are and yet nothing is simply what it seems to be.

These are examples of times when we have a glimpse into something greater and more whole than we normally experience. We do not simply imagine these moments and the truths they reveal; we are present to and participate in those truths.

In these moments one is, if for just the briefest instant, present and is given just that glimpse, that intimation, of the possibility of a fuller presence and a deeper humanity. The apprehension of Presence in one's presence reveals Presence in those around us. These moments spur us to become more than we thought we could be and spur us continually to become human and engage the Human Project.

## PARADIGMS

The mid-twentieth century philosopher, Thomas Kuhn, introduced the idea of paradigms in his groundbreaking monograph "The Structure of Scientific Revolutions"[6]. In a nutshell, his idea,

---

[5] From William Wordsworth's poem, "Lines Written a Few Miles Above Tintern Abbey."

[6] Thomas Kuhn, "The Structure of Scientific Revolutions" in *Foundations of the Unity of Science, Vol. 2.*

which was itself revolutionary, is that science does not—or at least cannot be shown to—advance asymptotically toward The Truth, *i.e.,* the absolutely correct and complete description of the empirical world. Rather, science—or, perhaps, the sciences—adopts what he called paradigms, prescriptive ideas about how the world works and uses those prescriptive ideas as guides to theoretical thinking until they are no longer adequate. At that point, science experiences a crisis until new paradigms are found that encompass the old insights, solve the crisis, and suggest new avenues for research. The development of Relativistic mechanics and Quantum mechanics out of Newtonian mechanics is such a paradigm shift.

One cannot, however, claim that the new paradigms are any more correct than the old. Such a claim would require that one already know what the correct description of the empirical world is and thus would beg the question. The most that one can say is that one paradigm is more or less adequate to the problems at hand.

I want to pick up this notion of paradigms that guide our understanding of our ability to make sense out of and be present within the world. My use of this idea, though, is somewhat broader than Kuhn's. He restricted the notion of paradigm shifts to science; I think that it also shows how the Human Project moves along.

Consider Kant's account of causality.[7] He said, in essence, that to make sense out of the booming, buzzing confusion of raw sense perception, our minds impose a framework of space, time, and causality on those disorganized perceptions. The most that can be said about this framework is that it is, in some sense, a map of

---

[7] The Critique of Pure Reason.

the world-in-itself[8], but not that it recapitulates the world-in-itself. According to Kant, we construct our experienced world within this framework. In contemporary language and thinking, this is the idea that the imposition of a framework of space, time, and causality on our raw sense perceptions is hard-wired within our brains.

I believe this to be correct. But notice something interesting. Though the imposition of such a framework may be hard-wired, the details of how that framework is constructed are not. Consider causality. In Kant's time a Cartesian understanding of causality was the paradigm[9]. It was thought that for any event, there is a single, distinct, discoverable, and knowable cause. If you saw an event, say a particle moving through space, you could assume that something caused it to move and that cause could be discovered. One had but to know a single distinct cause of an event in order to explain it. Newton, using this paradigm of causality, listed three essential ideas out of which he constructed his laws of motion and theory of gravitation:

1. A body in motion or at rest will continue in motion or rest unless acted upon by an outside force.
2. A force acting on a massive body produces an acceleration in that body.
3. For every action there is an equal and opposite reaction.

These paradigms were assumed to be completely correct until the early 20th century when physics began to look at the actions

---

[8] Kant's term for the world as it actually is, independent of any human interpretation or understanding. The German is *Das Welt an sich*.

[9] This paradigm was first clearly started by the Enlightenment philosopher Rene Descartes.

of extremely small bodies acting over extremely small distances, for example electrons moving around atomic nuclei. It turned out that these events were impossible to understand according to the Cartesian/Newtonian paradigms. Heisenberg, Bohr, and Einstein, among others, replaced Cartesian Causality with Quantum Causality in which every event is not assumed to have a discrete, discoverable, and knowable cause. Instead, these events were assumed to be more or less likely, and causality was conceived of as the probability of finding a particle at a particular place. The electron, for example was no longer seen as a distinct mass moving discretely around a nucleus, but as a kind of cloud defined by the probability of finding it at a particular spot near the nucleus.[10]

According to Newtonian mechanics, the position and momentum of every particle in the Universe can, in principle, be known, and if known then the position of any particle, at any point in the future, can, at least in principle, be calculated. In quantum mechanics, though, the very meaning of "position" and "momentum" has changed so that knowledge of one creates ignorance the other. Therefore, one cannot, even in principle, know the simultaneous position and momentum of any particle and therefore can predict only the probability of finding it at any given point and time. This does not invalidate Kant's epistemic paradigm, however. It only illustrates that the details of the causal framework are not hardwired in our brains.

Similarly, Einstein also upset the Cartesian paradigm when he proposed the Theory of Relativity. He tied together the notions of

---

[10] The Nobel winning physicist, Niels Bohr, once said that anyone who is not shocked by quantum physics has not understood it, or words to that effect. See Karen Michelle Barad's *Meeting the Universe Halfway*, p. 254.

space, time, and causality. Under the Cartesian paradigm, space and time were thought to be independent of causality. Einstein, though, reasoned that there has to be an upper limit to the speed at which a causal chain can propagate, namely the speed of light, and that insight not only solved a major crisis[11] in physics but also forever changed how we think about space, time, and causality. Yet Kant's insight that space, time, and causality are the essential blocks we use to construct the physical world remains. It is only the details of how we use those blocks that has changed.

## A PARADIGM SHIFT

I want to expand on Kant's insight about how our minds turn raw sense perceptions into observations. He restricted himself to our experience of the empirical world. It is my contention that this does not exhaust the ways we experience the world. It is the organization of these multiple modes of experience that moves us from merely biological creatures, *Homo sapiens*, to human beings. I think that this happens in at least four different dimensions of experience, the Empirical Experience (science), the Rational Experience (logic and mathematics), the Aesthetic Experience (art), and

---

[11] By the late nineteenth century physicists were making some very disturbing observations that were completely inconsistent with Newton's laws of motion. Some experiments even suggested that as objects accelerated, time slows and space contracts, an idea that makes no sense within a theory that assumes there is an absolute framework of both space and time.

the Holy Experience (religion)[12].

Notice that these are not independent of one another. Thus, for example, one can say of the proof of a theorem in logic or of a scientific theory that it is elegant or even beautiful. Pythagoras and his school certainly brought religion into mathematics, and surely the arts and religion are constantly interacting with one another. One can even think of art as having arisen from the attempt to express and excite the experience of the Holy. Thus, these experiences can be thought of as forming a kind of multi-dimensional space of human experience. And yet, it is crucially important to keep the dimensions conceptually separate. Failure to do so is the most important reason that, for example, the Creationists and the Evolutionists are unable to be reconciled with one another. They are dealing with conceptually different aspects of our experience of the world, and the failure to recognize this leads inevitably to confusion.

All of the various versions of Creationism, from the most extreme 6,000-year-old-universe advocates to advocates of Intelligent Design, make the mistake of assuming that if the Biblical account of creation is true at all, then it must be empirically true, and yet they reject nearly every accepted tenant of scientific verification. For their part, far too many Evolutionists make the same mistake in reverse. They assume that since the Biblical account of creation is empirically false, then it must be absolutely false, thus rejecting

---

[12] An argument can be made for other species of knowledge in addition to these four. Economics, government, and engineering have been suggested to me. I will restrict myself to these four, though, because I do not feel competent to comment on other possibilities. I will leave that task to others who understand them better than I.

religion (or at least Christianity) because it is not science.

I propose that 150 years of controversy and anguish could have been avoided by the simple expedient of recognizing that the truth of religion is *a different kind of truth* than the truth of science. Thus, the Biblical account of creation does not need to be scientifically true in order to be religiously true. The search for empirical verification of the Genesis creation story is a category mistake, just as the rejection of religion on empirical grounds is a category mistake. The Theory of Evolution is completely compatible with Christianity for exactly the same reason that it is compatible with poetry.

It is our facility in moving through this four-dimensional knowledge space that makes us increasingly present to and within the world, *i.e.,* makes us increasingly human. This is the Human Project. The Genus, Knowledge, is that which facilitates our movement in this Human Space.

Note that this is a kind of pragmatic version of truth. At the risk of repeating myself, John Dewey defines knowledge as "that which satisfactorily terminates inquiry"[13]. It is not entirely clear to me what he means by "terminates." If he means "stops" then it would follow that there is very little scientific knowledge since one never stops investigating even a well-confirmed theory[14]. Science does not stop. I think, though, that what Dewey intends is that belief becomes knowledge when its assertion becomes warranted, and the crucial question for Pragmatist epistemology is when an assertion is warranted. For example, Newton's assertion that $F = MA$ was warranted because every time he measured force, mass,

---

[13] John Dewey, Logic: The Theory of Inquiry, p. 8.

[14] See, for example, the work of Karl Popper.

and acceleration the equation held.

I am expanding on Dewey's notion of terminating inquiry a little. My version is that Knowledge is that which permits one to make sense of the universe—or at least that dimension of the universe with which one is concerned. It facilitates one's moving around in the space of human experience. When one achieves this, one is warranted in asserting the truth of something. Thus, Newton was warranted in asserting his theory of gravitation and mechanics because it made better sense of the experienced world than its predecessors. By the same token, Einstein was warranted in asserting Special Relativity, because it made the appropriate kind of order out of the crisis of the failure to detect events that were predicted by Newtonian mechanics.

Similarly, crises have appeared in the history of logic and mathematics. Aristotle was warranted in asserting his logic because it allowed him to reason better about the abstract world of thought. By the 19th century, though, as even algebra and geometry were being abstracted and alternative versions constructed, mathematicians were beginning to consider the underlying logical structure of mathematics. It turned out that Aristotelian logic was not adequate to this task. Thus, logicians such as Gottlob Frege, Giuseppe Peano, and others began to create a new logic. This effort was brought to fruition by Bertrand Russell and Alfred North Whitehead in their monumental *Principia Mathematica*.[15] Russell and Whitehead's success warranted the assertion of a new paradigm in logic. This new logic did not invalidate Aristotelian logic so much as it encompassed Aristotelian logic.

---

[15] Russell and Whitehead, in this book, were the first logicians to successfully reproduce arithmetic within a consistent set theory.

I believe that in both Art and Religion paradigms also play a crucial role and that these paradigms, when successful, facilitate our development as human persons. We become human as we gain Knowledge, *i.e.*, encompass more of the Human Space and gain facility in moving through it. As I shall argue, Knowledge is gained in at least the four dimensions of Science, Logic and Mathematics[16], Art, and Religion.

---

[16] The term "Logic and Mathematics" will get awkward with repetition. From here onward, I will shorten it to just "Logic" with the understanding that it includes mathematics as well.

# CHAPTER 2:

# Ways of Knowing: Logic and Science

As I began thinking about knowledge, I reflected on what turns out to be an important ambiguity that few seem to have paid much attention to. I thought about the question, "How do you know that?" and suddenly realized that it could mean two very different things. On the one hand, it could (and usually does) mean "What is your evidence? Why do you think you know that?" But on the other hand, it could also mean "In what way do you know that? What is the mode or manner in which you know it?" Thinking of the "how" in this latter way, led me to begin thinking that there may be more than one way of knowing. And that led me to realize that even though none but the most thoroughgoing skeptic would argue that there is no knowledge in logic and science, these ways of knowing are different. Each is a separate species within the genus Knowledge.

## LOGIC

There are surely many statements in logic that no one would argue against as knowledge claims. Consider, for example,

- $1 + 1 = 2$
- The Pythagorean Theorem

- The Symmetry of Equality (if $a = b$ then $b = a$).

How do I know these statements? The first might seem to be known on the basis of observation. If I put an apple on the table and you put another beside it, then there are two apples on the table. But suppose I spill some water on the table and you spill some more on top of my spill. Are there now two small spills of water or only one large one? So how do I know that the first is true because in the observational world it seems sometimes not to be? And I might lay out lots and lots of right triangles and count squares on their sides, but how do I know that the second will *always* be true? What happens when the hypotenuse of the triangle is seven centimeters? Or six light years? Or four nanometers? The third, at least, seems self-evident enough, but most of us have learned to be wary of self-evidence as a basis of knowledge. So how do I know statements like these three are true?

The answer is simple: I prove them. Knowledge in logic is valid proof, which is to say theorem-hood, and since logical validity[1] does not admit of degrees, when a theorem is validly proved, it cannot be unproved. So, on the one hand, there seems to be a sense in which logical knowledge really is absolute. Since the most common way of setting up a mathematical or logical system is axiomatically, it might at first glance seem as if theorem-hood, and thus knowledge, is inherent within a given set of axioms. Change the axioms, and you get a different set of theorems and thus a different system. Riemannian geometry is a different geometrical system

---

[1] A valid inference is one such that the truth of the premises guarantees the truth of the conclusion. It turns out that validity then is not dependent upon meaning but solely on form.

than Euclidean Geometry. Different things are true (provable) in the two systems, and so different things are known. Thus, on the other hand, logical knowledge seems not to be absolute after all but relative to an axiom system. We do not simply know a statement; we know a statement within an axiom system. However, things are not even that straightforward. It is possible for two formal systems to be equivalent yet have different sets of axioms.

Indeed, one of the tests of the strength of a logical system is how many different and equivalent ways one can set it up[2]. In fact, not all logical systems are set up axiomatically. There are other ways to do it. A logical system set up non-axiomatically is called a natural deduction system. Instead of axioms, one lays down sufficiently strong rules of inference.[3] When this is done correctly, it is possible to prove that the resulting system has exactly the same set of theorems as the axiomatic version of that system. This means that the two systems are equivalent, and from a purely logical point of view, the natural deduction version and the axiomatic version are but two different styles of presentation of the same system, different dialects of the same logical language, if you will. The theorems are not relative to the axioms at all but are in some sense implicit in the system itself.[4]

From the point of view of logic, a formal mathematical system is usually set up with nothing more than a set of axioms and some

---

[2] Logical systems are said to be equivalent just in case they have the same set of theorems, that is, the same things can be proved in them.

[3] Rules of inference set up standards for allowable inferences within a formal system, for example, "from $p$ and $p$ implies $q$ one may infer $q$."

[4] An interesting question in the philosophy of logic is just what a formal system actually is. However, interesting as that question may be, it is beside the point here.

rules of inference. But as we have seen, there is nothing special about this way of doing things. These systems can also be set up in a natural deduction style. I see no reason not to apply this observation to mathematical systems, for example, to geometry or set theory. Shouldn't it be possible, at least in principle, to do the same thing?

Different sets of axioms give, say, different geometries or different set theories. But if that is the case, couldn't one give appropriately powerful rules of inference and dispense with the axioms, thus creating a "natural deduction geometry" or a "natural deduction set theory"? I don't know of anyone who as actually done this, but I also don't know any reason why it wouldn't work, at least in principle. It would probably be spectacularly inconvenient to work with, but philosophically it would be very interesting to show that it could be done since it would add credence to the assertion that formal systems are not axiom dependent. In what follows, I assume that such a system is possible.

The conclusion that I draw from all this is that in logic and mathematics, while truth still resides within the logical system, it is not relative to a set of axioms. Instead, it is implicit in, or intrinsic to, the system itself. The epistemological implication of this is that to say that I know a certain thing in logic is not to say that I know it in any kind of absolute sense. It is rather to say that I know a system in which it is a theorem.

To see how this works, consider an example from logic. Virtually all logicians agree that whatever else must be true about implication, it must be transitive:

If $A$ implies $B$, and $B$ implies $C$, then $A$ implies $C$.

There are other properties of implication, however, that are more controversial. Consider, for example, the theorem of many systems of logic that true propositions are implied by all propositions[5]. This is so controversial that it is sometimes referred to as "The Paradox of Material Implication." Some logicians think this is absurd[6], and others see no problem with it at all. The latter group will construct their systems to include both transitivity and the Paradox; the former will construct theirs to include transitivity and exclude the Paradox. But even those logicians who reject the paradox know it, not because it is true and they are somehow inevitably stuck with it, but because they know a perfectly good system in which it is a theorem.

And this is not contradicted by the fact that they also know different systems in which it is not a theorem, systems designed specifically to avoid it. Knowledge claims in logic are, at the level of truth, claims about systems. Truth is intrinsic to a system, and so knowing something is, in a certain important sense, also intrinsic to a system. Once one knows a valid proof of a theorem, one knows that theorem forever. Such a knowledge claim cannot ever be overturned. The most one can do is to construct a different system in which it is not a theorem, and different systems do not contradict each other. The systems Anderson and Belnap construct do not contradict the more common systems that accept the Paradox; they are just different systems.

---

[5] Consider the implication, $p$ implies $q$. In many systems if $q$ is true, then the truth of $p$ is irrelevant to $q$. This is a result of the fact the valid inference is a function of form, not content, though many find it to be counterintuitive.

[6] See for example, Alan Ross Anderson and Nuel D. Belnap, Jr., *Entailment*.

## CHOICE IN LOGIC

The fact that different systems of logic do not contradict one another is a very important point. It means that one has a great deal of latitude in logic. One can choose in which systems one will work and in which systems one will not work. These choices are not imposed on the logician by anything external but by considerations idiosyncratic to the logician. For example, the so-called Intuitionists do not reject indirect proofs[7] of existence theorems in set theory because they think these proofs are somehow *logically* suspect. They reject such proofs because they think these proofs are *philosophically* suspect. Other logicians reject the so-called modal logics, not on formal grounds, but on philosophical grounds. Even as staunch a critic of modal logic as Willard van Orman Quine could be said to know, in the sense that I am using the term, theorems in Lewis' systems of modal logic, while arguing strenuously that these systems are useless as analyses of logical necessity[8].

To summarize, then, truth in logic is provability and one is warranted in asserting a theorem when one can prove it (or at least when one is aware of a valid proof of it). This makes knowledge relative to a specific logical system.

Let us return to the three statements we were puzzled about at the beginning of this chapter. How do we know them? Because we

---

[7] Indirect proofs of theorems work by showing that the denial of the theorem implies a contradiction. Since valid inference by definition preserves truth, the theorem itself must be true.

[8] Modal logics are systems of examining the formal behavior of logical necessity. There are many such systems. The English logician, C. I. Lewis, is famous for having created an intricate web of such systems.

can prove them. Notice that it is perfectly possible to create systems in which they are not true, and this fact does not contradict our knowledge of them. This is a very strong sense of knowledge, truth, and justification. Logic is a species within the genus Knowledge, which surely is not an unexpected conclusion.

## SCIENCE

Knowledge in logic, then, is deductive success in a formal system, and logical investigation is about extending knowledge claims, which is to say, proving new theorems. The situation in science is very different. The whole point of scientific investigation is precisely to overturn knowledge claims. Does that mean that there is no knowledge in science? If one believed that there is one and only one species of Knowledge and Truth, then it would seem as if one would have a very hard time avoiding that conclusion. But if we were willing to give up the claim that there is a single species of Knowledge, then one could say that in science there is no knowledge-in-the-sense-of-logic. But from that it would not follow that there is no knowledge in science in any sense whatsoever.

Think about an assertion of physics that most of us would claim to know, for example:

- $e = mc^2$
- $F = MA$

Are we right that we know these laws? If there were only a single species of truth and logical/mathematical truth were the paradigm, then we would be forced to answer that we cannot properly claim to know either because neither is logically true. From this it would follow either that there is, properly speaking, no scientific truth at all, or that there is scientific truth, but it is not knowable. Neither seems to be an acceptable claim. There does seem to be a sense in which the phrase "empirical knowledge" is not an oxymoron, even though knowledge claims in science are not intrinsic to any theoretical system and can be overturned. We do know that $e = mc^2$; we do know that $F = MA$. But how do we know them?

It all has to do with justification. There are two different levels of justified assertion. At the most basic level, one is justified in asserting a description of the world (an observation statement) when that description is accurate, *i.e.* when it actually describes what happens in the observable world. At a more abstract level, one is justified in asserting a generalization (a law or a theory) when that generalization is well supported by (that it implies) successful observation statements. In short, justification in science depends on consistency with the empirical world.

To be sure, in theoretical physics, knowledge claims sometimes appear to be little more than logical deductions, as in the more arcane and far reaches of relativity theory and quantum mechanics, but they are not. The knowledge claim in question may follow from a law as a matter of mathematics and logic, but this is not what makes it known. What makes it known is its utility and accuracy as a description of the observational, the empirical world, not the fact that it is a logical consequence of an axiom within a formal system.

All of this gets very tricky in detail, as even a quick study of the philosophy of science will reveal, but the basic structure remains in spite of the stickiness of the details. Knowledge claims in science are legitimate (hardly a controversial claim), and they are, in principle, different from knowledge claims in logic and mathematics (perhaps a somewhat more controversial claim).

The most obvious difference is that knowledge claims in science can be overthrown. Indeed, it is often precisely such an overthrow that represents the most spectacular advances in scientific knowledge. When this happens, what we used to know, we no longer do. For example, it was once known that the total mass of a closed system cannot change[9]. We no longer know this. What we now know is that the total mass of a closed system can indeed change but only in accord with Einstein's equations. What we now know is that the sum of mass and energy within a closed system cannot change.

Thus, a claim to scientific knowledge is validated by descriptive success. For example, I know that $e = mc^2$ because it follows from well-tested laws and accurately describes the empirical world, that is, it implies accurate observation statements. Scientific knowledge, then, also seems to be a species of Knowledge, again not an unexpected conclusion. But it seems that science and logic are different species, which might be an unexpected conclusion, and one that led me to further unexpected and important conclusions.

## LOGICAL AND SCIENTIFIC KNOWLEDGE COMPARED

Before going on, I want to point to some other differences between logic and science and one similarity. In mathematics and logic, we seek to understand certain abstract concepts by investi-

---

[9] More familiarly stated, perhaps, as "Matter cannot be created or destroyed."

gation of their formal behavior. If we want to understand sets, for example, we set up a formal system and see how that system works. The way to see how a system works is to see what theorems can be proved in it. Of course, different systems give different theorems, and so it might seem as if there is still a quandary. It may appear tempting to ask which of the competing and mutually inconsistent formal systems is the *correct* system that describes the behavior of *real* sets.

As interesting as that question may appear to be at first glance, it is, in fact, a red herring. The simple answer is that all of them are correct, assuming, of course, that they are all internally consistent. The differences are simply the differences of different kinds of set theories. To ask which of the different kinds of set theory is the *true* set theory is like asking which of the several alternative geometries is the true geometry. Just as I know that Euclidean planes work this way and Riemannian planes work that way, I know that constructible sets work this way, and that non-constructible sets work that way. The point is that knowledge in logic is deductive success within a formal system.

Science works very differently. The whole enterprise of science is the attempt to describe the empirical world. Physics describes how matter and energy interact; chemistry describes how atoms and molecules come together to form compounds; biology describes the world of living things; astronomy describes the universe beyond the earth; and so on. Scientific knowledge is the successful description of the observable world.[10] Unlike the situation in logic,

---

[10] I know that there is a lot of disagreement about the details of what counts as "a successful description," but it seems to me that these differences of opinion are not important for the point I want to make.

one does not choose among different scientific theories on the basis of idiosyncratic or philosophical considerations.

One must always ask which theory gives a better description of the observable world. It may not always be obvious which theory that happens to be, but science is not a formal system. Rather, it is an observational system, so that however formal theoretical physics, for example, may sometimes appear, the theory must always be referred ultimately back to the empirical world. The question that must always be asked is "Yes, but is this what the world actually looks like?" If the answer is yes, then a knowledge claim is justified. If the answer is no, then the claim is not justified. In short, knowledge in science is always relative to how well we can see the world, and what is known is not constant, but is always subject to revision.

Within logic, truth is coherence—internal consistency—and within science truth is correspondence—an accurate description or prediction of the empirical world. These reflections are what led me to suggesting the version of pragmatic theory of truth and knowledge described in Chapter 1. Within logic, valid deduction satisfactorily "terminates inquiry"; the system must be logically coherent. Within science, correspondence to the observational world satisfactorily, if provisionally, "terminates inquiry." Thus, the genus is pragmatic while these two species are coherence and correspondence. Both internal coherence and correspondence with the observational world turn out to be far more complex and difficult to describe than one might have thought, but the rather rough-and-ready account given here is sufficient to make my point. Knowledge in science and knowledge in logic are different and yet still legitimately knowledge.

There is a similarity between logic and science, though, concerning the context of discovery. Both logic and science are, in an important sense, independent of the investigator. What I mean by that is that it does not matter who the logician or scientist is. I do not mean that the scientist's own observations do not enter into the experiment. That the observer always changes the system being observed, at least at the atomic level, has been a commonplace since Heisenberg. It does not matter, though, that it was Heisenberg who first described the Uncertainty Principle, and it does not matter that it was Marie Curie who discovered radium. It does not matter that it was Russell and Whitehead who constructed the first consistent set theory strong enough to capture mathematics, and it does not matter that it was Kurt Gödel who first proved his famous theorem.

The knowledge that is gained in logic, mathematics, and science is independent of who first discovered it. Indeed, this very independence is what allows us to talk about "discovery" in the first place. This is a very important point that I will come back to as I consider other ways of knowing.

## Ontology in Science and Logic

There is one final point that I want to discuss. This concerns the issue of existence claims in logic and science—the ontology of logic and science (from the Greek words *ontos*, meaning *to exist* and *logos*, in this context, meaning *an explanation* or *an account of*). There is an intimate relationship between knowledge claims and existence claims—between epistemology and ontology. To a large extent, one's epistemology conditions one's ontology, because what we are able to know limits what we are willing to believe exists.[11]

People clearly make and deny existence claims in science, for example, "worm holes exist in space," "there is no such thing as an electromagnetic ether," and so on. One cannot, properly speaking, make scientific knowledge claims about something that does not exist. I cannot know anything about phlogiston or the ether or the magnetic monopole or anything else that does not exist. At most I can make hypothetical knowledge claims, "If there were phlogiston, then it would..."

And yet, it turns out that both science and logic deal largely with theoretical entities, things that in principle cannot be observed directly. One cannot see subatomic particles such as the Higgs boson, because they are far too small to reflect visible light. One can only see the effects of these particles. And this is exactly what physicists do with large particle accelerators such as those at Fermilab in Illinois and CERN in Switzerland. Physicists at CERN conducted the crucial experiment that revealed the predicted effects of the Higgs boson and announced with appropriate confidence that the Higgs must exist. But what could that claim actually mean?

It must mean something very different from what I mean when I assert that Uncle Harry exists. I can see Uncle Harry, hear him, touch him, and sometimes even smell him. No one can do these things with the Higgs boson. Since the answer to "how do you know" in the evidential sense is different when we speak of Higgs bosons than it is when we speak of Uncle Harry, it seems to me that the assertions are different.

---

[11] It can be argued that from a philosophical point of view, the major philosophical shift occasioned by the rise of science is that it removed ontology from the center of metaphysics and replaced it with epistemology.

The physicist's claim that the Higgs boson exists is based on the fact that its existence is required by a body of theory that has been well verified. The theory predicts that if the Higgs boson exists, then certain experimental results that are empirically verifiable will appear under appropriate conditions. It turns out that those conditions are very difficult to create, but they were created at CERN, and the empirical results predicted by the theory were observed. The conclusion? The Higgs boson exists.

Notice that pretty much the same thing could have been said of phlogiston in the early 18th century. The theory of heat in those days required that heat be a fluid that flowed from warm things to cold things. This fluid was variously called "caloric fluid" and "phlogiston," and the predicted phenomena seemed to be observed. Therefore, even such luminaries as the 18th century chemist, Joseph Priestley, asserted with confidence that phlogiston exists.

But as the 18th century progressed some disturbing phenomena were observed that were difficult to reconcile with accepted theory. Then in, 1824, Sadi Carnot published a book that presented a new theory that did not require phlogiston at all. Caloric fluid was replaced with a statistical aggregate of energetic molecules that collectively exert force on the sides of vessels containing a gas, and this force is what we measure as gas pressure. This turns out to have been one of the most important revolutions in physical science, comparable to Newtonian mechanics, relativity theory, and quantum mechanics.

For this discussion, the important thing to note is that what was once known to exist, phlogiston, was no longer known to exist. The epistemic/ontological situation regarding phlogiston pre-1824 is identical to the contemporary epistemic/ontological situation regarding the Higgs boson prior to the CERN experiment. The assertion of the existence of a theoretical entity is dependent on the accepted theory and the observations that theory predicts. Scientific knowledge, even as to what exists, is theory dependent.

I came to a similar conclusion about logic. We cannot see a number. What we see are individual things, and we count them; we do not see the number itself. We can see numerals, but numerals are only the names of numbers, not numbers themselves. And when we consider irrational numbers like *pi*, it becomes obvious that we do not see numbers, only the names of numbers.

The same thing applies to sets. We do not see sets. We see individuals that our minds group together. One might argue that we can see finite sets... so long as they are not too large. We can see the set of apples in the basket, but we cannot see the set of all the galaxies in the universe.[12] And when infinite sets enter the picture, our inability to see sets becomes obvious.

One group of logicians (called constructivists) asserts that to legitimately claim that a set exists, one must be able to show how that set is actually constructed. That's easy to see in the case of finite sets, say the set of left-handed baseball players, or even the set of all galaxies. But what about infinite sets? With infinite sets things get more interesting. The constructivists insist that one must be able to show how even an infinite set is constructed in order to assert its existence. Thus, the set of even numbers is asserted to exist because it can be constructed even though it is infinite.

But not all infinite sets can be constructed like this. Non-constructivists assert their existence because denying their existence

---

[12] Actually, I assert that we cannot see the set of apples. We see only the apples.

involves one in contradiction. The constructivists, on the other hand, argue that more is needed, but their assertion is not because they believe that such an indirect proof is logically incoherent but because it is philosophically suspect. This is exactly parallel to what I came to see about knowledge in logic. Logical knowledge is dependent on the logical system one chooses to work in, and that choice is a philosophical one, not a logical one. The same thing is true of existence claims in logic.

And so, I came to see that in both science and logic, existence claims are a subset of knowledge claims and are subject to the same limitations that all such knowledge claims are.

Knowledge in science, then, is different from knowledge in logic, and this difference is reflected in differences in both the sense in which their knowledge claims are said to be true and the sense in which belief in them is said to be justified. In short, it is clear that there is more than one species of both knowledge and truth.

# CHAPTER 3:

# Ways of Knowing: Art

When I realized that scientific knowledge is importantly different from logical knowledge, I realized that I had discovered a crack in what might be called "the unified field theory" of knowledge. Knowledge, I realized, really does come in different species. And since that is the case, I asked myself whether it might also be the case that knowledge extends into areas other than logic and science. What else can we say that we know? And how do we know these things?

There are surely dimensions to the Human Project other than science and logic, other ways in which we actualize our potential humanity, and it occurred to me that whenever we talk about truth, we are talking about becoming Human. We are talking, then, about Knowledge. We routinely speak of both artistic and religious truth. So, I asked myself in what senses might art and religion also be ways of knowing the world? And if they are ways of knowing the world, how do they contrast with logic and science?

Since people talk meaningfully about artistic or aesthetic truth, I assumed that they are not just blathering, and I began to wonder, even though the phrase may sound odd to some, what an epistemology of art might look like. If, for example, poetry is a species of Knowing, then a poem must move us forward in the Human Project in a way that is comparable to—though necessarily different from—proving theorems in logic and verifying (or, if you prefer, falsifying) laws in science. So, to begin I asked myself what it is that artists are up to. How does art make us more human?

## WHAT DOES ART DO?

A lot has been written about this by artists, by critics, and by philosophers. Consider the following two quotations. The first is from Audre Lorde's essay "Poetry is Not a Luxury" (in her book of essays, *Sister Outsider*):

> The quality of light by which we scrutinize our lives has direct bearing upon the product which we live, and upon the changes which we hope to bring about through those lives. It is within this light that we form those ideas by which we pursue our magic and make it realized. This is poetry as illumination, for it is through poetry that we give name to those ideas which are—until the poem—nameless and formless, about to be birthed, but already felt. That distillation of experience from which true poetry springs births thought as dream births concept, as feeling births idea, as knowledge births... understanding...[1]

The second is from Adrienne Rich's book, *What is Found There* (The emphasis is Rich's):

> *You must write, and read, as if your life depended on it....*

---

[1] Lord, *Sister Insider*, pp. 36.

To read as if your life depended on it would mean to let into your reading your beliefs, the swirl of your dream life, the physical sensations of your ordinary carnal life; and, simultaneously, to allow what you're reading to pierce the routines, safe and impermeable, in which ordinary carnal life is tracked, charted, channeled.

To write as if your life depended on it: to write across the chalkboard, putting up there in public words you have dredged, sieved up from dreams, from behind screened memories, out of silence—words you have dreaded and needed in order to know you exist....[2]

When I first read these lines from Lorde and Rich, I was stunned. "This," I said to myself, "is exactly what art does for us and what artists do." Art gives voice and expression to our awareness of the depths of existence and possibility without which we would languish in realms of perpetual sterility. Art is what we turn to in order to know that we are more than simply living biological entities, that we are living human beings. Art brings to birth our deeper understanding of who we are, how we are, when we are, what we are.

Art, when thought of in this sense, is clearly a species of Knowing, and it makes perfectly good sense to ask epistemic questions about art. Obviously, it creates a different kind of knowledge than the formal knowledge of logic or the empirical knowledge of science. It makes no sense to ask an artist to prove her creation or

---

[2] Rich, *What is Found There*, pp. 32-33.

to ask her for empirical evidence for her art. Of course. By why? Because aesthetic truth is a different kind of truth than the formal truth of logic and the empirical truth of science.

Aesthetic knowledge is knowledge of the possibility of being that moves beyond the facts of our biology and the limitations of the Law of the Excluded Middle (every proposition must be either true or else false—there is no middle ground). Art awakens us to dimensions of being we had been aware of only as phantoms moving dimly in the recesses of our souls. It gives expression—and thus reality—to what we had previously been able only to grope toward. Thus, when Rich speaks of "words you have dreaded and needed in order to know you exist," she is not speaking of knowledge of our biological existence. She is speaking of our human existence. We need to know who we are and could be as human beings, for good or ill. And art tells us that.

This is what I understand art in general to be about: it is the way we awaken one another and give expression to our potential to live a humane life, not as problem to be solved but as a life to be lived, as a revelation to be discovered, embraced, and expressed. Sometimes artists appear to approach artistic creation as a problem—and there are always numerous technical problems to be solved in the creation of any work of art. Thus, for example, a composer may contemplate how to write music using nontraditional modes or even how to use 12 apparently unrelated notes as a scale. Even in this situation, though, I suggest that the difference between noise and atonal music is that in the latter, the composer has transcended the mere technical difficulties of 12-tone composition and moved into the realm of expression. Anyone can define an arbitrary tone row; it takes an artist to turn that tone row into music.

This transformation from our problematic lives as Homo sapiens into genuinely human beings is what E. E. Cummings was pointing to in this stunning remark in his *i six non-lectures*.

> But (as it happens) poetry is being, not doing. If you wish to follow, even at a distance, the poet's calling...you've got to come out of the measurable doing universe into the immeasurable house of being.[3]

It is also the kernel of Kafka's reflection on books contained in a famous letter to a friend:

> If the book we are reading does not wake us, as with a fist hammering on our skull, why...do we read it? Good God, we would also be happy if we had no books, and such books as make us happy we could, if need be, write ourselves. But what we must have are books which come upon us like ill-fortune, and distress us deeply, like the death of one we love better than ourselves, like suicide. A book must be an ice axe to break the sea frozen inside us.[4]

These are two very striking ways of saying the same thing. Success in art is the revelation of what it is *to be* human as distinct from what it is *to do* humanly.

---

[3] Cummings, *i six nonlectures*, p. 24.

[4] Franz Kafka, *Letter to a Friend*. This is an anonymous translation that I found on the Internet.

## THE AESTHETIC OBJECT

To understand this, I have to spend some time reflecting on the aesthetic object. Years ago, my then teenage daughter, Meera, and I were driving one evening from Pittsburgh to Philadelphia. To pass the time, I asked her what a poem is. Now, by then she was quite used to my asking questions like this, apparently out of the blue, so she bit. And for most the trip we talked at length about poetry and the nature of the aesthetic object. We drew no concrete conclusions. The conversation was mostly at the level of puzzlements because every time we thought we had it pinned down, one of us would point out a problem. As we pulled into Philadelphia, we were left with these puzzles.

Consider this famous haiku by the great 12th century Japanese poet, Bashō:

> Into the old pond;
> A frog jumps
> And sounds the water.[5]

It is a poem, to be sure, but just what is the poem here? In spite of appearances, this turns out not to be a straightforward question after all. Is it these ink stains on the page? Surely not, for then Bashō did not write it—the printer of this book, did. The poem would not even be a single object since there are thousands of copies. Could it be the original in Bashō's calligraphy? Surely not, for then in destroying the original, we would destroy the poem, which exists in thousands of copies. Similarly, it could not be a reading of the

---

[5] My rendering, based on the word for word translation and commentary of Robert Aitken, *A Zen Wave*, pp. 25-29.

poem either. Surely the poem exists even when no one on earth happens to be reading it. What, then, is the poem? Is it an idea in the poet's mind? Surely not, for Bashō is long dead, and we hardly need to countenance disembodied minds and/or ideas to make sense of poetry. So, what is the poem?

The poem is not in—or about—some kind of information conveyed, for what information does poetry convey? Or music, dance, or painting, for that matter? Art is not concerned with information, at least not in any straightforward sense. Art is, to follow the ideas above, concerned with revelation, with discovery, with the ground of thought. The poem is contained in the "the words you have dreaded and needed in order to know you exist," that you exist as a human being and not simply as yet another biological thing, a very sophisticated paramecium. Indeed, the poem—or the dance or the painting or whatever other else medium one may employ to express oneself—is the answer to both the need and the dread—which are, perhaps, identical. Nor are these dreaded words the Japanese words Bashō wrote on a page, for it is still the same poem, even in translation. The dreaded and needed words are spoken, not with the lips but with the heart, and the heart does not speak in information.

## Information vs. Expression

Information is something that we tell each other. Art is expression. Suppose I smash my finger with a hammer. I might do two things. I might scream with pain, or I might announce to all and sundry that it certainly hurt. The first is expressing my pain; the second is telling people about my pain. Suppose someone very dear to me dies. The doctor tells me that she has died; I might express my grief, weeping with the pain of it. If, in my grief, I say, "Why did she die?" I am not asking for information. "She had a massive heart attack," is not the correct answer. I am not asking what the cause of her death was; I already know that. I am asking for comfort, and so the correct answer is a silent embrace and a shoulder to cry on.

When I want to convey information, I tell people things. When I want to reveal something, I express things. Language is useful for both, but the way language works is very different when we express things than when we tell them. When we enter the realm of art, we leave behind the realms of telling (the doing universe) and enter the realm of expressing (the house of being). Art is the expression of a universal hidden within a particular, of that which is so very and strictly personal that it touches and reveals the core of our existence as human beings and calls us to realize our potential humanity.

Art is nobility within the realm of expression, and the aesthetic object is what we express. This is why a poem cannot be turned into a magazine article. I can tell you what it is to be human, at the level of information, but to express it, to reveal it to you, to share with you the depth and power of being human, I must write or read a poem—or sing or play the cello or dance or any artistic endeavor. I must express rather than tell; I must leave behind the world of doing (information) and enter the house of being (expression), and the measure of the truth of this expression is the power of the ice axe it wields.

## AESTHETIC KNOWLEDGE

An example of aesthetic knowledge deepening a person's humanity occurs in the 1993 film *Philadelphia*. The film tells the story of Andrew Beckett, a young gay lawyer played by Tom Hanks, whose employers fire him when they discover that he is gay and has AIDS. Beckett sues his former firm for wrongful termination, but no lawyer will take his case. Finally, Beckett approaches Joe Miller, played by Denzel Washington. At first, Miller is quite homophobic and afraid of AIDS, and he, too, refuses to take the case. But in a moving scene he realizes that anti-gay discrimination is of a piece with racial discrimination and changes his mind. He is still homophobic, but believes that the law must protect everyone, even people he happens to dislike.

As the film progresses, Miller's homophobia slowly lessens. Near the end, Beckett and his partner throw a party, and Miller and his wife attend. At the party, he sees gay and lesbian partners expressing their love for one another and begins to understand that it is the same love that he feels for his wife.

After the party, Miller and Beckett begin to go over Beckett's up-coming testimony. Beckett has a deep love of opera, and he has put on a recording of various arias. As they begin the discussion, Maria Callas begins to sing the aria "La Mama morta" from the opera *Andrea Chenier*. This is Beckett's favorite aria, and he interrupts their discussion to listen and explain it. Connected to an IV stand by tubes delivering drugs to him, Beckett translates the aria and explains what is happening in the opera. By the end of the aria, he is weeping for sheer beauty of the music and virtually dancing with the IV stand. Miller listens, at first with impatience, but as

Beckett get more and more deeply caught up in the music, Miller's face softens, and he begins to understand the depth of Beckett's humanity.

When the aria is finished, Miller has become decidedly uncomfortable and leaves hastily, but he is haunted by the memory of feeling Beckett's humanity. When he gets home, he goes into his baby daughter's bedroom, picks her up and embraces her. He then goes into his own bedroom, gets into bed, fully clothed, and embraces his sleeping wife. The scene closes with his being awake and feeling deeply what he has learned. His homophobia has melted way in the heat of this newly learned truth about love. He has come to love Andrew Beckett.

What has happened? As the film moved forward, Miller was primed to learn something, but it took Beckett's devotion to the music to open Miller's heart fully. Through gaining an expressive knowledge of the music, he came to understand something that he had not grasped before: that Presence[6] lives and moves within the hearts of homosexuals as surely as it does in his own heart and that therefore he must extend his love and protection beyond what he had thought possible. Aesthetic knowledge had deepened his humanity.

Another example from my own life also illustrates the related phenomenon of aesthetic arrest. I am especially fond of the paintings of Andrew Wyeth. The Brandywine Museum, near Philadel-

---

[6] As pointed out in the above, I prefer the term "Presence" to "God." Briefly, the word "God" has come to mean so many different and incompatible things that it's use almost guarantees being misunderstood. I experience this "more than something" as a presence in my life, and so I point to that presence with the word "Presence."

phia, houses a large collection of the Wyeth family paintings, and I make a point of visiting it whenever I can. On one of these visits several years ago, as I was walking through the galleries, I turned a corner and found myself face to face with a new painting that I had never seen. It is a portrait of Jesus wearing the crown of thorns. Instead of being the usual robust, clean, and Northern European Jesus of most paintings, this Jesus is exhausted, dirty, and definitely Semitic. One eye is partially closed by a thorn pushing on its lid. Jesus is looking out of the painting defeated and abandoned. The title of this painting is *Alone*.

I could hardly move. I stood in front of the painting for about ten minutes, utterly unaware of the people moving around me. When I finally tore myself away, I discovered that my cheeks were wet with tears. It is difficult for me to articulate what I learned from that painting. Indeed, if it could be articulated, Wyeth would not have had to paint it.

I now understand aloneness in a very different way than I had before discovering it. Being arrested by this painting changed my life by deepening my grasp of what it means to be alone and forsaken. It presented me with an artistic expression of existential aloneness. I experienced this as a kind of awakening, in the Buddhist sense of awakening. This new understanding of aloneness now permeates my life and motivates me to reach beyond, to transcend human isolation and the walls of fear that create that isolation and its companion aloneness.

This is the experience of aesthetic arrest, the experience of being frozen by a work of art. When we experience aesthetic arrest, we learn more about what it is to be human. In short, we encounter Knowledge in the form of artistic knowledge.

## ART COMPARED TO SCIENCE AND LOGIC

If science tells us about—describes—the empirical world, art expresses the emotional, moral, and spiritual world. Just as successful description is the measure of success in science, the measure of success of a work of art is its success as expression. Knowledge claims in science are based on success in telling; knowledge claims in art are based on success in expressing. Let us look at some of the implications of the difference.

As I pointed out in the last chapter, logic and science do not in depend on whom it is that happens to make the discovery. Information is, in this sense, objective. But art does depend on the artist because expression depends critically on who it is that doing the expressing.

Because the artistic way of knowing is an expressive way of knowing rather than a discursive way of knowing, the artist plays a crucial role in aesthetic knowing that is radically different than the role played by the logician, the mathematician, or the scientist. Only Bashō could write Bashō's haiku. It matters who wrote it, because the poem is *his* expression of what *he* knows in *his* bones about human—humane—life. It succeeds as art—expresses aesthetic truth—to the extent that his expression evokes *our* deeper understanding of what *we* know in *our* bones. Art assumes that there is a level of understanding and truth that we all share but which, by its very nature, cannot be told but only expressed by the artist. Aesthetic expression, then, lies in a relationship between an artist and an audience, and aesthetic truth emerges out of this relationship. Indeed, it can be argued that there is no genuine art without both artist and audience.

This leads to a further question: There is an important sense in which knowledge claims in formal systems cannot be overturned. If a proof is valid, then it is valid even when something else, something inconsistent with it, is true in a different formal system, like the logical systems I mentioned in the previous chapter. But knowledge claims in science can be overturned. Indeed, some believe that this is exactly what scientific investigation is about. What a scientist knows today may not be known tomorrow. Can knowledge claims be overturned in art? Can what one person expresses be contradicted by what another expresses.

Thought of as expressions, it would seem that aesthetic knowledge claims cannot be overturned. After all, it is hard to see how one expression—one poem, say, or one painting—could contradict or render another invalid. The point of different artistic expressions is not to contradict others or to compete with them, but to supplement them or enlarge the field of aesthetic expression and thus deepen our understanding of what it is to be human.

Think, for example, about radically different poems, say Basho's haiku above and "Beowulf." Does the one invalidate the other? Does the one render the other, in some important sense, false? Clearly not. Since both are valid artistic expressions, both speak from the depth of one human (the artist) to the depth of another human (the audience), even though they speak in very different terms.

By the same token, different aesthetic theories are not really in competition with one another. The aesthetics of the saga does not compete with or invalidate the aesthetics of haiku. One aesthetic might supplant another, as when Romantic aesthetics supplanted Enlightenment aesthetics, but it cannot render another invalid, just ineffective, or inappropriate to the cultural circumstances of the moment. But the truth expressed by, for example, Dryden or Pope is not overthrown by the truth expressed by Wordsworth or Keats any more than Schoenberg overthrows Brahms or Monet overthrows Gainsborough.

This is why it is critically important that we constantly create new art. The truths expressed by Dryden are not importantly different from the truths expressed by Wordsworth, but the adequacy and appropriate mode of their expression is different because culture is a living thing and changes. One might even say that one of the reasons culture changes is exactly because its artists have been effective in wielding the artistic ice axe. It dulls with repeated use and needs to be replaced or sharpened.

## FALSEHOOD IN ART

A closer look at the issue of falsehood, though, is important. I once talked about these issues with a colleague, and she objected that while she could understand what it would be for a telling to be false, she could not understand what it would be for an expression to be false. She could understand what it would be for a sentence to be false in a formal system or in science, but she could not understand what it would be for something to be false in art. But the possibility that something be true seems to require the possibility that it be false as well. So, what would falsehood be in art? What would a false poem be?

Looking at this slightly differently, consider. One can make a mistake in a proof and end up making a false knowledge claim: the supposed theorem doesn't follow after all. One can make a mistake in science and end up proposing a law that is false: the observation statements predicted from it do not describe the observable world. But how can one make a mistake in art? If we are talking about knowledge and truth, do we not need to make room for mistakes and falsehood?

A poem is false if it expresses something that the poet does not feel. It is not so much that the poem expresses something that I cannot share or that does not reveal myself to myself. It is rather that the poem, itself, is a kind of lie, and its expression is empty, devoid of artistic content. I am not talking about content in the sense of information but content in the sense of deeply held and felt revelation. One makes an artistic mistake (as distinct from a technical blunder, as, for example, when one uses a trite rhyme or a clichéd image) when one expresses falsely, when one's words are not, in fact, the words one needed and dreaded. Every artist has done this, usually inadvertently, though sometimes on purpose. It is inevitable, and it is why the first version of a poem, dance, symphony or painting is almost never the final version.[7] Great artists have no qualms about learning from these mistakes and then discarding them. Brahms destroyed scores by the score.

## ONTOLOGY IN ART

Within logic and science, existence claims have the same kinds of restrictions as knowledge claims. In fact, it might be argued that existence claims in logic and science are a kind of knowledge claim

---

[7] Consider, for example, Anne Lamott's advice in *Bird by Bird* to young writers to just sit down and write out that shitty first draft.

and so must have the same kinds of restrictions. What about art? What kinds of existence claims are made in art? Indeed, are there existence claims made in art? What would an aesthetic existence claim be?

We now see that aesthetic knowledge lies in a very different arena than science and logic. It lies in the arena of expression rather than the arena of telling. Aesthetic truth lies in the ability of a poem to express to us (or, perhaps, for us) the spiritually and morally human, as opposed to the ability to tell us something about the biologically human. Biology tells us what it is to be Homo sapiens; art expresses what it is to be Human.

This is what Cummings meant by coming into the immeasurable house of being. It is what Rich meant by writing as if your life depends on it, and what Lorde meant when she talked about poetry giving birth to the felt nameless and formless. It is Kafka's ice axe. Given this understanding of art, what kind of existence claims could possibly make sense in art? Art does not say that something exists; it expresses that existence. It does not describe existence; it does not say "This such-and-such is so-and-so." It expresses what that existence means, how that existence matters, not physically, but spiritually and morally.

Let us consider a specific poem, for example, this short section from T. S. Eliot's "Burnt Norton":

> At the still point of the turning world. Neither flesh nor
> fleshless;
> Neither from nor towards; at the still point, there the dance
> is,
> But neither arrest nor movement. And do not call it fixity,

Where past and future are gathered. Neither movement
from nor towards,
Neither ascent nor decline. Except for the point, the still
point,
There would be no dance, and there is only the dance.[8]

At a superficial level it may look as though he were claiming that the still point is real, and he even uses the locution "there is only the dance." But there is something much deeper going on here.

Eliot's idea is that human life is like a dance; we circle and circle about a certain center which is unchanging. Just as dance is movement and stillness, human life circles around this stillness at the center, occasionally even resting in it. It is this stillness at the center, at the core, that gives our lives vitality, strength, movement, beauty, meaning and all those things that we cherish, and which carry us beyond biology into humanity. Does Eliot claim that this core, this still point, is physically real? Clearly not since he is not *claiming* anything at all. This still point he talks about is not real like sealing wax, cabbages, and kings are real, nor is it real like numbers and constructible sets are real. Rather, he is expressing his experience of the profundity of human life, a profundity that feels more real and more substantial to him than simple biology.

It is as if he has found something that gives his life meaning and purpose, and instead of offering it to us, he is expressing for us what it means, how it fulfills him and brings his humanity out of hiding. The idea is not that the still point is a place located in time and space, or that it is something that is needed to make a

---

[8] T. S. Eliot, Collected Poems, 1909-1962, p. 177.

formal system operate. It is, rather, something that allows Eliot to know that he is a human being. These are words that Eliot "dreads and needs in order to know that [he] exists," (we might say words that Eliot needs in order to Know that he exists) not as a biological specimen but as something with moral and spiritual significance. This discovery births thought in him, thought to which he gives utterance and expression in the poem.

In a very important sense, when all is said and done, art does not make existence claims for the very good reason that it does make any claims at all. It is expressive, not discursive. When one starts claiming things, one leaves art. Claims convey information, and thus belong to the realm of telling, not expression. I conclude, then, that the relationship between epistemology and ontology seems to pertain to discursive knowledge only, not to expressive knowledge.

One might suppose that art expresses one simple statement: "It is possible to be human." I think, though, that even this is misleading. The Human Project is far more complex than this simple statement would suggest. There are far more ways to be human than any of us can dream of in our philosophies. Let us, then, rest content with the understanding that art assures us that there is more to humane life than biology, and it is therefore as essential to the Human Project as science or logic or mathematics. Without art, humanity withers into mere biology. Or, as a bumper sticker I rather like has it, "*Earth* without *art* is just *eh*."

# CHAPTER 4:

# Ways of Knowing: Religion

By now, I had realized that science, logic, and art, inasmuch as each advances the Human Project, is a species of Knowledge. Each is a separate way of Knowing, a way we experience and come to find our human place in the world. The next step for me was to understand how religion is also a way of knowing the world. If religion advances the Human Project, then it must be yet another specie of Knowledge. But does it advance the Human Project?

There are many who argue that on the contrary, religion not only does not advance the Human Project, but in fact it actually hinders it. They point to the atrocities that have been committed in name of religion from time immemorial as evidence for this claim. Without religion, we would not have the Hundred Years' War, the Inquisition, genocides without number, and so on. In view of this indisputable historical fact, how can anyone claim that religion advances the Human Project?

These people have a point. Yet I think they confuse the institution of religion from the very human impulse that gives rise to religion. The various institutions of religion are not religion. I think every human being feels, however dimly or denied, an impulse toward what is called religion, even though they may vehemently reject every religious institution. This is the truth behind the slogan "I am spiritual but not religious," I am not interested here in any specific religion, but in religion itself, religion as one of the core institutions of human culture. The first question, then, is what is necessarily shared by all religions, in virtue of which they *are* religions. (This question comes from my training in analytic philosophy.)

## WHAT IS RELIGION?

I began my considering these questions with a thought experiment. I supposed that I was an astronaut-anthropologist and was sent to a newly discovered planet that happens to have an advanced civilization. My mission is to understand and describe this civilization in terms that humans back on Earth will understand. Among other things, I'd need to look at the various institutions within that civilization and figure out how to describe them in human-like terms. Some of them would not be difficult. I could look at how they distribute goods and services and describe this in economic terms. I could look at how they regulate their society and make communal decisions and describe this in governmental terms. And so on.

What would I look for to describe their religion—or even to decide whether or not they have religion? I would need first to know what it is that makes religion "religious." The criteria I used would need to cast a web both wide enough and fine enough to capture the religions on earth from Animism to Zoroastrianism. This is clearly not a simple or straightforward task, but it is exactly what I need for this study.

One might initially be tempted to say that religion is about deity or the divine or, to revert to traditional language, God. One might think that religion is the social institution that concerns itself with that society's understanding of and relationship to God. Unfortunately, though, that is not even true on earth. The Buddha considered the question of God's existence to be irrelevant and carefully avoided engaging in that conversation. He said that such conversations are pointless and thus at best a distraction from his real message of the healing of human suffering. To this day, Buddhism is, for the most part, indifferent to questions of divinity[1]. Or consider Unitarian Universalism. While there are many Unitarian Universalists who do indeed accept some notion of divinity, there are also many who do not. Unitarian Universalism is not, in any straightforward sense, about divinity. Yet, both Buddhism and Unitarian Universalism are, as far as I can tell, quite clearly religions. So, it cannot be that it is concern about God that defines religion. It must be something else. What is that something else?

It is not an accident, I realized, that holiness, wholeness, and healing are not only etymologically related but are also central concepts to religion. I suggest that religion is about the healing of our human brokenness. It begins with the discovery that we are broken in our lives—every one of us, without exception. This brokenness is what The Buddha called the First Noble Truth: it is impossible to live through our lives without *dukkha*, usually rendered as "pain" or "suffering" and what I think of as existential aloneness. Religion is about how we face the fact of that aloneness. My astronaut-an-

---

[1] This is not strictly true. There are branches of Vajrayana, for example, that at least appear to have adopted and worship certain of the old Tibetan gods, and occasionally one encounters Buddhists of nearly all schools who revere The Buddha and certain Bodhisattvas as if they were gods. Yet it remains true that The Buddha himself dismissed talk of gods as irrelevant and very clearly described himself as nothing but an awakened human.

thropologist needs to look for those institutions within the alien culture that deal with becoming whole, *i.e.* with holiness.

## WHOLENESS, EGO, AND SPIRIT

So, I began to look more closely at this wholeness business. Consider the story of The Fall of Adam and Eve. In spite of what is often said about it, I suggest that, at its deepest, it is not at all about sexuality or even obedience. Loosely put, here is the story:

> God created a perfect environment—The Garden of Eden—and placed Adam and Eve within the garden. He told them that they could eat whatever they wanted with two exceptions. They could not eat of the fruit of the Tree of the Knowledge of Good and Evil or of the fruit of the Tree of Life, because, He told them that if they did, they would immediately die[2].

> All goes along fine until one day Satan comes along and suggests to Adam and Eve that they eat the fruit of the Tree of the Knowledge of Good and Evil. They point out that God had told them not to eat it because if they did, they would die. Satan replies that they won't die. God said that because He knew that if they ate that fruit, then they would become as wise as the gods themselves. So, Adam and Eve go ahead and eat it.

---

[2] It does seem odd that the eating of the fruit of the Tree of Life would prove fatal, but that another story.

And what happens? Satan seems to be right; they did not die. They suddenly realize, though, that they are naked. They make aprons to cover their nakedness. But, of course, an apron does not cover all of their bodies, but only their genital regions, the places where they are truly different from each other.

God comes along, and they hide. God says, "Where are you?" And Adam replies that they heard him coming and hid because they were naked and ashamed. This is correct enough, but it reveals to God that they must have eaten the forbidden fruit. And so He expels them from the garden forever.[3]

There is a reason that this story has become central to both Judaism and Christianity. It could be argued that the entire Torah and the Bible are about how to return to the Garden. I think that the story is about how we grow into a mature understanding of our spiritual journey and in that growing understanding come to realize an apparently uncrossable divide between ourselves as individuals—ourselves as ego—and ourselves as participants in one another—ourselves as spirit. It is not, then, about our sexuality, though it uses awareness of sexual differences mythically to make this point.

Our ego is that part of our personality that is concerned with our being separate and autonomous. It addresses the question "Who am I that is not all those other people and things out there?"

---

[3] For a more traditional version of this story, see the first three chapters of Genesis.

It begins when we are born, and the umbilical cord is severed. Suddenly we are no longer part of our mother's body. Now we must stand alone, for ourselves. We stop at our skin, so to speak, and begin to understand that we are different from the rest of the world. We are who we are; we are our self. This is the ego. Unfortunately, there is a catch to it.

All of a sudden, this wonderful ego discovers that it is not simply alone, but *unbearably* alone. The great triumph of the ego is the realization that it stops at the skin, and the great tragedy of the ego is the realization that it stops at the skin. It is as if the ego says to itself, "There are all those others out there, and they stop at their skins, too. Therefore, they cannot feel what I feel; they cannot know what I know or think what I think or even perceive what I perceive. It is a marvel that I can even communicate with them. And what about my death? If I stop at my skin, then I must live irreducibly alone, for my whole life, and then die alone forever."

This is Adam hiding from God. And when God asks Adam where he is, he gives the correct answer. It is not, "I'm over here up to my elbows in the bulrushes." God, being omniscient, knows perfectly well that Adam is up to his elbows in the bulrushes. The correct answer is "I heard you coming and was ashamed because I am naked, so I hid." What makes this the correct answer is that Adam confesses that he has realized that he is different from everything else, including God, and this condemns him to existential aloneness, isolation, separation, alienation, hidden from the great healing wholeness—holiness—that is God—or, in my language, Presence. And this is the answer every one of us must, at some point in our lives, give. We are different; we are separate; and we are alone.

At the risk of repeating myself, though our sexuality makes an excellent metaphor or image for difference, this story is not really about our sexuality. It is a story about our selves and what happens to every one of us as we live our lives. Consider these examples of existential aloneness:

- Your own ideas are so clear and obvious to you, but no matter how clearly you try to explain them to others or how obvious you try to make them, those others stubbornly fail to understand, let alone agree.
- Your discomfort, depression, frustration, or fatigue are so real and powerful to you, but no matter what you say to others, they just don't seem to understand your feelings.
- By the same token, no matter how hard you try, you cannot explain to someone how you love them. Words just don't do it, but what else is there?
- Turning things around, you want, perhaps desperately, to understand someone else's ideas or feelings, and you just can't seem to get it.
- Someone you love wrestles with clinical depression and is suicidal. All you want to do is to crawl inside of them and embrace that place where they are suffering and heal it, or at least make it stop hurting, but since you both stop at your skins, you can't.

The list goes on and on. Existential aloneness. Who is there who does not know the aching sense of being alone in the universe? And what would we think of someone who didn't?

It is at this point that we begin to discover spirit. If the ego is about how we are separate, then spirit is about how we are connected, joined, not separate. It answers the question, "Who am I that I am related to all those others out there?" It is the yin to the ego's yang. When we dwell in ego, we know that we are different; when we dwell in spirit, we know that we are related, joined, connected, that we dance with one another and that this dance creates an us, a togetherness, a unity.

Spirit, then, lives in love, the kind of love called *agape* in Greek and *ubuntu* in Zulu.[4] We live alone, to be sure, but not irreducibly alone, for we are also tied together as one whole being. And we will indeed die alone, but if we understand the spiritual truth that we are all one beneath the skin, then we die into love. What the Torah and the Bible offer us are answers to the question, "How can I live within spirit without rejecting my ego?"

Notice that I am *not* suggesting that either ego or spirit is in any way a disembodied being temporarily trapped somehow inside our flesh. Instead, they are ways of conceiving of our selves and of relating both to our selves and to the world. Both are essential to our understanding of how it is that we exist: we are separate, and we are connected. After all, it takes binocular vision to see depth.

Human brokenness is what happens when ego suppresses spirit. When ego takes over, it is triumphant, but ultimately it becomes terribly and tragically alone. This aloneness is human brokenness, existential aloneness, and it is the human condition. This is the Buddha's *dukkha*. As astronaut-anthropologist I need to look around and find whether these beings experience existential aloneness and if so, how they address it. Their religion is about the healing of their brokenness. This is why it is also about holiness,

---

[4] *Ubuntu* is the recognition that we become human as we realize more fully how we belong to each other.

*i.e.,* wholeness. Clearly, this healing allows us to move beyond the merely Homo sapiens and become more fully human, and thus religion offers us a species of Knowledge.

The heart of spiritual healing is the discovery that even though we are autonomous—and filled with a worth and dignity that is inherent in our hearts and souls—we are also linked together by that which we neither control nor determine and thus we are interdependent. A metaphor may help to understand how this can be. Consider the mycelium that joins the mushrooms in a fairy ring[5]. When viewed on the surface, the mushrooms appear to be separate; when viewed from underground they are connected by the mycelium and are thus joined. Imagine that we are joined by a kind of spiritual mycelium. Religion is the work of opening ourselves to the nurture offered by this spiritual mycelium and in that nurture discovering that we are not alone after all. What we so often feel as an irreducible aloneness is, in fact, but one way of seeing ourselves. We are broken when we turn our backs on each other and try to exist within the hubris of thinking that there is nothing greater than we[6].

## THE NATURE OF RELIGIOUS TRUTH AND KNOWLEDGE

These ideas became central to my thinking about religion. In this context, I use them now in order to understand the idea of re-

---

[5] A fairy ring is a circular growth of small wild mushrooms.

[6] The word *hubris* comes from a Greek word that means *wanton violence*. To fall into hubris is to commit an act of violence against oneself.

ligious truth and therefore religious knowledge[7]. It is common and uncontroversial to hear people speak about logical and empirical (scientific) truth. It may be a little more controversial but still fairly common to hear people talk about artistic truth. In addition, people talk about truth in religion as if it makes obvious sense. Some speak as if religious truth is somehow the ultimate and absolute truth, unchanging, eternal, and unquestionable. The ancient Christians— and many Pagans as well—talked about a special kind of religious knowledge they called *gnosis*, and many Protestant Christians talk about "the saving knowledge of Jesus Christ."

I began to ask myself, "What if I suppose that these statements are not just empty verbiage but actually say something? What if they make sense? What if they are expressing something important? What might that be, and where might assuming that they are important lead me?" They are clearly neither empirically nor logically true, and they do not appear to me to be aesthetic expressions. So, I had to ask myself how religion moves us along on the Human Project. As always, I began by looking at the word itself.

The etymology of the word *religion* is not entirely clear, but a common suggestion is that it may come from the Latin word *religāre*, which means *to tie fast*. Religion is the great tying together. This makes sense to me. It connects religious truth to my understanding of spirit. To become whole is to have the brokenness of the heart tied back together. Following the discussion of truth, then, religious truth is that which enables or fosters the healing of the heart. It is that which brings together into a coherent whole what can be thought of as the partedness of life. It is that which points us

---

[7] Where there is truth surely knowledge cannot be far behind.

back to Eden and shows the way home. Religious truth is the tool for the healing that makes religion religious. As St. Paul put it, "For now I know in part, but then I shall know even as I am known."[8] As the Buddha put it, "Know the truth and find peace."[9]

Both St. Paul and The Buddha are telling us something about what happens when we become whole again. We come to know something, and this knowledge changes us. Christians call this variously salvation or sanctification; Buddhists call it enlightenment. Christians speak of the forgiveness of sin, and Buddhists speak of awakening. It may appear as if they are talking about two very different things, but the difference seems to me to be far more linguistic than substantive. At bottom, both are talking about transcending existential aloneness and encountering that form of love that I understand as *ubuntu*, a love that testifies to Presence and reveals the depth and sacredness of relationship in the formation of a human being. This encounter with *ubuntu* is a life-changing event.

The sacredness of relationship is why Jesus equated love of God with love of neighbor and said that this love is the very essence of Torah. Religion is not about texts; it is about healing broken relationships. It is also why The Buddha said: "However many holy words you read, however many you speak, what good will they do you unless you act on them....Read as few words as you like and speak fewer but act on the law." This law is, "In this world hatred never yet dispelled hatred. Only love dispels hatred."[10] Hatred

---

[8] First Corinthians, Chapter 13, verse 12.

[9] Thomas Byrom, *The Dhammapada*, p. 7.

[10] Ibid, p. 4.

cannot dispel hatred because hatred has to do with enforcing separation and difference, driving apart that which is inherently whole. Hatred is concerned with the breaking of the human heart. Love dispels hatred because love has to do with bringing together into a whole that which belongs together, seeing as whole that which is whole. Hatred is violence; love is the healing of violence. Hatred endangers our humanity; love restores our humanity. Love is concerned with the healing of the human heart, and thus it is at the center of religious knowledge. To love, to embrace *ubuntu*, is to know religiously.

When a Christian says, for example, "I know that my redeemer liveth," what does he or she mean? This is clearly a knowledge claim, but equally clearly it is a radically different kind of knowledge claim than one finds in logic, science, or even art. "I know that my redeemer liveth" means "I have discovered healing for my existential aloneness in an equally existential understanding of Christian mythology. I have a deep and personal—a spiritual and existential—commitment to that mythology, and it lifts me from my ego into my spirit and makes me whole again. It binds me back together. This is *agape* [*ubuntu*], the love of God, and this knowledge is salvation."

Clearly this suggests an intimate connection between religion and art. If art gives expression to that which heretofore had been only a dimly perceived possibility and religion is that which brings forth a healing that can only be dimly grasped by the broken heart, then it is through art that the religious impulse gets its clearest and most profound expression. This is the beating heart of mythology. For the Christian it is the Christian mythology that expresses the possibility of human holiness—human healing—the possibility of living a human life standing under the Christian banner. For the Muslim it is Muslim mythology that expresses this possibility. For the Buddhist it is the Buddhist mythology, and so on for all religions.

By *myth*, of course, I do not mean the all too common and terribly shallow understanding of the word. I do not mean *misleading falsehood*, and I do not mean *unsophisticated unscientific attempt to explain the observable world*. When I use the word *myth*, I mean *religious knowledge expressible only through art*[11]. It is not an accident, after all, that most of the world's greatest religious geniuses have been storytellers and poets.

Jesus provides us with a good example. When he was asked which of the Laws is the most important, he replied that there are actually two, love God and love your neighbor. Then, when asked who our neighbors are, he thought a moment and said, "Well, there was a man going down along the Jericho Road who fell among thieves…" Jesus told a story. He could have said, "Everyone is our neighbor," but that would have missed the power of this truth as a religious truth. He would have missed the power of the story, the myth. In saying these words, that are true enough, he would have left out the words that we "dread and need in order to know that we are alive."[12] He would have left out the *religious* truth that he was teaching, leaving only a namby-pamby half-truth that has little or no healing power. And his message would likely have been forgotten.

---

[11] See, for example, Joseph Campbell's understanding of myth.

[12] Rich, op cit.

Lao Tzu also provides an example. *The Tao Te Ching* opens with this sentence:

The tao that we call "Tao" is not the Tao.[13]

He could have said, "Strictly speaking, you cannot name the Tao," and that would have been true enough. But this, too, would have missed the essential point. It would have missed the deeper truth that Lao Tzu was expressing. Instead, Lao Tzu began a poem. He dredged up the dreaded words he needed and wrote as if his life depended on it, and those words have had the power to heal for 2600 years, across both cultural and linguistic translation.

This is what mythology does, and this is why there is, always has been, and always will be such a profound relationship between religion and art. Indeed, it can be argued that art always begins in religion, even though typically it eventually branches away from the sacramental to live a life of its own.[14] One might even think of the relationship between art and religion as comparable to the relationship between logic and science. Knowledge in logic and science is essentially propositional, "knowledge that." Knowledge in art and religion is not propositional but transcendental, knowledge that carries us beyond our present state. It is, if you like, "knowledge of."

---

[13] The translation is mine, as are all passages I quote from the *Tao Te Ching*.

[14] Some would turn this around, saying that religion began in art. These origins are indeed tangled and so lost in the mists of history that we will probably never know which gave birth to which. The question of priority is not important for my purposes, though. The important point to note is the fact that art and religion are intimately related.

## How Religious Knowledge Is Like and Not Like
## Scientific and Logical Knowledge

Another way to think of this is to consider the difference in belief. Knowledge implies belief. To know in logic and science is to believe *that* something is true. To know in religion is to believe *in* something. In the primary sense at least, one does not believe *in* Newton's Laws of motion; one believes *that* they are true. On the other hand, one does not believe *that* Jesus' teachings heal existential aloneness; one believes *in* the healing power of Jesus' teachings.

The confusion between these two essentially different sorts of knowledge has led to enormous confusion and suffering, especially between science and religion. It has led some people to assume that religion is bad science and others to assume that science is destructive of religion. Neither is true, though far too often people act as if it is and tragically reject the truths offered by one or the other. Some comparisons of the differences are in order and will show how mistaken such a confusion really is.

In science there is an agreed upon standard of knowledge—or at least an agreed upon standard of discovery. Do the crucial experiment. It either does or it does not verify the law in question. If it does, then we have to deduce further observation statements and see if they, too, are true. If it does not, we have to modify or even abandon the law. Everyone (at least everyone who understands the scientific method) agrees with the procedure and, eventually, with the results. If I measure the amount of energy released when matter is "destroyed" and it consistently turns out to be different from Einstein's prediction, then Einstein is wrong.[15] Period. End of discussion.

In the actual world of scientific investigation, of course, things are not often this straightforward. Conceptually, though, this is what's going on. Sometimes the difference between what is observed and what is predicted leads to adjustments and tinkering, and sometimes to wholesale revisions and even the abandonment of heretofore widely accepted laws. The point, though, is that there is an accepted standard that all agree upon and that leads ultimately to consensus, even though the road to consensus is often rather rocky. Nothing even remotely comparable happens in religion.

Religious truth represents success in the religious task, which is to say it brings healing to broken lives. One of the things that characterizes liberal religion is the realization that efficacy is not owned by one and only one religious tradition. The more conservative one is the more likely one is to claim that salvation—or enlightenment, or sageliness, or whatever else one may call it—is to be found only in one tradition, namely, one's own.

I would argue that claims of religious efficacy must be understood autobiographically—they are about the life of the claimant—in spite of the fact that they often appear prescriptive—that they prescribe the mythology that others ought to embrace. It seems patently obvious that if, for example, Buddhism did not heal broken hearts in some very important sense it would not have survived for 2600 years. And if Buddhism works, then, for exactly the same reason, so do Islam, Judaism, Hinduism, Christianity, *etc.* The objective efficacy of the various religious traditions—and therefore at

---

[15] Or there is something wrong with my experimental design or equipment.

one important level also their truth—is not what determines which of them I might embrace, and this is represents a very different standard than one finds in science.

I am not free to choose among competing sets of scientific laws in anything like the way I am free to choose among religious systems. I am simply not free to choose, say, the phlogiston model of heat or the ether theory of electromagnetism. I am, though, completely free to choose Buddhism or Christianity, or any other religion that works for me[16]. Our choice among religious systems is idiosyncratic in ways that choice among empirical systems can never be.

Religious knowledge is, in this regard, more like logical and mathematical knowledge, though there are important differences between religious knowledge and logical knowledge even in this regard. As I argued above, I certainly can choose which of various systems of logic or mathematics I will work in. In set theory, for example, some logicians choose to restrict themselves to constructible sets and some do not. This choice is not based on formal considerations, i.e. the consistency and coherence of the system in question, but on what are essentially philosophical considerations. Those who restrict themselves to constructible sets do not think it is legitimate to claim existence for a set that one does not actually know how to construct. Thus, they will not accept indirect proofs of existence theorems. This does not mean that they think that such proofs are not *logically* valid. Quite obviously they are. It means

---

[16] Note that this is not the absurd claim one hears occasionally in Unitarian Universalist circles that one can believe anything one wants. It is the assertion that one is free to embrace—believe in—the religious mythology that actually does heal one's brokenness.

that they think that such proofs are *philosophically* suspect.

The difference between the choice among formal, logical systems and the choice among religious systems is this: the choice among logical systems is a philosophical, an *intellectual*, matter, but choice among religious systems is an *existential* matter. Philosophical considerations are idiosyncratic in a sense, but they are also public and intersubjective. I can be convinced by someone's philosophical argument. Choice among religious systems is not a matter of philosophy so much as it is a matter of personal commitment. One is rarely, if ever, argued into choosing a religious system. Rather, one chooses a religious system on the basis of personal experience. Thus, religious choice is idiosyncratic in a far more robust sense.

This realization led me to the obvious question of whether or not the truths of one religious system are actually compatible with the truths of another, the other side of which is the question whether one religion can contradict another. If the acceptance of a religion does not depend on intersubjective criteria but on an inner commitment to its mythology and is, in this sense, autobiographical, then the various religions are not contradictory in spite of their very real differences in worship practices, scriptures, mythologies, *etc.* What can happen (and does happen with truly distressing regularity) is that one religion insists that it has a monopoly on ways of healing the heart and soul.

Such a claim is pretty clearly false. Buddhism works; it heals broken hearts and relationships and moves people into becoming more Human. Christianity also works. Judaism works. Taoism works. Religious Humanism works. And so on. Genuine religion works. It is absurd to suggest that until Jesus or The Buddha or Mohammed or whomever else, there was no genuine religion in the world and that it sprang full-blown at one and only one point in space and time. It is just not a question of who has the "right" religion. It is a question of which religious system works in this cultural context, at this time, with these people.

Occasionally one hears arguments among scholars of comparative religion about whether or not, say, salvation (Christian) and enlightenment (Buddhist) are the same thing in other words. In one sense, they are clearly different, because what heals a Christian—brings a Christian to stand under the vision of his/her wholeness—is not the same thing that heals a Buddhist. The language is different; the cultural context is different; the attendant mythology is different; the cult and worship are different. If I may borrow a metaphor, the Christian sees the moon sighting along one finger (The Christ) and the Buddhist along another (The Buddha). In a very important sense, then, they are different.

On the other hand, it seems to me equally correct to point out that both The Christ and The Buddha point to the same moon.[17] At the same time, then, the teachings of Jesus and The Buddha do not seem to be all that different after all. The holiness that they both reveal is the same holiness, even though they talk about that holiness in vastly different ways and understand (intellectually) holiness differently. Why does it matter how one achieves this healing, so long as one achieves it? Why does it matter which finger one sights along so long as one sees the moon of healing? Beyond

---

[17] See, for example, Thich Nhat Hanh's book *Living Buddha, Living Christ*. There are also some very interesting recent conversations across religious lines searching out the common threads that unite them rather than the differences that separate them. See, for example, *The Ground We Share*, by Robert Aitken and David Steindl-Rast.

autobiography, why does it matter in what mythic language one is most comfortable talking about the holiness of life? The important thing is not so much how one understands holiness intellectually but how (and whether) one stands under holiness. It is the difference between understanding (an intellectual stance) and standing under (a commitment stance).

None of this should be surprising. The wholeness that religion brings people springs from a level of experience and reality to which the Law of the Excluded Middle simply does not apply. Thus, the opening sentence of the *Tao Te Ching*, and thus the prohibition against uttering the name of God. Since God cannot be named trying to do so is to fall into idolatry. Therefore, a specific religion can but point to holiness with the finger of its mythology. One myth cannot contradict another any more than a symphony can contradict a painting, or a Japanese haiku can contradict a Norse saga.

## SOME FAMILIAR QUESTIONS

Asking myself some of the same questions that I've previously explored in earlier chapters, I considered first whether or not religious knowledge is dependent on or independent of the knower. In logic and science, it does not matter who knows, or who discovers the knowledge. Who cares whether Kurt Gödel or I first proved the theorem? Who cares whether or Einstein or Marilyn Monroe first proposed General Relativity? In art, on the other hand, it matters critically who the artist is. Only Dylan Thomas could write Dylan Thomas' poetry, and no one but Beethoven could write his symphonies. Art can be imitated but it cannot be duplicated. So, what about religion? Does it matter who knows in religion?

Beyond the vagaries of charisma, personal style, and cultural readiness, it really doesn't seem to matter whether it was Siddhartha Gautama or someone else who sat under the Bodhi Tree and received Perfect Enlightenment. Anyone could have done it—he said so himself. Siddhartha Gautama's actual existence does not even seem important. It is the teachings and the practice that are important, not the person.

Does Jesus' message depend in some important way on the historic, flesh and blood Jesus, the individual man living in Judea at the beginning of the first century of the Common Era? Suppose someone were to discover definitively that Jesus never lived. Would that make a difference in the power of Christian message to heal? It certainly would for some people, because it seems terribly important to some that Jesus actually lived, died, and was physically resurrected.

This may be the test case because if it matters that it was Jesus, this particular person, who founded Christianity, then maybe it matters in some way that I do not understand that it was Siddhartha Gautama who founded Buddhism. So, I looked at this carefully. Why should it matter that Jesus, the young carpenter from Nazareth, was The Christ? Would Christianity be as powerful a mythology had The Christ not been Jesus of Nazareth but John the Baptist instead? Is it because there was something about this specific person and his having lived that saves? Is it because it is easier for some people to commit themselves existentially to the mythology if they also believe that the object of the myth actually lived? I think that it is the latter and that therefore the issue is really more about the believer rather about than the founder. Christians do not believe (religiously) *that* Jesus lived. Rather, they believe *in* the living Jesus. In any event, it seems to me that this is the only case in which it might matter who the founder actually was.

Then I thought about both Taoism and Hinduism. Most scholars have serious doubts that Lao Tsu was a real person. Most Taoists, though, don't much care. Whether he existed or not, we have the book, and we have the practice. There was no single founder of Hinduism, no one even remotely close to a Jesus or a Mohammed. Therefore, it cannot matter who brought the inspiration, the message, the release form samsara of Hinduism. Everyone knows that while Arjuna was a real person, *The Bhagavad Gita* is a made-up story, an historical novel, if you will. Yet it carries a healing message to those who can hear it in the pages.

It does not seem to matter, then, at least as a philosophical generalization, who the original religious knower is. It does not matter whether it was Siddhartha Gautama or Thich Nhat Hanh or even me who sat under the Bodhi Tree and received Perfect Enlightenment. That it happened to be that specific individual in about 650 BCE is an accident of history. We are all capable of Perfect Enlightenment. So, the religious knowledge brought by a spiritual leader does not seem to be dependent on who that spiritual leader was or even whether or not they actually lived. It could be anyone, just as it could be anyone who first proposed General Relativity. In this sense, religious truth and knowledge is not dependent on the knower, and I conclude that at this level at least, religion is more like logic and science than it is like art.

But that's not the whole story. At another level, while it may not matter who the original knower was or even if there was a single original knower, it does seem to matter who the current knower is. At the level of the individual believer it matters a great deal, because no one can heal another. My salvation is tied uniquely to me. My enlightenment is mine and cannot belong to another, which suggests that religious knowledge is also highly individual. The Buddha said,

> No one purifies another. Never neglect your work for another's however great the need. Your work is to discover your work and then, with your whole heart, to give yourself to it.[18]

I might be initiated into religious knowledge, but because the brokenness in my life is *my* brokenness and cannot be shared by another, the healing knowledge that *I* gain and that heals *my* brokenness is also uniquely mine.

If my enlightenment is tied in some very special way to me, then my religious knowledge is very different from my knowledge of General Relativity. Scientific knowledge can be transmitted; religious knowledge cannot. All that can be transmitted is a method for achieving it. This suggests that, while scientific knowledge is totally independent of the knower, religious knowledge is independent only when seen from a larger perspective, in the macrocosm. In the microcosm, in the heart of the individual, religious knowledge belongs uniquely to the enlightened. Thus, "No one purifies another."

Consider the Four Noble Truths of the Buddha:

---

[18] Byrom, Op cit, p. 62.

1. Life is filled with *dukkha*[19];
2. *Dukkha* is created by attachment;
3. It is possible to be freed from attachment and thus from *dukkha*;
4. The path of freedom lies along the Eightfold Way.[20]

Why—or how—are these true? Buddhists sometimes speak as if they are empirical truths, but I don't think so. At the very least, this "empirical" is different from the empiricism of science. What is called for is knowing these truths in a way that is radically different from knowing that, say, $E = mc^2$.

The Buddhist is not concerned at all with one's ability to speak the Noble Truths with the lips. Any fool can do that. Enlightenment is not memorization. And the Buddhist is not interested in one's ability to manipulate the Noble Truths or to predict new observation statements based on them. It is not in any way a matter of externals. And the Buddhist does not depend on someone else verifying or falsifying enlightenment. Instead, the Buddhist is interested in the words that are spoken, not publicly, but privately, in the heart, and in the way that this knowing, these heart-words, change one's life. This is clearly and in principle not a public matter. It is not an intersubjective thing, but something that is purely within the individual and cannot be transmitted to another.

What, then does the Buddha do for us? The Buddha helps us

---

[19] Dukkha is a word that has no easy equivalent in English. It is often translated as pain or suffering, though that is somewhat misleading. It has the sense of spiritual suffering. I think of it as the suffering, even sometimes despair, that accompanies what I have called existential aloneness.

[20] The Eightfold Way is Buddhist spiritual practice.

to be in a situation in which enlightenment, purification—religious knowledge—becomes possible. The Buddha helps us to set ourselves up so that religious knowledge becomes apparent and explodes upon us and heals us. But, as the koan says, "If you see the Buddha on the road, kill him." If you depend on the Buddha to give you anything, then you have fallen into yet more attachment. The point is that one must not be attached to anything, not even the Buddha, not even enlightenment itself. Thus, the Buddha tells us, "the raft is not the shore,"—the vehicle of enlightenment is not enlightenment. "The tao we call 'Tao' is not the Tao."

## RELIGION AND ONTOLOGY

Finally, I considered the ontology that follows from this epistemology. Think about the claim, say, that God exists. What are we to make of such a claim? Evidently this is a very different claim than the claim that, say, non-constructible sets exist, or the claim that quarks and queens, kegs and kings exist. It is even a different kind of claim than the artist's expression. The claim that God exists, when it is not simply a reporting of one's theological stance; it is an alignment with, or a commitment to, a certain mythology. It is a standing under; it is an existential commitment.

Again, we see the importance of the distinction between telling and expressing. The claim that God exists is not telling us anything about the furniture of the world. God is not to be included in the list of everything that is, our old, familiar list that includes neutrinos, sealing wax, cabbages, kings, and maybe even non-constructible sets. The assertion of God's existence is a part of a religious mythology. Therefore, it does not assert that God is in the list of things that exist; it asserts that the speaker is committed to a particular mythology. And since mythology is a form of art, it expresses rather than tells. We see, again, the intimate connection between religion and art. The major difference is that in art, the whole thing lies in the expression, whereas in religion, the expression is but a tool serving the deeper need for healing.

Notice that the apparently opposite claim that God does not exist is also not a claim about the furniture of the world. It is also a commitment to a kind of mythology, one that may or may not be religious. The atheist who denies the existence of God is not telling me anything; they are expressing how and where they find—or perhaps do not find—the wholeness (which in more conventional theological langue would be called "the holiness") of life. It follows that these two statements, that God does exist, and that God does not exist, are not, in spite of appearances, contradictory. How could the expression of the religious insight of one person contradict the expression of the religious insight of another? They cannot, just as two poems cannot contradict each other. Instead, the expression of these insights is autobiographical rather than prescriptive. That the Buddhist does not find healing in Jesus' ministry, message, or mythology does not contradict the Christian's finding it. Or vice versa. My autobiography cannot contradict your autobiography.

## Coda

Religious belief is belief, or faith, in a deep existential commitment to a mythology, and the commitment to this mythology moves us from brokenness to wholeness, from alienation to relationship, from ego to spirit. This is what it is to know religiously. This epistemology is the foundation of the metatheology for Part II. It is also the crux of understanding how to break the circle of hatred that stands behind, for example, racism.

It is all about *ubuntu*. *Ubuntu* makes us human beings and moves us beyond the isolation of simple ego-centered separation into an unfolding and fuller life of spiritual connection. It is not something that comes all in one flash, like a lightning strike. To be sure, there are flashes of deep insight and liberation that sometimes strike like lightening. But if one's religious experience stops with that flash, something dies. As Buddhists insist, enlightenment is not an event but a process. The Buddha continued his spiritual practice even after his enlightenment because even he was not finished.

Religion is not something that one gets and is then finished with and can go on to something else. Religion does not immunize us from broken-heartedness. Surely the point of Buddhist practice is not to turn The First Noble Truth into The First Noble Falsehood. It is rather to show how to transcend the brokenness of life that is, in any event, inevitable. As the Chinese say, "After Enlightenment, the laundry"; after Enlightenment, the First Noble Truth is still true. The Christian version of this is the observation that Christians are not perfect; they are forgiven—again and again and again.

The point is that we grow into a constantly deepening *ubuntu*. The metaphor of concentric circles is helpful. We begin fully immersed in isolation and existential aloneness and begin to move outward, expanding our ability to express ubuntu and live our lives standing under Presence. It moves to immediate family, to extended family, to cohort, to those who seem to be like us, to our nation, to all humanity, and some few manage to expand the circle to embrace all sentient creatures. This is Buddhahood.

The goal of total embrace within *ubuntu* is best thought of, perhaps, as one of those teleological[21] ideals that draw us onward, ever beyond us yet giving us the impetus and determination to move onward. This goal is nothing less than the Bodhisattva Vow, the vow to follow the Buddha ideal of putting off entry into the perfect enlightenment of Nirvana until all sentient beings are enlightened. And one makes this vow even while knowing that total fulfillment is not possible.

Such ideals are like the hills on the horizon that beckon the explorer ever onward to see what has not yet been seen. Precious few, if any outside of mythology, ever actually achieve this goal, and even those few that do must continue the effort to hold that love in their hearts. It is said that Kwan Yin, the Bodhisattva of Compassion, wept because even she could not bring enlightenment to everyone.

Total success is not the point. The point is to achieve whatever success one is capable of. In this way it is again like art. Several years ago, after retiring, I began to take singing lessons at the age of 64. Whatever might have been possible had I begun learning to sing as a child, it is clear that I will never be able to sing at a professional level. But even though I will never be more than a mediocre singer, a high level of singing stands in front of me. Achieving it, though, is not the point. The point is to learn to sing as well as I am able to sing at this point in my life, holding the ideal as motivation and example. The surest way to miss achieving world-class artistic

---

[21] "Teleological" comes from the Greek word *telos*, which means "end," "goal," or "result." Thus, a teleological ideal is one that points us to a goal.

achievement is to aim at it. Knowing what is possible for some to achieve, one creates the deepest art one is capable of and lets world-class-ness take care of itself.

In the same way, knowing that Buddhahood is within everyone, I work for the deepest realization I can achieve, and let Buddhahood take care of itself. Knowing that salvation is available to all, I work to achieve whatever reconciliation with God—Presence—I can achieve, and let salvation take care of itself. Knowing that there is no Golden Age of the Future, I hold the ideal of justice and freedom in my heart and work for whatever level of social justice I can actually achieve, guided by a realistic vision of what is possible. This knowing is not the knowing of logic, science, or art. It is the knowing of religion, a knowing that emerges out of faith, out of deep and existential trust.

Logic, science, art, and religion are all different ways of knowing the world in which we live. But they differ from one another, because each represents a different way we move along the trajectory from merely biological creatures to human beings. This is the outline—the framework—for my epistemology. With this epistemology in mind, I now turn my attention to the structure of religion—the scaffold, if you will, upon which it is built. Putting the hat of my astronaut-anthropologist back on, I ask myself how religions are constructed. What is the framework they all depend on?

# Embracing Presence

# PART II:
# Why Do You Believe That?

## TOWARD A METATHEOLOGY

"By your faith you are made whole."
—JESUS OF NAZARETH

# PROLOGUE III:

# From Academia to Ministry

Shortly after I arrived at CIT, I began attending a Presbyterian church that was within walking distance. The church building itself was rather cold and the members were somewhat distant, but since I found the preaching to be stimulating and the music to be satisfying, I continued going.

As many churches did, this church scheduled a memorial service to coincide with Kennedy's Requiem Mass. I went, expecting some solace and comfort, some resolution to my turmoil. I found nothing of the sort. Instead of comfort, I found mere simplistic formalism. Instead of a sharing of grief and horror and anger, I found an empty emotionlessness. Instead of groping toward understanding, I found smugness. Years later, after 9/11, I would remember this and try to do better.

I walked out of the church asking myself, "What the Hell was that all about?" All I had received was smug and formulaic cant. There was nothing to address the sorrow, or confusion, or anger, or fear, or any of the other emotions I was feeling. I never returned to that church. There was nothing for me there, and that led me to wonder whether there was nothing for me in Christianity anymore.

At Christmas break, I looked at the Apostles' Creed, which was recited every Sunday at the church I grew up in, and I realized that I could no longer, in good conscience, repeat it. I simply did not believe it. I did not believe that Jesus was divine. I did not believe that he was bodily resurrected. I did not believe in a Trinitarian theology. When I went to church with my parents, I stood with the congregation but did not speak.

The following summer I looked again at the Confession of Faith to which I had given assent when I joined the church seven years earlier and realized again that I could not give assent to any of the articles of faith that it contained (none of which do I remember any longer). I wrote a long letter of resignation from the church that examined each article in detail and explained why I could no longer give assent to any of them.[1]

But what I had left back in 1963 was Christianity, not religion. Shortly after I resigned from my childhood church, the woman I was dating and eventually married (Marnie Singer) introduced me to Unitarian Universalism, and it made perfect sense. Here was a religion in which I was not told what to believe but was encouraged to discover for myself what I actually did believe. At least that was the rhetoric of it; the practice of it, I discovered, did not always live up to the rhetoric as well as one might hope. (But then human institutions rarely always live up to their own rhetoric.) I soon began to think of myself as a Unitarian Universalist, though I did not join any church.

By the early 1970s, Marnie and I were married, had two young daughters, and were living in Edwardsville, Illinois. One evening I was driving a babysitter home, and the conversation turned to, of all things, religion. I remarked that we were not members of any church but thought of ourselves as Unitarians. She exclaimed, "So

---

[1] A few years later, I found out that my letter was used by that church as the core of an Adult Religious Education class.

are we!" As luck (or fate or something) would have it, there was a small Unitarian Universalist church in Alton, IL, about 20 miles north of Edwardsville, and our babysitter was active in the youth group.

Less than a week later, she called us and asked if we would be willing to chaperone a youth overnight at the church. Marnie and I had been talking about wanting to start our daughters in a religious education program, so we agreed. And that got us back to church. The Alton church did not have many young children, and so its Religious Education program was too minimal to meet our needs. So, after about six months, we began attending the St. Louis church instead. It was a bit farther away (about 30 miles) but had a much larger religious education program.

One Sunday we were driving home from church, and I was complaining about how uncomfortable I was as an academic. Marnie thought a minute and said, "Well, when you were in high school, you considered becoming a Presbyterian minister. Why not become a Unitarian Universalist minister?" Though the idea had not occurred to me, it was such an obviously correct suggestion that that it hit me like the proverbial ton of bricks. In the fall of 1976, I entered Starr King School for the Ministry, the Unitarian Universalist seminary in Berkeley.

One day in a class I was taking in seminary we sat for a time in meditation. I suddenly felt a deep need to find a way to reconcile science and religion, and I realized that the key to reconciliation would be to find a way to make scientific knowledge and religious knowledge compatible. But I had no idea how to do that.

## MINISTRY

I graduated from Starr King in 1979 and was ordained May 20, 1979. Over the years, I served seven churches, though twice I served two churches simultaneously, each less than full time. These churches were in Durham, North Carolina; Lynchburg, Virginia; Burke, Virginia; Gaithersburg, Maryland; Philadelphia, Pennsylvania; Palo Alto, California; and Santa Barbara, California. All were in transition in one way or another, and four were in deep crisis. My ministry, especially with those four, was to heal and move them through their transitions to a healthy and stable place.

It was rewarding, if difficult, work, and it took its toll. By about 2003 I began to notice that every year when vacation time came around, I was more exhausted than the year before and when vacation was over, I was less rested than the year before. This, I realized, was not sustainable, and I began to think seriously about retirement, even though I was only 58.

As I thought about retirement, I began to think that there were three things that I needed to be in place before retirement would be feasible. The first, and most obvious, is that the money had to be there. I could not retire unless my wife (Anne Anderson) and I had enough invested to sustain us through the next 25 or 30 years. After the deaths of our parents, we thought that we had enough.

The second requirement was that I had to know what I was going to do in retirement. Otherwise, I would simply be bored and want to go back to work. In 2003 I had only a vague notion of what I wanted to do, and a vague notion is not good enough. I needed a concrete plan, so I began to think my way to that.

The third requirement was that I had to be done with ministry, or at least parish ministry. If I still felt called to the parish, I would ache to go back to it. In 2003, I still felt called to ministry even though I knew that retirement was beckoning. I wasn't sure how I would know when I was done with the parish, but I did begin to pay attention.

Over the next few years requirements two and three began to come into focus. What did I want to do in retirement? Two things began to present themselves. The first was that I wanted to write; the second was that I wanted to deepen my spiritualty.

Several writing projects presented themselves. First, I wanted to organize some of my poetry into books. This led to two small volumes, *Full Circle*, which is a collection of sonnets, and *How To See Deer*, a collection of poems in various forms. The next project has to do with my family's history of slaveholding and involvement in Jim Crow.

Both sides of my family are Southern, my father's ancestors having come to the Virginia Colony in about 1655, and my mother's ancestors having come to Jamestown in 1609. My nuclear family in Delaware was the farthest north that any had branch of either family but one had lived. I had heard vague references to a Collier plantation somewhere near Hampton, VA, but no one had ever talked about our having been slaveholders. I began to feel an increasing need to find out the truth of our family's involvement in slavery. This culminated in my book, *The Great Wound: Confessions of a Slaveholding Family.*[2]

The third emerged from my memory of realizing in seminary that the way to reconcile science and religion is to create a new

---

[2] All three of these books are self-published and are available from me directly or through Amazon.

epistemology that could accept knowledge in both spheres without conflict. As I thought about that and reviewed some of my writing over the years, I realized that I have been unconsciously wrestling with this for years, and I was beginning to have a solution. The result is this book.

And finally, I am deeply influenced by both Taoism and Zen, and I have been sitting zazen more or less regularly since about 1997. I knew that I want to let go of the less and embrace the more, but I also knew that I needed more than just that. I have been reading the *Tao Te Ching* since the 1970s and have thought of it as my scripture. But I cannot read Mandarin, and so I also knew that, since I had to depend on translations, there was much in the book that I was missing. I also knew that it was unlikely that I would ever become fluent enough in Mandarin to read the book in the original, and that had been a source of frustration.

Then in 2001, Jonathan Star published a character-by-character literal translation, and I discovered his work in about 2003. "Do you suppose," I asked myself, "I could use that to give myself, not really a translation, but a rendering of the book?" That would probably not be possible while serving a large church, as I was then, but maybe I could work on it in retirement. And so, requirement two came into focus.

One more retirement project presented itself all unexpectedly after my actual retirement: learning to sing. For now, suffice it to say that it has changed the way I understand who I am. I sang in the church choir for about 10 years, and that singing became the focus of my corporate worship.

That left number three. Somewhere around 2004, I began to feel a kind of restlessness in my ministry. It was not exactly that I was bored with it or that it had become too easy. It was something else, something that I could not quite put my finger on. It was not unlike the feelings I had when I was trying to be a physicist while knowing in my heart that I would never be a scientist. And so, I decided to sit with that restlessness and see where it would take me. Eventually I began to realize that I was increasingly just going through the motions. My heart was not really in it anymore, and I was not giving my congregation the ministry that they deserved. I was done with parish ministry.

The three requirements were in place, and in 2007 I retired. I have not regretted that decision, though there were some anxious moments. Two are worth mentioning. The first was when I realized that I could not reasonably afford COBRA, yet I was three years away from Medicare. I had to join the ranks of the medically uninsured. But I was healthy enough to make it through to 65.

The second was the Great Recession of 2008-2009. It hit with full force just a few months after Anne and I had committed ourselves to a major remodeling project. It was a serious worry, and we did lose about a third of the value of our investments. But we had good financial advice, and we weathered that storm reasonably well. And the remodel project went ahead.

## Convergence
### The Writing River

By the time I entered college, I had pretty much given up on writing poetry. Even I saw that what I was writing was not really poetry at all, but simply re-arranged prose, so why not just stick with the prose? I did. A few attempts at writing short stories followed. They were an interesting experiment, but never really went anywhere. They did reveal a bit of talent for description, however, and that was something worth knowing.

I also pretty much gave up on ever being able to produce music, though I did not give up my love of music. In those days The Pittsburgh Symphony played in a hall that was within walking distance both Pitt and CIT, and they offered a very good deal on season tickets to students. I jumped at the opportunity both times I lived in Pittsburgh. That fed my love of music, but I still ached to be able to sing.

The University of Pittsburgh had (and I assume still has) an excellent university bookstore, and I used to hang out there quite a lot. One of the unusual sections was an entire room devoted to arts books. One day when I was in graduate school, while perusing the books there, I ran across Donald Keene's two anthologies of Japanese literature.[3] They begin with selections from oldest collection of Japanese poetry, the *Manyoshu*, and continue up to the mid-twentieth century. I bought both volumes and was hooked. It took me several months, but I read both anthologies cover to cover. I was especially taken by the short forms: *tanka*, a mere thirty-one syllables and which dominated Japanese poetry for centuries, and haiku, which became the poetry of Zen.

The impact of Keene's anthologies has turned out to be much larger than I imagined at the time. First, it re-ignited my wanting to write poetry, this time using a Japanese model. I did not really understand the model, though, and actually just stumbled along.

---

[3] Donald Keene, Anthology of Japanese Literature, and Modern Japanese Literature.

Years later, I would adopt a short, evocative form of English poetry that was inspired by the short Japanese evocative verses I read in Keene's anthology. It was these poems, few of which were actually successful, that opened to door to English poetry for me. Second, Japanese culture is steeped in a Buddhist sensibility, and this literature became an introduction to the Buddhism that years later came to direct my spiritual life and practice.

There are a lot of professions in which writing is an essential component, and ministry is one of them. We write sermons, prayers and meditations, weddings and memorials, newsletter articles, and all manner of other things. For some ministers this is something to be put up with, a necessary unpleasantness, but for me it was a necessary joy. It was one of the parts of ministry that I truly loved. Before long, I found myself writing my meditations and prayers in the form of poetry. The Japanese-like poems that I had been playing with earlier turned out to be too short, but I persisted and turned to longer forms, eventually settling on sonnet-length poems as the appropriate length.[4]

## The Music River

A mentor of mine once remarked that worship floats on a sea of music. Even though I was unable to sing at all well and could not play any instrument, I believed (and still believe) that he was right. I used to craft my services on a pattern of alternating words and music, and I worked as closely as I could with my church musicians.

---

[4] Several of these sonnets are in *Full Circle*.

I sang (very poorly) by myself, wishing I could sing better but assuming that I never would. For my entire ministry, my inability to sing was, at best, an embarrassment to me. There were times when the sound tech would forget to turn off my mike when we sang a hymn, and my terrible singing was broadcast across the congregation. As it turns out, my voice is one that carries, and there were times when it carried above the others who were singing even without being amplified. There were times when, at ministerial gatherings, my colleagues would gather and just sing together, but I refused to join in because I was embarrassed about how badly I sang. And so it went.

It was not until I retired that I learned to sing properly. The Santa Barbara church hired Ken Ryals as its new choir director the year after I retired. The first time I saw him in action, I said to myself, "Ken, the student must be ready, because there is the teacher." As soon as I could arrange it, I began taking singing lessons from him. When I explained my issues to him, he nodded and was able to coax a voice out me. I will never be an excellent singer or an intuitive singer. It was too late for that, but he was able to get me beyond my paralysis and embarrassment. I am now an acceptable singer who is, at best, a mediocre singer. And that is enough. Ken allowed me to break down the dam that closed off the river of music, and I will always be grateful to him.[5]

---

[5] Ken died suddenly in the summer of 2020 of a heart attack. The loss to me, to the church, and the huge community of his friends is enormous.

# PREFACE:
# A Short Primer on My Metatheology

When I realized that knowledge encompasses not only science and logic, but also art and religion, I began to wonder about how religious knowledge is structured. At first, I thought that would be theology, but then I remembered my astronaut-anthropologist, and I realized that I wanted was not a theology at all. Theologies are specific to specific religions. Thus, there is Christian theology, Hindu theology, and so on. What I was looking for was a framework on which theologies could be hung. I was looking for a metatheology.

I began to think of various theologies as books people write about their religious beliefs. These books fall together into categories and sub-categories. Christian theology, for example, splits into Catholic and Protestant theologies. The former contains the theologies of Augustine, Thomas Aquinas, and so on. The latter contains the theologies of Luther, Calvin, and so on. And within these sub-categories, there are the theologies of individual Christians, some written and some unwritten.

I think of a metatheology as a sort of library that houses all of these theologies. What I was trying to do was to build such a library. The epistemology that I outlined above is the foundation upon which the library could be built. With this realization, it was time to begin erecting the building. First, though, I need to gather my building materials: the relationship between theology and religion, an adequate way to talk about the Divine, and the African concept of *ubuntu*.

Many people make the mistake of thinking that interdependence is about ecology, safeguarding the earth, environmental action, and the like. To be sure these things do arise out of a grasp of the interdependence things. But I have come to realize that, as important as these things are, the idea of interdependence is far deeper than this. I believe that it is a profound theological concept that is imbedded, sometimes invisibly and sometimes quite obviously in the theologies of the world's religions. For just one example, it appears in Buddhism as the idea of mutual co-arising.

Imagine thinking of interdependence as the essential principle of human life. Imagine taking it so seriously that to say of someone that they are a good person is to say that they embody interdependence. Imagine having a word for this. This is what the Zulu (and many other African) people believe, and there is a word for this in the Zulu language: *ubuntu*. An embrace of *ubuntu* is what created the possibility of the Truth and Reconciliation Commission (the TRC) that made such enormous strides toward the healing of South Africa. *Ubuntu* also lies at the center of Archbishop Desmond Tutu's theology. In his book about the TRC, *No Future Without Forgiveness*, he says this:

> When we want to give high praise to someone, we say…, "So and so has ubuntu." Then you are generous, you are hospitable, you are friendly and caring and compassionate. You share what you have. It is to say, "My humanity is caught up, is inextricably bound up in yours." We belong in a bundle of life. We say, "A person is a person through other people." It is not "I think therefore I am." It says, rather: "I

am human because I belong. I participate. I share."[1]

Without *ubuntu*, there can be no humanity, only creatures that are biologically human, but that are morally and spiritually bereft, Homo sapiens, but not truly human. It is ubuntu that creates human beings, not biology. The whole concept of culture requires *ubuntu*. Consider how much we learn from and teach each other: language, art, religion, technology, law, sports, morality. The list is endless, because it includes all of the institutions of a culture. I have heard people argue that human qualities like kindness spring from our biology, but what springs forth in a young child's life is, at most, an urge, a compulsion to act in certain ways. It is other people who teach the child when and where and how to direct those urges and compulsions. So even if kindness itself is biologically determined, how to be kind is taught.

## THEOLOGY AND RELIGION

The image many people have of theology is that it is a dry and dull academic study that is utterly irrelevant to the real lives of real people. Not surprisingly, I have a different view. I think that religion always arises, not in the mind, but in people's lived experiences.

In this, I follow Ralph Waldo Emerson and the American Transcendentalists. For example, in his famous "Divinity School Address" Emerson says this:

A… secret, sweet, and overpowering beauty appears to

---

[1] Desmond Tutu, No Future without Forgiveness, p. 31.

man [sic] when his heart and mind open to the sentiment of virtue. Then is he instructed in what is above him. He learns that his being is without bound; that, to the good, to the perfect, he is born, low as he now lies in evil and weakness...

The sentiment of virtue is a reverence and delight in the presence of certain divine laws... The laws refuse to be adequately stated. They will not be written out on paper, or spoken by the tongue... Yet, this sentiment is the essence of all religion...[2]

Emerson is telling us the same thing: religion begins in experience, the experience of something that overpowers the mere and the temporary and enlivens the soul.

Nevertheless, we human beings are a curious lot. We want to understand what has happened to us, and beyond simply understanding, we want to communicate that understanding to one another. And so we try to fit our experience into our language. We do that in two different ways: with carefully thought out and rational language, and with poetry and story. The latter becomes religious mythology: stories and rituals that express a depth of truth that lies beyond the power of discursive language to separate this from that. The former is theology: the experience of the divine filtered through language arrived at after rational reflection, "life passed through the fire of thought," as Emerson famously wrote in his "Divinity School Address."

---

[2] "Divinity School Address," contained in *Three Prophets of Religious Liberalism*, Conrad Wright, ed. Boston: Beacon Press, 1961, pp. 91-92.

The essence of theology, then, is rationality. And yet, that very rationality is always in service to something deeper and more profound than the human mind. As a result, all theology is inherently inadequate to express the whole of the experience. It can take us only so far, and beyond that there is silence. Ludwig Wittgenstein's remark in the closing lines of the *Tractatus*, "Whereof one cannot speak, thereof one must remain silent,"[3] is relevant here. This is when poetry, story, and myth must take over. And yet even here, the expression is not the experience; the map is not the terrain. For an understanding of the religious experience, then, we need both theology and poetry.

## A Word about *God*

Before proceeding, I need to return to the discussion of the word *God* I opened in the Preface to Part I. It is, perhaps, the most critical word in Western religion. It is also, perhaps, the most controversial word in the English language. Hardly any word is more fraught with confusion than the word *God*. It means so many different things to so many different people that any use of it almost guarantees being misunderstood. It is important to find a way to refer to that which is, in some important sense, greater than any single being and is yet the foundation that grounds existence itself. *God* can do that, but it can also refer to a hypostatized human being, a supreme being, if you will, that may or may not live in the sky. It can also refer to a lot of other things, most of which are unintended but arise from the

---

[3] "Wovon mann nicht sprechen kann, darüber muss mann schweigen," Proposition 7. Tractatus. Logico-Philosophicus, C. K. Ogden trans.

context of the reader's social and personal history.

The problem, of course, is that we are trying to name a concept for which the naming function of language is inappropriate. Naming picks out that which is named and separates it from the rest of the universe. Thus, "ball" indicates a thing that is more or less round and typically light enough to pick up and toss back and forth. Toothpicks are not balls. When we say, "Mary picked up the ball and threw it to Tom," we know that she did not pick up and throw him a small, light stick of wood or plastic used for the cleaning of teeth. But what could the name *God* differentiate?

On the one hand, people sometimes think of God as utterly beyond all that is, approachable only through an act of divine grace. The technical theological term for this understanding of *God* is *transcendence.* On the other hand, people also think of God as that which gives being to all that is, permeating everything like salt pervades sea water. The technical term for this is *immanence.*[4] In neither case, though, is God a thing among things and thus is not a nameable part of the universe. But if God is not a nameable part of the universe, how are we to talk about God?

All of the Great Religions have had to deal with this problem. For example,

- In Judaism, one is simply forbidden to name God. How does one name that which has no name? To do so would be to make of God a thing and any such named god would be an idol.

---

[4] It is worth noting that the word *to transcend* comes from a Latin word meaning *to travel across* and the word *immanent* comes from another Latin word meaning *in place.* To approach the transcendent God, one must travel across the gap between that God and us. The immanent God, however, is the God that is in this very place.

- In Islam, to emphasize Allah's infinite attributes, there are 99 symbolic "names," none of which are the "real" name.
- In Taoism, one uses the word *tao* as simply a kind of place-holder.

Unless I make up a word, I doubt I will ever find a term to unambiguously point people to this unnamable more than something[5] that grounds our existence and is the focus of our most intense religious concern. The British theologian, John Hick attempted to do just this, to make up a new term.[6] However, I find his suggestion, while interesting, rather awkward. Even if one does succeed in making up an adequate term, I suspect that the made-up word will quickly accrue too much concrete meaning and will ultimately collapse into confusion, much like *God* has collapsed. Yet, we still need a term to point us to the Unnamable.

I have found that the best way to do this is to consider one's experiences of this "more than something" at the core of existence and to ask what those experiences have in common. Then use a term that comes closest to that commonality, knowing that it will not be entirely adequate. For me, that term is "Presence," and this is the term I have adopted.

People experience God—Presence—in their own, idiosyncratic way. If it is true, as Jung insisted, that "bidden or unbidden, God is present,"[7] then it would seem that God is manifest to each person in whatever manner that person can understand. For some God man-

---

[5] This phrase is borrowed form e. e. cummings.

[6] John Hick, An Interpretation of Religion: Human Responses to the Transcendent.

[7] Jung was quoting Erasmus, and he had this motto carved onto the lintel of the doorway to his study. I believe they were both right about this.

ifests as Love; for others, God manifests as Power; for still others as Life; and so on for virtually every person on Earth. Myriad are the ways God manifests, and myriad are the ways God is experienced. I invite people, then, to translate my term, *Presence*, into whatever religious language they are comfortable with. Occasionally, when the context of my subject suggests that *God* is the most appropriate word, I will revert to the word *God* and point out that fact.

## Ubuntu

*Ubuntu* lies at the center of my meta-theology. A more common English word for this is *interdependence*. I prefer using the word *ubuntu* rather than *interdependence* for a number of reasons. First, interdependence has become so intertwined with ecological action that I want a word that will not lend itself to such a narrow understanding. Ubuntu is far wider. Second, I want to call us to a deeper grasp of what counts as humanity and how we create one another in our humanity, and *interdependence* does not seem to have that connotation.

Third, I also want to call us to taking this idea far more seriously than people typically do. The idea of the "self-made" person is still too strongly held in the cultural subconscious, and there is no such thing. I think a new word will help to break us free of this unfortunate idea. Fourth, interdependence is seen as a fact while *ubuntu* can be thought of as a quality that reveals the inherent humanity of someone. And fifth, I think *ubuntu* is simply a far more graceful word than *interdependence*.

The idea of *ubuntu* is not foreign to Euro-American culture even though the word is foreign. For an example that I am rather fond of, consider the fictional community of Port William, Kentucky, created by Wendell Berry in a series of novels, novellas, and short stories. In his story, "The Wild Birds," he has a character say this:

> "The way we are, we are members of each other. All of us. Everything. The difference ain't in who is a member and who is not, but in who knows it and who don't. What has been here, not what ought to have been is what I have to claim. I have to be what I've been, and own up to it, no secret faults."[8]

"We are members of each other." "I belong. I participate. I share." The idea is the same.

This notion is so critical to the possibility of becoming human, that I think of it as a form of love. When we love, no matter how it is that we love, we become able to cross the barrier between self and other and are able to participate in the humanity of the beloved. In *ubuntu*, we extend that participation in ever-increasing circles. It is in this that we become more and more human, for to be fully and deeply human is to transcend the self-other dichotomy. What I call The Human Project is the project of developing *ubuntu*. Without *ubuntu* there is no humanity, and we are condemned to live lives of lonely isolation and ever-deepening emptiness.

---

[8] In Berry's collection of the same name, pp. 136-137.

## CHAPTER 1:
# Faith-Based Religion

Thinking about all this, I realized that I am not really building a theology. Instead, I am constructing a meta-theology, a kind of library that can house many theologies. I do not think there is a universal, one true theology. Instead, I think that our theologies are personal, autobiographical, more or less rational reconstructions of deep religious experiences we have had in the course of our lives. This outline is a kind of blueprint for constructing a personal theology.

I begin with by laying a foundation: religion is a way of knowing the world, a way that is importantly different from and not in the least incompatible with science. The model I use for building my library is systematic theology with its divisions into soteriology, theology, missiology, ecclesiology, pneumatology, and eschatology.

These are not exactly household words. Not many people think of themselves as sitting down with a friend and having a serious conversation about, for example, soteriology. Actually, I suspect that it happens far more often than people realize, though I doubt they would have thought of these conversations as soteriology. All of us deal in the issues of systematic theology without ever using this technical theological language. For example, who has not asked themselves what it is that keeps them from realizing their fullness as a human being, what is it that blocks them and breaks their hearts? Yet that is soteriology. Or again, surely each of us has pondered many times what we are called to do and be in this world we live in. This is missiology. And so on for each of these seemingly intimidating and decidedly academic words. We all do systematic theology, usually without realizing this is what we are doing.

To my surprise, I have found that many people resist the suggestion that we think theologically. This resistance is, I think, often based on having been taught religious beliefs of one sort or another prescriptively: "Believe this or else!" The "or else" ranges from ostracism to eternal damnation. This is not a good way to teach genuine religion. It is not even a good way to present the importance of theological and religious thinking. I am offering something else.

I do not think of the reflections that follow as in any way pre-scriptive. I am not suggesting that this is what anyone else must, should, ought, or even does think and believe about religion. On the contrary, these reflections are autobiographical; they record what *I* have come to think and believe and how these ideas are part of *my* story. Rather than prescribing belief for others, these reflections are an invitation to others to reflect on and tell their own religious stories. This is what really what makes these ideas meta-theology rather than theology. God—Presence—is beyond the reach of any individual mind, and so the fuller story of God[1] contains all of our individual stories.

The rest of this chapter contains a necessary discussion of religion itself. Is it based on an acceptance of a prescribed creed? Is it based on a correct way of acting in life? Is it based on a deep,

---

[1] Theology is, as the word suggests, the story of God.

existential trust? And where do love and *ubuntu* fit into all this?

## THE CENTRAL QUESTION

I used to think that the central question to ask someone about their religion is "What do you believe?" And like many people, I also used to think that religious belief is a matter of intelligence and rationality, and that belief, properly understood, is a step toward knowledge—which, I thought, is the real aim of human intelligence. To ask someone what they believe, I thought, was to engage them in an intellectual discussion about their religion, perhaps leading to a heady discussion of theology. In short, I thought that religious belief is a belief that something or other is the case. As we saw earlier, I have come to realize that I was wrong. Religious belief is belief *in*, not belief *that*. And this makes all the difference.

I suspect, though, that many, if not most, people also think that belief is the central issue of religion. If you ask someone what they believe, the chances are that they will give you a statement of belief, a creed or a personal credo. This is what is behind trying to talk people into belief. The idea is that if I can get you to *say* that you believe my creed, then you really *do* believe it and I have converted you. If this were so, then religious belief would be about what one says one believes. It would be about saying the right thing. But religious belief has little or nothing to do with what people say; it is about what heals their broken hearts.

## ORTHODOX RELIGION AND TAKING REFUGE

I think that there is a wide-spread and profound confusion about what orthodoxy is and this confusion leads to an equally profound misunderstanding about the nature of religious belief. So, consider orthodoxy. It is true that that the word *orthodox* itself comes from the Greek meaning *right belief,* but the rightness of belief is not as straightforward as one might think. The English word *right* is highly ambiguous, and this ambiguity has led to these misunderstandings. *Right* has at least these very different meanings:

- True or correct, as opposed to false or wrong, as in "the right answer to the question"
- Effective, as in "the right way to practice the violin"
- Morally correct, as in "the right thing to do"
- Proper or appropriate, as in "the right dress for the occasion"
- A direction, as opposed to left, as in "turn right at the corner"
- An inherent privilege, as in "the right to free speech."

There are several more meanings, but these six will suffice to make the point. Which, of all the possibilities, do we mean when we speak of right belief? Clearly, the last three are irrelevant.

The moral correctness is, I think, not to the point. I would argue that morality often arises out of religion and rarely religion out of morality. Belief that is not right is not immoral.[2] That leaves the first two, and they yield very different understandings when

---

[2] There are, of course, those who would argue this point, but I do not want to get into that argument here.

applied to religious belief. The first, right-as-opposed-to-false belief, yields a propositional form of belief, the assertion of the form "I believe that…" I think this is what most people understand belief to be. This is certainly how belief is understood in science, but as I argued above, religious belief is belief *in* rather than belief *that*.

Some etymologies are helpful here. The first Latin word of the Nicene Creed is, appropriately enough, *credo*, which is usually translated as *I believe*. Linguistically this is an accurate translation. The problem is that it does not go far enough. To the extent that the contemporary English word *to believe* is propositional, it has lost a great deal of the strength of *credo*. *Credo* comes from a Proto-Indo-European root that means *heart*. In fact, the English word *heart* comes from the same root, as does the word *courage*. Belief, in this religious sense, seems to have something to do with the heart and with courage.

Further and even more revealingly, this Proto-Indo-European root was once combined with another root which meant *to place* and formed a distinctly religious term that literally meant *to place in the heart* and indicated a religious form of trust. Religious belief seems to have something to do with putting something in one's heart and thereby giving it a very deep and profound trust. Belief has to do with the courage that arises from that deep and profound trust.

Let us look, then, at the English word, *belief*. Our word *belief* comes from another Proto-Indo-European root that means *to love* and, again, has the flavor of trust. The concept of trust is clearly central to religious belief. The very core of religious belief is a profound trust that is laid in the heart, grows from love, and engenders courage.

Finally, consider the word *trust*. Interestingly enough, it shares a root with the word *truth*. This relationship between trust and truth therefore is the core of religious knowledge. This shared root means *firm* or *steadfast*, which suggests to me another religious word, the word *faith*. *Faith* comes from the Latin word *fidēs*, also meaning *trust*. Again. Trust lies at the heart of religion, but not just any old trust. Religious trust lies in that in which we hold ourselves firm, steadfast, that in which we place our faith.

These etymologies[3] suggest to me that there is more to belief than simply assent to a proposition. They suggest an essential link between religious belief and faith, where faith is understood as a deep and profound trust, a trust that I would call existential in the sense that it lies at the foundation of our existence as human beings.

I find Buddhism to be helpful in understanding this link. The central assertions of all branches of Buddhism, the so-called "Three Jewels," or "Three Refuges" are these:

- I take refuge in the Buddha
- I take refuge in the Dharma
- I take refuge in the Sangha.

At the moment, I'm not interested in exploring the Buddha, the Dharma, and the Sangha.[4] What I am interested in is the notion of taking refuge. What does it mean to take refuge in something?

A refuge is that which gives help, comfort, and protection in times of trouble or danger. It is that to which we turn when all else

---

[3] Readers who are interested in following the etymologies in this book more carefully and fully are referred to the *American Heritage Dictionary, Fourth Edition.*

[4] The interested reader should see my *Finger-pointing Essays.*

has deserted us and which we know in our hearts will not fail us. When we lose our courage, our refuge is that to which we return to find that courage once more. It is shelter; it is inspiration; it is insight and renewal. To begin weaving all these threads together, then, our refuge is that in which we place our deepest and fullest trust. Our refuge is that in which we have faith—not blind and uncritical faith, but profound and existential faith. Our refuge is that which we trust with our very selves, with our integrity, and with our humanity. It is that which gives us the courage to exist, to be in the world. Our refuge is where our heart is, and where our heart is, there we are, also.

Searching for a concrete example of this, I turned to contemporary Religious Humanism. Though this language is certainly atypical among them, I think that Religious Humanists could be said to take refuge in the Rational. This does not mean that they take refuge in our rational facility, what used to be called ratiocination, that is, the rational faculty of the human mind. Rather, it means that they believe that there is an order that pervades the universe and that this order is comprehensible through the exercise of human reason, which exercise finds its most exquisite expression in science. Religious Humanists find inspiration, comfort, shelter, confidence, courage, and trust in the Rational, in this universe-pervading order. They place their faith in the Rational, and it grounds their religious lives.[5]

The question of whether or not this refuge sought by Religious Humanists is prescriptively correct is not to the point. What *is* to the point is that these Religious Humanists do place their faith, take

---

[5] This is, I think, a contemporary version of 18th Century Deism.

their refuge, in the Rational, just as Buddhists place their faith, take their refuge, in the Buddha. Just as it is both futile and inappropriate to try to argue Buddhists out of their faith in the Buddha, so is it both futile and inappropriate to try to argue Religious Humanists out of their faith in the Rational. To try to drive another out of his or her refuge is to steal the faith of another, which is the ultimate admission of a lack of faith, a lack of trust, a lack of courage, and a lack of heart. It is to misunderstand the place of faith in religion and to fail to honor the diverse ways that people experience Presence in the depths of their hearts and souls.

The notion that faith proceeds from belief puts the cart before the horse. It is quite the opposite. Since belief is the expression of faith, it is faith that creates belief. This is yet another reason why what I used to think is wrong. The central religious question to ask of someone is not "what do you believe?," but rather, "in what do you have faith? In what do you take refuge?" In his book *Stages of Faith*, James Fowler put the question in this way:

> On what or whom do you set your heart? To what vision of right-relatedness between humans, nature, and the transcendent are you loyal? What hope and what ground of hope animate you and give shape to the force field of your life and to how you move into it?[6]

To Fowler's questions I would add these:

> What gives meaning and purpose to your living? Where do you find comfort and strength? What has the power to still your fear and to open your heart to the living of your life?

---

[6] James Fowler, *Stages of Faith*, p. 14.

# Chapter 1: Faith-Based Religion

In what do you take refuge?

It is important to notice two things. First, any verbal answer to these questions is but a pointing to something deeper than the words. The real answer, the answer behind this answer, is the commitment, the faith, itself. If one says, for example, "My faith is in God," the true answer is their faith, not the words they use to express their faith. Thus, *Credo in unum Deum* is, when properly understood, not a proposition at all. It is not a telling. It is the expression of a profound commitment. In the same way, "I love you" is not an assertion of fact but an expression of love. And this is why trying to talk someone into religious belief won't work. One can compel another to say the words, but one cannot compel another's existential commitment. One may as well try to compel another to love them.

Second, the answer to any of these questions may or may not be something that appears conventionally religious. Any honest answer, conventionally religious or not, is, in a deeper sense, necessarily religious. It is, by definition, religious or, if you prefer, spiritual.[7]

Without refuge—faith—we are left only with despair. We have all left the Garden of Eden behind. We have discovered that there really is evil in the world and that we are, each and every one of us, quite capable of doing evil things, even with the best of intentions.

---

[7] Arguments about the religious versus the spiritual leave me cold. Our spirituality is nothing more nor less than our ability to discover our refuge and to move back and forth from refuge to living, from faith to life. Religion is about healing the broken heart, something that cannot be done without a place of spiritual refuge. One must not confuse the *concept* of religion with the *institution* of religion.

The world really can be a frightening place. Living is a beautiful thing, but it also hurts. As the young Prince Siddhartha discovered, suffering, pain, old age, and death are all too real in our world. When we discover this truth, it is inevitable that we also discover the fear of living. The Buddha called that fear *dukkha* and made its discovery the beginning of Buddhism. Religion begins when we take seriously the question of what we are going to do about *dukkha*... or sin or alienation or... Where will we find refuge? Where will we find the strength to trust our lives and the lives of other people? How will we open our hearts once again to the love and the beauty that also dwell in the world?

When we turn and look back at the Garden and see the angel brandishing the Flaming Sword at the entrance and know that we will never dwell there again, there is a terrible temptation to allow the heart to shrivel in fear and to give in to a mourning that will never find comfort. There is a temptation to try to control the world around us so that our pain can be covered in a great cloud of power and isolation. This, though, is an illusion. It will not work. There is no comfort to be found in isolation, in separating ourselves from the world that has hurt us and turned our hope to fear. There is no refuge in walls that divide and drive hearts asunder. Prince Siddhartha had to leave his castle to find enlightenment and become The Buddha, and Jesus had to leave the carpenter shop, go out into the wilderness, and then return to live among his people.

Properly understood, then, orthodoxy is about religious belief. It is not about repeating the right (correct) creed; it is about taking the right (effective) refuge, making the right commitment. I think, though, that most people still make the mistake of thinking that religious belief is about orthodoxy in the sense giving of assent to the correct propositions, *i.e.* to assent to a creed. This is an example of the mistaken idea that truth speaks in only one voice, the scientific voice. Since this propositional understanding of belief dominates so much of Western religious thinking, speaking differently about belief is to invite confusion. What I am looking for is a different basis for religion, one that does not depend on the correctness of belief, but answers to the idea of belief itself as existential commitment. Orthodox religion does not ordinarily do that.

## ORTHOPRACTIC RELIGION

Buddhism can be understood in a way that suggests a different possible model for belief. The idea of taking refuge is central to Buddhism, but the three branches of Buddhism differ in what they consider to be the appropriate way of taking that refuge. The three branches of Buddhism are Theravada, the Buddhism of South Asia; Vajrayana, the Buddhism of Tibet, Nepal, and Mongolia; and Mahayana, the Buddhism of Southeast Asia, China, and Japan.[8] They all share the same core: The Three Jewels, the Four Noble Truths, and the Eightfold Way. They differ primarily in how they teach their followers to follow the Eightfold Way, in how to practice the Buddha's teachings, The Dharma.

Note that each step in the Eightfold Way begins with the same word, "right." Buddhism does not understand "right" to mean "correct" but rather to mean "effective." Thus, the thing that distinguishes

---

[8] There seems to be a fourth branch emerging in the West that synthesizes these three. It is, though, still in its infancy, and it remains to be seen how successful it will be.

the three branches of Buddhism is differences in how each suggests they can be carried effectively into one's life. It is generally (though probably not universally) recognized in Buddhism that what is effective in one context or for one person need not be effective in another context for another person. The three branches generally acknowledge each other as perfectly legitimate ways of practicing Buddhism. For example, the Dalai Lama, who practices Vajrayana, has enormous respect for Thich Nhat Hanh, who practices Zen, which is a branch of Mahayana, and vice versa. Each recognizes that the other has achieved a high level of enlightenment.

This way of understanding religion can be thought of as orthopractic, that is, as the right (in the sense of effective) religious practice (*ortho*-, right, plus the Greek *praxis*, to apply). The difference between Mahayana and Vajrayana is found in what they find to be effective ways to practice Buddhism. Mahayana offers right (effective) practices to those who find those practices to be effective; Vajrayana offers other practices to other people. For example, in Zen one meditates in front of a blank wall and contemplates a koan; in Vajrayana, one meditates in front of a more or less complex painting and contemplates the mandala. Neither Mahayana nor Vajrayana insists that it offers the exclusive, "one true" version or practice of Buddhism. Orthopractic religion does not—or at least need not—demand exclusivity.

## ORTHOFIDEIC RELIGION

Nevertheless, all three branches insist that their practitioners take refuge—place their faith—in the Buddha, the Dharma, and the Sangha. This placing of faith is not about giving assent to three propositions; it is about opening one's heart and soul, with or without assent to propositions. This suggests to me that there is actually a third option that is being pioneered in the West by Unitarian Universalism.

There is no creed in Unitarian Universalism to which one is asked to give assent. Nor is there a generally accepted way of practicing Unitarian Universalism. Thus, it is neither orthodox (in the conventional sense) nor orthopractic. There is no "ortho-word" that characterizes Unitarian Universalism, so let me suggest a made-up word: *orthofideic*, from *ortho-* plus the Latin *fidēs*, meaning faith or trust. Orthofideic religion is religion that is based on right (effective) faith. Unitarian Universalism, I submit, is exploring what an orthofideic religion might be.

In Unitarian Universalism, one is free, and in fact encouraged, to find for oneself the best way to articulate one's faith, to assert one's credo. Equally one is both free and encouraged to find for oneself the most effective way to carry that faith into life, an effective way to practice one's faith. As might be expected, there is little agreement within Unitarian Universalism about how to explain this faith. Perhaps it can best be characterized as a deep and profound trust in the interdependence of life and existence, a trust that finds its most exquisite expression in Love. The question, though, is how to understand this concept of Love.

## THE CENTRALITY OF LOVE

Unfortunately, English has an impoverished vocabulary for talking about love. The same word has to cover everything from strong attraction though intense eroticism to the love of God. It is as if we have thrown up our hands in despair, in effect agreeing with C. G. Jung's remark at the end of *Memories, Dreams, Reflections* that no matter what we say of Love it will simultaneously be too much and too little.[9] We English speakers seem to have abandoned the field to poetry. Also, unfortunately, in America at least, there is a decided distrust of poetry, and that makes it very difficult to talk and think articulately about Love.

Let me try, though, because I think that Love properly understood is at the center of all genuine religion. Without some understanding of what I am talking about when I say "Love," it will be difficult to understand the metatheological framework I am trying to build. Two examples are Jesus' insistence that love of God and neighbor is the essence of Torah and the Buddha's insistence that love alone dispels hatred.

Unlike erotic love, the love that I am speaking of is not an emotion. It is not something one feels. It is a state of being, a way of standing in the world. It is the state of being in which we reach an existential understanding, when we stand under, the truth that each and every one of us is connected and of equal value and worth. Love is an existential understanding that we are, in a very profound sense, one, and that the apparently unbridgeable divide between me and thee is merely a way of seeing things that is not as ultimate

---

[9] Carl Gustav Jung, *Memories, Dreams, Reflections*, pp. 353-354.

as it appears to be. As the Buddhists say, I and thou are not two, even while I and you are two. As Jung correctly points out in *Memories, Dreams, Reflections*, one must be prepared for paradox when one is talking about Love. Yet this is actually no more paradoxical than the conclusion in quantum mechanics that light is composed simultaneously of waves and particles, or that I am simultaneously father and son.

Sometimes Love emerges and announces itself as a bond between two hearts that is so powerful and sacred that they become as one. This bond is the love the Greeks called *Eros*, and it is what creates a genuine marriage. Sometimes Love emerges and announces itself as a bond between hearts that move in different ways but find the power of their companionship and are held fast by that power. They are two souls supporting, sustaining, and nurturing each other's separate lives. This bond is the love the Greeks called *Philia*, and it is the center of true friendship.

Sometimes Love emerges and announces itself as an unconditional binding of people into the world. This bond recognizes neither east nor west, neither race nor class, neither male nor female, neither gay nor straight nor any other category invented by humans. Instead, it sees one vast and sacred web of holiness spun through every glorious and beautiful heart. This bond is the love that the Greeks called *Agape*, and it is the heart of faith. However, it may emerge, however it may announce itself, Love is always precious, sacred, holy, and greater than any of us are able to understand or grasp alone.

Think a moment of The Buddha's remark, recorded in *The*

*Dhammapada*: "See yourself in others, then whom can you harm?"[10] The point is not that in order to refrain from harming others one must see oneself reflected in others as images in a mirror. The point is that when one sees others and self to be *inseparable*, one understands with the heart and soul—one stands under the truth—that in harming another one necessarily harms oneself. "Then whom can you harm?" This is Love expressing itself as *ubuntu*.

Why, then, did Jesus insist that loving God and loving our neighbors is the same thing? Do not be confused by the word *God* here. To recapitulate a point made above, it is not a way to pick out a thing, a being, supreme or otherwise, that can be listed among the things of the universe. "God" is not like "…sealing wax, cabbages, kings, God, and Uncle Harry." The word is simply a finger that points us to that which both pervades the universe as salt pervades seawater and is the foundation upon which the universe constantly emerges.

To love Presence is to stand under the truth that it moves within and through one's being. Indeed, there is a sense in which we are nothing but Presence emerging into time. To love one's neighbor as oneself is to stand under the truth that one cannot separate oneself from one's neighbor, cannot conceive of one's integrity without invoking the integrity of all others that live. These two truths are nothing but different versions of the same more profound truth. Each is a paraphrase of the other. If one's integrity is but Presence emerging into time, and if one's integrity is entwined with the integrity of all, then it follows that everyone's integrity is also Presence emerging into time. How could one stand under one truth without

---

[10] Thomas Byrom, *The Dhammapada*, Chapter 10.

also standing under the other? They are equivalent, different ways of grasping and giving our flesh to the same profound idea.

What did The Buddha mean when he said that only Love can dispel hatred? The essence of hatred (and therefore also of sin) is the separation of people. When we think of others as separate from us, we begin to think of them as manipulable and disposable. We allow ourselves to violate their integrity, thinking mistakenly that our integrity will not be harmed when we violate theirs. This is hatred, apartheid, the denial of *ubuntu*. It cannot be healed—dispelled—except by standing under a different truth, namely that our integrity and the integrity of others are so intertwined and interdependent that I and Thou are unthinkable without each other. This is Love; this is the embrace of *ubuntu*. *Ubuntu* draws back together that which hatred tears apart, healing the pain of hatred and dispelling its power.

This notion of *ubuntu* is so central and fundamental to my thinking that I can define it only by pointing at it. These ideas cannot be unraveled into a simple linear thread. Trying to do so is like trying to project a sphere onto a plane: something is always and necessarily left out. And so, I repeat myself from time to time without apology.

## Sighs and Songs

You say that what I have said before
I say again. Well, then. I repeat myself.

So does the wind, blowing in from the sea,
Carrying fog through the forest and down
The mountainside in slow explosions.

So does the grass, dancing its stately dance
With the stammering wind. It would not be grass
If it did not repeat itself, if it did not continue.

The wind does not give offense, nor is it lost
In its constant sighs and endlessly repeating song.
How can one deny the profound grass,
Whispering over and over, talking to the wind?

And so, if I say again what I have said before,
It is not me who speaks. It is the grass; it is the wind.[11]

---

[11] Collier, *Full Circle*, p. 27.

CHAPTER 2:

# Soteriology

*From what do we need to be saved?*
*What will save us from that?*

## JUST A LITTLE MORE ON HOW I THINK
### ABOUT THEOLOGY

Theology is a slippery topic, easily mistaken for proselytizing. There is an enormous temptation for people to think that the theologian is—or at least thinks he or she is— "telling it like it is" and that the implicit message is "This is *The Truth*, so you'd better understand it and believe it." This is an error. Unfortunately, I find theologians often taking themselves to be making prescriptive statements about right belief. In fact, the most they are actually saying is that the beliefs they are expressing encapsulate what works for them religiously. There is another way of understanding theology that does not commit the theologian to be telling people what to believe.

Theology is about something else. Theology is about how people reflect on, construct, deconstruct, reconstruct, and come to understand their own deepest and most profound religious and spiritual experiences. Understood this way, theology can be conceived of as a kind of autobiography rather than as a prescription. It is people saying, "Here is how *I* understand the profundity of the human experience, how *I* think about what it means to be human in general, and to be me in particular." One person's autobiography cannot contradict another's. Understood this way, differing theologies cannot, in spite of appearances, be in contradiction, and they are not prescriptive in the sense of telling others what they ought to believe.

In response to this idea of theology as autobiography, people sometimes point out that some theologies talk about a universal love—which I sometimes refer to as Love and sometimes as *ubuntu*—and others seem at least to allow for, if not actually to require, the rejection and hatred of some classes of people. That certainly appears to be a contradiction. In response, I can do no better than to quote Karen Armstrong in her book *The Great Transformation*:

> The test is simple: if people's beliefs—secular or religious— make them belligerent, intolerant, and unkind about other people's faith they are not "skillful" [able to heal broken hearts]. If, however, their convictions impel them to act compassionately and to honor the stranger, then they are good, helpful, sound. This is the test of true religiosity in every single one of the major religions.[1]

The fact that people so often fail this test either by their actions or by their rhetoric does not imply that the essential understanding of theology as autobiography is wrong. It means that people's actions and rhetoric are not always consistent with the Love to which all of the great religions point us.

Here is a peculiar thing, though. Knowing another's autobiography can only enrich one's understanding of one's own life. Thus, sharing theologies, at least at this level and in this sense, can only

---

[1] Karen Armstrong, *The Great Transformation*, p. 392.

enrich our understanding of our own lives and theologies, even though we understand our lives in radically different ways. I do not pretend to be telling—or even suggesting—that anyone "ought" to accept my theology or that anyone "ought" to understand his or her life as I understand mine. Instead, I am simply sharing the theological reflections that have helped me to come to understand my life. How can it hurt to understand the life of another person?

Approaching theology, though, is rather like cleaning up my desk: it is not obvious where to begin. In spite of the fact that systematic theology is often broken into distinct branches or facets, it has always seemed to me that the whole is in fact undifferentiated. As a result, I feel as if I need to say everything at once—which, of course, I cannot do. This means that, again like cleaning my desk, it probably doesn't matter where I begin so long as I do begin.

## The Questions

Sometimes people start with what I think of as theology-proper or reflections on God, or ultimate reality—Presence. In the conceptual order of things, that might be appropriate, but in the temporal order of my own life, that was not the beginning. I began my own serious theological thinking with reflections on the difficulties and dangers involved in becoming human.

Having been raised in a Calvinist church, I was well aware of our all too human propensity to sin and the need for divine intercession to deliver us from that sinful nature. This was, of course, the very essence of soteriology. However, I never did understand how Jesus' death and resurrection accomplished that.[2] Jesus died a terribly painful death, but so did most people the Romans executed. No one could explain to me why this painful and terrible death was any different from the rest.[3] I could not bring myself to believe that Jesus, once dead, came back to life. So, the resurrection had to be a metaphor, yet the very suggestion that it was a metaphor was met with derision and dismissal. As a result, I was left with only human sinfulness and no understanding of how to escape its talons.

As noted in the Prologue, I left Calvinism in particular and Christianity in general in the early 1960s, a time of particular turmoil in America. The Civil Right Struggle, the Vietnam War, and the beginning of the Environmental Movement weighed heavily on me. I struggled with trying to understand how people could be so heedless of their impact on the lives of one another. And I asked myself what could be done to change that. These reflections are what is known technically as soteriology (from the Greek *soterion*, meaning "deliverance").

Soteriology is one of the central concerns of all religions, most mythologies, and virtually all deeply reflective people. It proceeds from two basic religious questions: "Why is evil so pervasive?" and "How can we escape it?" Though the term is far from being in common usage, this concern is surely something that faces almost all human beings at some point in their lives. All of the Great Religions have their own version of these two soteriological questions. The Christian version is this:

---

[2] I still don't.

[3] See Brock and Parker, *Proverbs of Ashes,* for a good rebuttal of many of the various attempts to explain this.

- From what do we need to be saved?
- What will save us from that?

The Buddhists version is this:
- What causes *dukkha* (spiritual suffering)?
- What will release us from *dukkha*?

The Jewish version is this:
- What estranges us from God?
- What will overcome this estrangement?

The Muslim version is this:
- What is the source of injustice?
- What will overcome injustice?

Even Religious Humanists ask themselves the soteriological questions, though the questions are often so hidden in their unique religious language that they are often not recognized as such. Perhaps a Religious Humanist version would be this:
- What blinds us to the order pervading the Universe?
- What will cure this blindness?

Trying to find a more or less neutral formulation that is more appropriate for the metatheology I am trying to build, I have come to put the questions to myself in this way:
- What endangers our humanity?
- What will protect us from that danger?

## THE DANGER

I remembered that walk out into the thunderstorm when I was sixteen. And I remembered how isolated and alone I felt in my adolescence. And began to think about the stores of The Fall and the Expulsion, and I suddenly began to realize that these stories are not really about two human beings, Adam and Eve. They are stories that tell me something important about myself.

To recapitulate the previous discussion briefly, we are born into a kind of undifferentiated haze of wholeness in which we do not notice that there are differences in the world. Yet all those things out there on the other side of my skin really are out there, different from me, each with its own consciousness, awareness, likes and dislikes, needs, thoughts, and feelings. The understanding of this radical difference comes upon us slowly as we grow from infancy through childhood. It is in early adolescence that we typically begin to understand the power and importance of this differentiation of self from other. This dawning understanding is usually more or less simultaneous with our awakening genital sexuality.

We notice two things and are never the same again. One is that we really *are* ultimately different from every other thing on earth, and they from us. The other is that this difference creates the reality that we are moral beings, and that morality is not so much about following more or less arbitrary rules handed down to us from some authority but about taking responsibility for bridging the gap between self and another.

I discussed the story of the Fall of Adam and Eve and their Expulsion from the Garden above in Part I, but since these stories are the mythic versions of the Jewish soteriological question and are well-known to most of us, I want to return to that discussion. God's creating Adam and Eve in the story is comparable to our birth. The undifferentiated haze of wholeness into which we are born and in which we do not notice that there are differences in the world is the Garden. Even though there are lots of things on the other side of the infant's skin, they do not recognize this, and their journey into adulthood is the journey to understanding and overcoming difference.

In the Expulsion part of the story, Adam and Eve eat of the Fruit of the Tree of the Knowledge of Good and Evil, and the very first thing they notice is that they are naked. Their nakedness reveals their difference, and they see this difference as ultimate, believing that it cannot be bridged. I left the Garden when I began to realize that all those things out there on the other side of my skin really are out there, different from me, each with its own consciousness, awareness, likes and dislikes, needs, thoughts, and feelings.

The understanding of this radical difference comes upon us slowly as we grow from infancy through childhood. It is in early adolescence that we typically begin to understand the power and importance of this differentiation of self from other. Since it is usually more or less simultaneous with our awakening genital sexuality, our sexuality is a good metaphor. At some point, though, it dawns on us that we really *are* ultimately different from every other thing on earth, and they from us. At that point, when we notice this difference between self and other, we also begin to realize that if this difference really is ultimate, we are condemned not only to being alone inside of our skins but also to being unbearably alone. At that point, we are never the same again.

The understanding of the ultimacy of difference creates a kind of existential aloneness. It is with this aloneness that we are expelled from the Garden of Eden. Childhood is over; adulthood begins. It is also the beginning of the religious quest, the quest to return to the Garden, this in spite of the fact that deep in our souls there is the lurking fear that we can never return, that The Garden is closed to us forever. It would seem that, like Sisyphus, we are condemned to a hopeless quest, the quest to wander forever in search of something that, not only can we never find, but also, we know we can never find.

That, it seems to me, is the ultimate danger to our humanity.[4] To become genuinely human it appears we must first discover that which condemns us to an aloneness that appears to be so ultimate as to be unbreakable. The project would appear to be defeated even as it gets going. Our very existence condemns us and opens to us the possibility of alienation and despair. For Augustine the concept of sin was just this alienation and despair. I think he was right about that. Sin is not transmitted to us through a sexual act on the part of our parents. It is transmitted to us the moment when we recognize our separation from the rest of creation. This, not sex or even disobedience to God, is the Original Sin.

Another way of thinking about this is to think about violence. We have, I think, a rather shallow view of violence, thinking of it largely in terms of physical violence. Yet the phrase "physical violence" is not redundant, since there are forms of violence that have nothing to do with physicality. Violence is anything that violates the essential integrity, the wholeness and, if you will, the holiness of another being. In human terms, it is the violation of the humanity,

---

[4] For a more extended discussion of what it is to be human and of what I call the Human Project, see Part I, Chapter 1.

the personhood, the worth and dignity of another human being.

Clearly, when we abuse others physically, we are violating them, doing violence, but there are many other ways we can violate one another, from the failure to respect others' ways of thinking and being in the world, to failure to show compassion and empathy. Here are a few examples to illustrate my point:

- Demeaning a person's sexuality or gender expression is a violation of their humanity and is a form of violence.
- Failure to recognize one's complicity in acts of violence perpetuates those acts and thus is a form of violence.
- Accumulating far more wealth and resources than one needs while refusing to ameliorate the poverty of others violates their humanity and is a form of violence.

All forms of abuse are violent. This means, of course, that we can even be violent to ourselves through a failure to respect our own integrity, worth, and dignity.

The deepest form of violence is slavery[5]. It is not simply that to enslave another one must do violence to the body of the enslaved, as evil as that violence is. It is also that one must violate the soul of the enslaved, a violation that requires the simultaneous violation of one's own soul. This makes the violence of slavery both physical and spiritual, and this spiritual violence is continued and deepened, even when the physical violence is stopped.

In a 1982 sermon, Bishop Desmond Tutu wrote:

The evil of apartheid is perhaps not so much the untold misery and anguish it has caused its victims (great and

---

[5] See Collier, *The Great Wound: Confessions of a Slaveholding Family*.

traumatic as these must be). No, its pernicious nature, indeed its blasphemous character, is revealed in its effect on God's children when it makes them doubt that they are God's children.[6]

It follows from this that violence and apartheid are the same thing. The violence that moves people into despair, numb to Presence within them, thinking—or just being afraid—that they are less than human, less than God's children, is, quite simply, apartheid.

This despair born of numbness to Presence is found not only in the victims of violence, but also in its perpetrators. Thus, Howard Thurman writes this in his essay "Jesus and the Disinherited":

...hatred destroys finally the core of the life of the hater. While it lasts, burning in white heat, its effect seems positive and dynamic. But at last, it turns to ash, for it guarantees a final isolation from one's fellows. It blinds the individual to all values of worth, even as they apply to himself [sic] and to his [sic] fellows. Hatred bears deadly and bitter fruit. It is blind and nondiscriminating. True, it begins by exercising specific discrimination. This it does by centering upon persons responsible for situations which create the reaction of resentment, bitterness, and hatred. But once hatred is released, it cannot be confined to the offenders alone. It is difficult for hatred to be informed as to objects when it gets under way... Hatred cannot be controlled once it is set in motion.[7]

---

[6] Quoted in Michael Battle's Reconciliation: The Ubuntu Theology of Desmond Tutu, p. 162.

[7] Howard Thurman, *Jesus and the Disinherited*, p. 86.

Violence, then, is blindness to the image of God—Presence—within the soul of another. It is anything that denies or lessens human identity. It is anything that diminishes the humanity of human beings and tends to render them no longer human but merely *Homo sapiens*.[8] But such blindness is ultimately self-defeating because it requires blindness to oneself as a child of God, blindness to the true image of God within oneself. How could I see God clearly within my own soul and fail to see God within the soul of another? Is not the God within me is the same God as the God within thee? Thus, to lessen another's human identity is to lessen my own. To exclude another from his or her humanity is to exclude myself.

Understood in this way, then, violence includes all forms of political, economic, and moral oppression, to be sure, but it also includes far more. The list is nearly endless. For example, organizing the world into groups that are "in" and "out," like separating people into "the races of mankind," is a way of deciding who are the "real" people, the genuine human beings. Doing this invites us to violate others, for those who are "out" and therefore not "real" appear to be fair game. It becomes acceptable to treat them less than humanely—to violate them—if not overtly and physically, then psychologically and spiritually, in our consciousness, in our hearts, in our souls.

When we violate another psychologically, we inure ourselves to the suffering of another; we permit ourselves to demean them; we accept their pain as unimportant or even as appropriate in the world. And in the process, we violate them again. We violate one another whenever we treat another as less human, less holy, than

---

[8] Much of the work of Toni Morrison is an exploration of this within the context of American slavery.

ourselves. This is the core of the Golden Rule, in whatever form. Breaking this rule is the essence of violence; following it is the essence of the Hindu doctrine of *ahimsa* (nonviolence).

It is worth noting that this idea is found in many places. For example, it is essential both to Martin Buber's distinction between the I-Thou and the I-It relationships in his seminal book, *I and Thou*, and to understanding the implications this distinction has for how people treat one another. It is also implicit in my commentary above on The Buddha's words about Love dispelling hatred. I suspect that any theology that takes the idea of human relationship to be fundamental will ultimately come to this same conclusion, though the language in which it is couched may differ considerably.

I think that violence is the result of falling into a kind of despair. It happens when we become so alienated and terrified of our aloneness that we try desperately to cross that uncrossable divide through force, and to make others live, not their lives, but our lives. It is as if we try to obliterate the separation by obliterating other people. That, though, is impossible, and so violence simply creates deeper aloneness and despair, which, in turn, invites more desperation and violence.

## THE ANSWER

If there were no answer to the second soteriological question, pessimism would be justified. To be human really would be to be Sisyphus. So, I now had to turn to the second question: What will protect us from alienation, despair, violence, apartheid—sin? It would have to be something that has the power to allow us to cross, or, as the word suggests, to transcend the barrier of our skin. It would have to be something that could reveal to us that while it is true that we stop at our skin, it is also true that we do not stop at our skin. Is there something that has that power?

I have found that the answer is yes. When I was sixteen years old, I had my first truly mystical/spiritual experience. This was my experience of disappearing into the remnants of a thunderstorm.

The experience has stayed with me, sometimes in an attenuated form and sometimes as real as this moment. Walking into that evening, I felt a profound Love enter my soul, a Love that was not simply an emotion, even though I did feel it deeply. It was also, and far more importantly, a palpable Presence that linked itself in my heart to itself in the world. I felt this Presence as a blessing. In a way that is even more intimate a knowing than one knows another in the deepest sexual experience, I knew that while aloneness is certainly real, it is also transcended by a Love that binds the universe into an indivisible whole. I also knew that the experiencing of this Love and giving it the flesh of my living is the way to open my soul to the humanity that until that moment had been but a promise yet to be redeemed.

At the age of only sixteen, of course, I could not have described this experience in this language, though I did know that my life was forever changed. What I had I experienced was Presence. Each of us discovers it in our own way; this was mine. How it is discovered is not what is important. What is important is that it *is* discovered. And what is Presence? It is a transcendent Love that permeates and deepens all of human existence. And since this Love permeates human existence, it draws us all together and links us in an interdependent whole. The realization that we are, in this sense, one is the foundation of moral agency.

When they ate that famous metaphorical apple, Adam and Eve discovered that human beings are moral agents. It is important that the forbidden fruit was not really an apple. The tree was not even The Tree of Knowledge or the Tree of the Knowledge of Evil. It was the Tree of the Knowledge of *Good and Evil*. The metaphor is clear. Knowing good and evil requires knowing two things. Knowledge of evil requires knowing that we are alone within our skins, for separation and alienation is the essence of evil. Knowledge of good requires that we understand that being alone does not condemn us to being separate, for relationship is the essence of goodness. The discovery of existential aloneness coincides with the longing to be in relationship with the other. Knowledge of good and evil is the beginning of moral action, and moral agency proceeds from *ubuntu*.

The key to relationship with the other is the realization of and encounter with Love. This is why we are, in fact our "brother's keeper." This is why the Torah enjoins us to love our neighbor as ourselves, for in Love, in Presence, our neighbor *is* our self. This is why Jesus of Nazareth believed that it is impossible to love God without loving our neighbor and why The Buddha said that only Love dispels hatred, only Love overcomes evil.

This, then, is the beginning of my metatheology. What endangers our humanity? Our greatest danger is separation, alienation, despair, violence, and apartheid. What saves us from this danger? *Ubuntu*—saves us, the Love that transcends the barriers between us.

## Night, Tarnished

A melancholy sweeps over me as the sun
Drops its light behind the sea. The light
Shimmers, dims, trembles, fades, and is gone.
My mood darkens with the sky's vast darkness.

Sometimes the light of hope is as dark
As the sky this night. It falls to the sea and is drowned.
The deep waters of despair close over it,
And with a hiss that snaps shut the lock,
Darkness closes over me.

And here I stand. Alone. Empty-hearted.
Wandering the empty shore, the cold sand,
Aimlessly waiting for I know not what.

The moon will rise with its beautiful light.
But oh, how dark and long is the night!

## Night, Polished

Standing on the bluffs tonight, I look into the sky.
The darkness is beautiful, lit by silver stars
That dance and sway to a distant, elegant music.
A crescent moon hangs among the stars
And seems, looking about the world, to smile.
The breeze is gentle; the waves lap the shore
Below the bluffs with a hypnotic sound,
As if to call my heart back to Life.

Something rises in my heart that fills me
With joy. It is like a song sung to me
By no one, a poem written by no hand,
A gift that cannot be taken but only given.

I know the sun will swallow this music with its light,
But oh, how long and beautiful is the night![9]

---

[9] Collier, *Full Circle*, pp. 9, 27.

CHAPTER 3:

# Theology
### *What Is Ultimate Reality?*

There are at least three senses in which people use the word *theology*. In ordinary, non-technical usage, it refers to almost any more or less serious talk about religion. In more technical usage, it refers to two things. On the one hand, it refers generally to careful and rational thinking about religion. On the other hand, it refers more specifically, and as the word itself suggests (from the Greek words *logos*, in this context, meaning *an account of*, and *theos*, meaning *God*), to a systematic discussion of the concept of deity, God, Ultimate Reality, Presence.[1] One could even say, (somewhat oddly) that theology is part of Theology.

Most people would say that God[2] is the central concept in religion, and it is arguable that this is true of the Religions of The Book (Judaism, Christianity, and Islam). One might think that the notion of a non-theist Jew, Christian, or Muslim is an oxymoron. On the other hand, I have known people who described themselves as Christian Humanists while disavowing belief in God. In any event, certainly Confucianism and many sects of Buddhism are, at most, indifferent to the idea of deity. As the Buddha is credited

---

[1] To distinguish the more general use from the more specific use, I call the general use *Theology* and the more specific use, *theology*.

[2] Through most of the first part of this chapter, I revert to the more conventional and familiar word *God*.

with saying, "I do not teach that there is a God, and I do not teach that there is not a God. I teach release from *dukkha*."[3] Nevertheless, since the notion of divinity is so central to most of Western religious thinking, it does seem to me appropriate to take up this topic next.

I do so with no small degree of trepidation. In the first place, the idea of God is difficult to hold in one's mind. In the second place, there is a certain irony in the fact that the subject of God is one of those ideas that has aroused enormous amounts of ill-will, anger, dissention, and even violence. Untold millions of people have lost their livelihoods—not to mention their lives—for believing the "wrong" thing about God, whatever the current and local "wrong" thing may happen to be. While I am not afraid of this level of gross intolerance among my readers, I am well aware that the idea of God is one that arouses people to passion, paradoxically even among people who reject it.

## The Importance of God

That said, I do think that far too many people dismiss the idea of God rather too lightly. One sometimes hears people saying that the idea of God is a false one, or, at the very least, that there is little (or no) evidence (meaning "empirical evidence") to support the assertion of God's existence. In the extreme, one sometimes even hears people say that the idea of God is simply mystical mumbo-jumbo that has no place in a sophisticated, rational view of the

---

[3] This is a paraphrase of a comment recorded in the Cula-Malunkya-suta. Quoted in Walpola Rahula, *What the Buddha Taught*, p. 14.

world. This extreme view is clearly nothing but *ad hominem* and thus utterly irrelevant, but the call for empirical evidence for the existence of God deserves some attention. It contains the epistemic assumption that, outside of mathematics and logic, when one asserts the existence of something, one is making an empirically verifiable assertion. Thus, to assert that God exists, one must have empirical evidence. This is based—again—on the idea that the only sense of truth acceptable is the truth of science.

I argued earlier the lack of scientific evidence either for or against God's existence is irrelevant since assertions about God are not scientific assertions but religious ones. Therefore, their truth cannot be evaluated by scientific method and cannons but only by religious ones.[4] One does not ask whether a religious assertion is independently verifiable but whether or not it heals the broken heart. It seems obvious that the answer to this question is that the religious beliefs expressed in both assertion of God's existence and the denial of God's existence can and often do heal broken hearts. Thus, both are religiously true and are not in actual contradiction.

It is a monumental arrogance and a classic example of a Strawman Argument to assert that God is nothing more than the Great Old White Man in the Sky with a long white beard and funny robes and then to dismiss the idea of God as either childish or irrational or unsophisticated. Surely that is not the idea that inspired *The Upanishads*, a body of religious poetry that has moved people and changed their lives for at least 3,000 years.[5] Nor is it the idea that

---

[4] By the same token, of course, scientific assertions cannot be evaluated according to religious notions of truth. Both of these points are all too often lost sight of.

[5] See for example, *The Upanishads: Breath of the Eternal*, Swami Prabhavananda and Frederick Manchester

so captivated the Baal Shem Tov that within a generation he and his Hassidic followers were able to rekindle the spark of living fire within Eastern European Jewry. And it is certainly not the idea that has healed millions from lives of addiction and despair.

So, what is it that can so thrill people that the poetry they write under its influence is revered for millennia and retains its power to inspire even when transported into utterly foreign cultures and languages? What is this thing that can so utterly transfix and transform people that it enables them to regenerate a dying culture and heal broken hearts and souls? What is it that can fill empty lives and give people the strength to face the demons of their past and defeat them?

Whatever that is, it is surely neither childish nor irrational nor unsophisticated. It must tap the very wellsprings of profundity, and we turn our backs on it at our own great peril. I sometimes find an idea that at first appears silly to me and easily dismissed but on closer examination reveals the power to engage some of the best minds that have ever lived. When this happens, an appropriate humility demands that I assume that I have missed something important and that I need to take another, closer, look. The idea of God is such an idea.

Consider this problem that I have occasionally. Every now and again I find myself at a gathering of people at which the conversation turns to religion, and someone will ask me whether or not I believe in God. I'm stuck. How could I possibly answer a question like that? A simple yes or no won't work, because before I could answer yes or no, I'd have to know which conception of God my questioner is asking about. There are some conceptions of God I can give assent to and others to which I cannot and still others that have never even occurred to me. Without a long preliminary conversation any answer I could give would surely be misleading at best.

## SOME COMMON MISCONCEPTIONS

Let me begin the discussion, then, with some of the more conventional conceptions. First consider the common notion of God as a, or perhaps *The*, Supreme Being. This notion is often, though misleadingly and incorrectly, thought to be represented by the figure in the long white robe with the flowing white hair and beard on the ceiling of the Sistine Chapel. I think that the idea of God as Supreme Being is little more than anthropomorphism since it takes all those qualities that we most admire about human beings and blows them up into bigger-than-life images. It's as if one thinks that God is just another human being, only a lot more.

The trouble with this is that what counts as the best that humanity has to offer is pretty clearly culture bound. For example, is God brave, courageous, and fierce, or is God compassionate, peace-loving, and forgiving? Could we have it both ways, with God both fierce and peace-loving? Perhaps, though, God is neither; perhaps God is something else entirely, embodying qualities embraced by cultures radically different from ours. Could there be lots of Gods, one (or more) for each culture? How could that be? How could there be multiple *Supreme* Beings?

To embrace the Supreme Being notion of God, it seems to me, would be to assert the supremacy of one culture over all the others that hold different human qualities to be the most admirable.[6] But that just begs the question. How could we know which human qualities are supreme without knowing already which human qualities are God-like? A quagmire ensues.

One variation on this is to let go of human qualities entirely and argue that since God is the Supreme Being, we cannot know what sorts of qualities God may or may not possess. But then I fail to understand what the phrase "Supreme Being" means. It would seem to me that by definition any being, supreme or otherwise, must be part of the furniture of the universe and would have to appear on the list of things that exist. But I fail to see any hierarchy in the list. To say that some things are "better" than others, we would have to know which things are more God-like. But how could we know this without begging the question again. If God created *all* things, is it not an arrogance to suggest that some things God created are better than others (with, of course, human beings at the top of the list and generally white human beings at the top of the top of the list)? Did God make a mistake creating the things that I don't happen to like, for example, mosquitoes? How could that be? Quagmires abound.

Another variation is to suggest that God is an abstraction, a sort of religious theoretical entity like negative numbers and dark matter. There are huge philosophical arguments about the ontological status of theoretical entities. How does one tell whether an entity that one cannot perceive actually exists? Indeed, what does it even mean to say that they exist? I am not talking of entities like the far side of the moon that could be perceived were we in a position to

---

[6] This seems to be what in fact Euro-centric colonialism actually believed, with, of course, European culture at the top.

perceive them. I am talking about an entity that in principle cannot be perceived directly but only through their effects on things that can be perceived directly. Theoretical entities, then, are things like dark matter or the interior of black holes or electrons.

How do we know they exist? We have to infer their existence from phenomena we can actually see, and that means our knowledge of their existence is always dependent on current theory. If the current theory is overthrown, the assertion of the existence of any entity, the existence of which is inferred from that theory, is thrown into doubt. This happens all the time in science. Consider, for example, the story of phlogiston or the electromagnetic ether. Our knowledge of the existence of theoretical entities, then, is always dependent on whatever else we know. So, we are faced with a very real question of whether or not their actual existence is dependent on there being humans.

For example, do, say, negative numbers have an existence that is independent of human beings? Were there negative numbers, say a billion years ago? Will there be negative numbers when there are no longer any humans to think about them? These questions seem rather arcane when we are talking about mathematics and logic, but they become very serious in science. Were there (will there be) electrons when there were (will be) no human beings to observe their effects? This turns out to be a surprisingly difficult question to answer.

In any event, it does seem to me that all entities that are, in principle, not directly observable are human constructs, created to make sense of the world *we live in*. Thus, the suggestion that God is such a theoretical entity seems a rather peculiar notion in spite of what might at first appear to be an attractive way of thinking. Our knowledge of God's existence would then be, like our knowledge of electrons, dark matter, and black holes (and phlogiston, comes to that), dependent on whatever else we may know. If we were to give up a theory that implied God's existence, then God would suffer the same fate as phlogiston.[7]

I conclude that God is not any sort of being at all, supreme or otherwise, and that this precludes all anthropomorphic ways of thinking and talking about God. For example, God does not will this or that. God does not "have a plan" or listen to human prayers or direct the course of history. God does not get angry, watch over us, get jealous, judge, hate, get bored, or anything else that we human beings do. All of these things are just projections of what we do onto that which we neither understand nor comprehend. Some people say that this would leave us with nothing at all, but I don't think so. I think there is more to the story.

I began to wonder why there is such a strong taboo in Judaism and many other religions against uttering the name of God. I think that there is more to it than simply being a bit of left-over ancient name magic. It is really about avoiding the mistake of turning God into a thing, an idol. One cannot utter the name of God because God has no name. As pointed out previously, to name something is to separate it out from everything else that is. It is thus to limit that thing, saying it is this but not that. Suppose, though, God has no limit. How, then, could one name it? How would one separate

---

[7] Of course, we could suggest that God's existence is mythic in the sense developed above in Part I, Chapter 3, but that would lead to the conclusion that there must be multiple Gods since there are multiple mythologies. It would also lead us to conclude that since the power of myth depends on there being humans, God's existence is also dependent on there being humans. But then what of the supremacy of God? Yet another quagmire.

it from everything else? It follows that to name God is to make of God an idol, a mere thing.[8] It is to hold up something that one substitutes for the genuine, unlimited God. The famous opening line from *The Tao Te Ching* point succinctly to this problem:

The Tao we call "tao" is not the Tao.

The name we call "holy" is not holy name.

Yet the use of the word "God" to mean some sort of existing being is so pervasive that to use it in another sense is to invite confusion.[9] It is also a term that some people find to be so offensive that it stops them from going any deeper in their understanding of religion or their own lives. But one cannot simply give up on the whole theological enterprise because of this problem. To refuse to use a word is not the same thing as to reject an idea or a concept. The word, after all, is not the concept. The words are not as important as that to which the words point. The experience of awe and the wholeness of the heart are what religious language expresses, however one may choose to think or talk about them. These experiences can be found in every life if one takes the trouble and care to recognize them. From here on, then, to avoid both confusion and the giving of offense, I shall try to keep the use of the word "God" to a minimum and, as I noted earlier, instead use the term

---

[8] The first definition of the word *idol* in the American Heritage Dictionary is "an image used as an object of worship," and it comes ultimately from a Proto-Indo-European roots meaning "to see." Thus, in its original usage, an idol is something visible that is the object of worship, *i.e.* a mere thing that is worshipped. It seems to me a small step from this to including non-visible worshipped things as idols. For example, power becomes an idol when it is worshipped. As I have argued, not all things are visible. To reduce God to a thing, then, is to create an idol.

[9] See also the discussion of *God* above.

"Presence." I hope the reason for preferring this term will become clear as we go along.

## A DIFFERENT UNDERSTANDING

To me, a deeper and more profound understanding of Presence begins when we encounter two things: awe and healing, or, to use more conventional religious language for the same thing, mystery and holiness. These two terms need a little explanation. Mystery is not, as is sometimes derisively suggested, a bogus explanation for that which science cannot yet explain, with emphasis on the "yet." Science does not remove mystery from life. And holiness is not a quality that insulates some people from being sullied by the material world—or that some people think insulates themselves.

Mystery, properly understood, is what a parishioner of mine some years ago once called, coining a wonderful word, "the awe-struck-fullness of the world." Mystery is that which excites awe, the realization within the heart—or, if you will, within the soul—that we are tied together into a fullness, a depth and profundity, and a sheer beauty that pervades the universe without being part of it. This is interdependence as a religious reality. The Hindu metaphor for this is a good one: Mystery pervades the universe without being part of the universe as salt pervades the sea without being water. Awe is the apprehension of mystery expressed as a blessing that descends upon the universe like song. This is Presence-as-Transcendent.

Holiness is simply the quality of being whole. It is that which dwells within each of us in virtue of which each and every one of us is loved and cherished, just as we are, in our own being. It is the sacredness that we hold in our own hearts. Our apprehension of our own sacredness has the power to move us from the alienation of violence and separation to the wholeness of Love. Holiness is the font of internal worth and dignity within each of us. Indeed, I would even say that this worth and dignity is who we truly are. It is our integrity. This worth and dignity, then, is nothing but Love expressing itself in our living. Thus, there is a sense in which one can say that we are also creatures of Love, and since Love is but the expression of Presence, at the most profound level, our being is an expression of Presence. This is Presence-as-Immanent.

There is a myth in Hinduism that I think expresses these ideas quite beautifully. Shivanataraj, Shiva Lord of the Dance, creates all things, it is said, with his divine dance. As he dances, each thing comes into existence, lives for a while and then falls again into his All-Consuming Flame. But Shiva, in all of his manifestations, is simply an avatar of Brahman[10]. Our reality is, more properly, understood, the dance of Shivanataraj. Thus, each thing is but Brahman expressed through the dance of its avatar, Shiva. We are Brahman twice removed. Thus, we are, each and every one of us, holy. Enlightenment is but our awakening to this true nature and living our lives in its light.

---

[10] Hinduism is actually and in spite of appearance, a monotheistic religion. The only true god is Brahman. All of the thousands of lesser "gods" and "goddesses" are but aspects or expressions or avatars of Brahman. All is ultimately Brahman (or more properly, Brahaman/Atman), Brahman pervading all like salt pervades the sea.

## THE IMMANENCE AND TRANSCENDENCE OF PRESENCE

This discussion raises the question of immanence and transcendence. If one replaces the word "Tao" with the word "God" in the *Tao Te Ching*, one finds oneself contemplating something that is so utterly outside of the universe ("the ten thousand things") that it cannot even be spoken of. And yet, as *The Upanishads* ("...though you do not see Brahman in this body, He is indeed there"[11]), St. John ("Those who love, love God, for God is love"[12]) and the Baal Shem Tov ("Whatever is above is also down below"[13]) remind us over and over, there is nothing wherein there is no trace of Presence.

There is no place wherein Presence is not hiding; there is no place where Presence cannot be found. There are no "God forsaken" places. Presence is both utterly beyond our power to name and speak of, and it is about us at every moment. It is both above us as the clouds are above the earth and filling our lives as blood fills our bodies. (Religion is no stranger to paradox.) The first concept, Presence as Tao, is referred to as Transcendence; the second, Presence as filling existence, is referred to as Immanence.

Presence-as-Transcendent is beyond the universe in the sense that it is the background that creates possibility of the universe. It is that without which nothing that is could be, and yet is not of this world, as Shivanataraj dances the world into existence but is not part of this world himself. The great 20th century theologian, Paul

---

[11] Swami Prabhavananda and Frederick Manchester, trans., *The Unpanishads*, p. 70.

[12] The First Letter of St. John, Chapter 4, verse 16.

[13] The Baal Shem Tov, quoted in Elie Wiesel, *Souls of Fire: Portraits of Hasidic Masters*, p. 32.

Tillich, called this "The Ground of Being." It is Presence-as-Transcendent that Michelangelo sought to express in his famous painting on the Sistine Chapel ceiling as God reaches across the void between Earth and Heaven granting a spark of life to Adam. Knowledge of Presence-as-Transcendence is manifest as awe.[14]

Presence-as-Immanent is so totally within the universe that it cannot be escaped, cannot be lost, cannot be discarded, though it can easily be forgotten or ignored or lost sight of. This is Presence that is constantly with us, constantly reminding us of the integrity our lives are built of, constantly showing us the possibility of healing in the real circumstances of our lives. It is Presence-as-Immanent that we encounter in those moments of unexpected insight and wonder. It is Presence-as-Immanent that opens the doors and windows of our lives to the winds of healing. It is Presence-as-Immanent that we know when we experience the ties that bind us together with each other and with all that is. Knowledge of Presence-as-Immanent is manifest as *ubuntu*, as is all other forms of Love.

I am at a loss when I contemplate the question, "which of these ways of understanding Presence is correct?" The seeming paradoxical answer that I simply cannot escape is that both ways are correct. Lao Tzu writes of the Tao that is so utterly beyond this world that it cannot even be named but only pointed at, like a finger pointing at the moon (to mix a Buddhist metaphor with a Taoist insight). And he is right; Presence is like that. In an accidental paraphrase of a famous Navajo song, *The Upanishads* speak of Brahman [Presence] as "upon the right, upon the left, above, below, behind, in front,"[15]

---

[14] To see just how powerfully Michelangelo expressed this, you have to see that fresco in person.

[15] Swami Prabhavananda and Manchester, op cit. p. 46.

and they speak of Presence without which there is neither love nor beauty nor healing nor even life in this world. And they are right; Presence is like that.

So, is Presence actually two, a transcendent one and an immanent one? No. There is only Presence, now understood as transcendent, now as immanent. Neither idea captures Presence completely, because both are only human constructs expressed in human language with all of its limitations. Immanence is Presence seen as process, and transcendence is Presence seen as eternal. Immanence is but transcendence leaving its footprints in time; transcendence is only immanence projected outside of time and into eternity. To grasp Presence one needs both concepts, just as one needs both eyes in order to see depth.

It is like music. The musician—either the performer or the composer—is not the music, though without the musician there could be no music. Yet we hear the musician in the music. Who would fail to hear Pablo Casals in his performance of the Bach Cello Suites? Who would confuse a Bach cantata with a Beatles' song?

The suggestion that we embrace both transcendence and immanence may appear at first blush to be paradoxical. But I have found that in the realm of mystery and awe, paradox abounds because any attempt to capture the part of human experience that carries us beyond the power of the rational to apprehend runs afoul of the limitations of language rather quickly. Poetry and paradox become essential to the expression of the experience of Presence. Divinity, Ultimate Reality, what I call Presence, is not a thing to be discovered like a desert island or a subatomic particle. It is the existential core of one's being, the foundation of one's faith (existential trust), the central reality of one's being. At least this is how I have experienced it, and how I continue to experience it in my life and how I seek to express it in the way that I live.

But why would anyone accept either conception of Presence, let alone both? Think for a moment of the famous ontological argument for God's existence, usually attributed to St. Anselm. In Anselm's formulation, it runs like this:

> God, by definition, is the most perfect being, that than which no greater can be or be conceived. But a being that is both conceivable and exists is greater, more powerful— more perfect—than one that can be conceived but does not exist. Therefore, God exists.

In more contemporary and less formal language, the argument is this. God is, by definition, absolutely perfect and therefore ultimately powerful. But failure to exist implies powerlessness. Since God cannot be both ultimately powerful and powerless, it follows that God must exist. As a point of simple logic this argument is entirely valid—that is, if the premises are granted, then the conclusion cannot be denied except upon pain of contradiction. Yet it seems to me that the ontological argument misses the point, as all such rational arguments must miss the point. By the same token, many of the arguments for atheism are logically valid as well, but also miss the point. I cannot emphasize too strongly that experience precedes rationality, and religious belief is a matter of experience.

I have never known anyone who was turned either from or to theism solely on the basis of a logical argument. Valid though these arguments may be, they rest on the assumption that religious belief is like logical or scientific belief. But neither belief nor disbelief is a logical, rational matter. It is far more like falling in love than it is like learning set theory or relativity theory.

Again, belief is more fundamental than theology. Belief is based on direct experience while theology is a rational reconstruction of direct experience. We cannot simply believe anything we want to believe. We can believe only those things that we discover we must believe, only what the circumstances and experiences of our lives require that we believe. Assent can be compelled, but belief cannot. It can only be discovered. Why anyone would opt for the theist paradox, then, is not the correct question to ask. The correct question is what kind of experience would lead one to embrace such a paradox as the most adequate expression of their religious belief.

And now I was almost ready to get back to the question I started with, whether or not I believe in God—in Presence. First, though, I needed to remind myself of a fundamental point I have made several times already. When one makes a knowledge claim in religion, one is not making an empirical claim, and this is true even when one appears to be making such a claim. Religious knowledge, as I pointed out earlier, does not turn on scientific evidence but on the embrace of a certain religious mythology.

And again, I am not using the word "mythology" here in the unfortunately common sense of a story that is either intentionally misleading or used to cover ignorance. I am using it in the sense of Joseph Campbell to indicate an expression of the profound foundation of one's faith, that wherein one finds healing for existential aloneness.[16] Even apparent existence claims in religion are ways of committing oneself to a mythic system.

---

[16] See for example his *The Power of Myth*.

## So Then, Do I believe in God?

With this in mind, I can answer the original question: Do I believe in God, in Presence? It should be obvious, though, that I find this to be an unfortunate formulation of the question. First, it needs to be restated: What kinds of experiences have I had that lead me to take my refuge in Presence? And how do I express that refuge? What is my religious mythology? Clearly the mystical experience I had at the age of 16 is one such experience, but that is not enough. Many people have that kind of experience, and it leads them in entirely different directions.

That experience, as striking and profound as it was, is not the only religious experience I have had. They do not happen often, but as I reflect on them, I realize that they are far more common than I originally thought. These experiences turn out to be both as inexplicable and unexpected as the mystical experience of my youth and as ordinary as waking up in the morning.

The inexplicable and unexpected experiences come upon me in meditation and in a few extraordinary moments. Sometimes during zazen or, even simply standing in front of the sea as a storm comes ashore, I am drawn outside of myself. I am caught up in a beauty that embraces far more than my ordinary consciousness could encompass. In those moments, I know Presence as something that guarantees that my soul is part of a greater wholeness and that any apparent barriers between me and Creation are but illusions through which my life dances.

The ordinary experiences are those moments when I am able to pull aside the veils and see between the cracks, hearing a distant or not so distant music weaving itself in and through my soul. In these moments, I am held ever so gently, as a mother cradles her baby's head while nursing it.

Examples of these moments are rife if we simply pay attention. Consider those moments of deep compassion when the suffering of another so touches you that you must act. Consider those moments when you are so caught up in love that your very soul spills over with love. Consider moments of aesthetic arrest that give birth to tears. Consider moments of deep, sharing friendship, or soul-filling laughter, or the delight of watching the free and easy play of a child. In these moments, we know Presence as something that nurtures and completes the soul, assuring us that we are not alone and that we are loved profoundly, unconditionally, and completely. We know that we are enough.

As different as these kinds of experiences are, though, there is one thing that they have in common. They all pull us beyond the particularity of ourselves. They show us, in ways that are both unmistakable and unshakable, that all of those things out there, on the other side of our skin, are really not so very different from us. They, too, are loved profoundly, unconditionally, and completely; they, too, are part of a greater wholeness; their lives, too, dance through those illusory barriers. They, too, are enough. All of these experiences are experiences of Presence expressing itself as *ubuntu*, and they move us toward the realization of our own humanity within the humanity of all. Indeed, they move us beyond the limits of humanity itself toward the unlimited and illustrate the truth that not only are we all one, but also, we are all infinite.

Why do I believe in—take refuge in—Presence? Because I have experienced it in my life and because this experience is, for me, the fulfillment of the promise of my birth. It is the return to Eden, not as an undifferentiated child but as a realized adult, knowing that I am both separate from all that is, and I am inseparably bound up in all that is. It is as the Zen saying has it:

> Before one begins the practice of Zen, rivers are rivers and mountains are mountains. After one begins to practice, rivers are no longer rivers and mountains are no longer mountains. But after one fulfills one's study, rivers are once again rivers and mountains are once again mountains."[17]

This is the Return to the Garden.

In the light of these experiences, I understand that there is no paradox. Presence is both transcendent and immanent, both within my soul and beyond my being. What, then, shall I do with this vision? I cannot unsee it. I cannot hide it or horde it away in a closet. I cannot pretend that it is not there. All I can do is to allow it to inform my life. All I can do is follow it. All I can do is live my life in the light of its mystery and stand in awe of its power to heal and fill my soul. All I can do is take my refuge within it.

## A Non-Theist Understanding of the Religious Experience

Having said this, I also remember another saying attributed to The Buddha: "Whether or not there is a God, there is still the question of your Enlightenment." It occurs to me that this vision, as I have called it, which I have understood as the ground of a

---

[17] Attributed to the 9th century CE Zen Master Ching-Yuan Wei-Shin.

mythology rooted in Presence, should also be understandable in an agnostic, perhaps even atheist, mythology as well. To see how, I must be careful to understand what such a theology might look like.[18]

To begin with we must be careful to avoid three common and rather shallow traps. First, the agnostic/atheist might claim that there is no evidential ground either for or against an assertion of God's existence. I agree with that claim without finding it very interesting, because, as I have argued, the assertion of God's existence is not an empirical assertion. The assertion of Presence is what I think of as a refuge statement: an autobiographical declaration of where one takes one's refuge, the assertion of what sort of mythology one adopts and finds healing of existential aloneness.

Second, the agnostic/atheist might be asserting that there is no reason to accept that there is beauty, richness, and healing in the world. Such a claim would be patently false. And third, the agnostic/atheist might try to be arguing that I, who have had the vision, didn't really have it. That would be like those who have never tasted mangoes claiming that they really don't taste any different from peaches.

To be making an interesting claim, the agnostic must be offering a way to understand the vision that both recognizes its importance and power and does not appeal to Presence. One way that this is sometimes done is to try to explain the mystical, religious vision in terms of human brain chemistry and physiology, thus "explaining it away." On this view, the mystical vision is "nothing but" a certain pattern of neural firings, a certain, in principle describable, state of

---

[18] I am, after all, constructing a metatheology, not a theology.

the human brain, and therefore it has no external referent.

The problem with this is two-fold. In the first place, it leads to solipsism. Precisely the same claim could be made about any experience whatsoever, including the experience of such manifestly existent things as our friends, sealing wax, cabbages, and kings. When I experience a cabbage, for example, it could be said that the experience is "nothing but" a pattern of neuron firings in my brain, a certain neuro-physiological state. If such an explanation of the experience of external objects does not "explain away cabbages," then nether does it "explain away" the object of the mystical, religious experience. You can't have it both ways.

In the second place, suppose it were true that one could give a complete neuro-physiological account of the mystical experience. Nothing would follow from that description alone. The experiences themselves would remain as powerful and moving as before, and as important to those who have them. To see this, let us think about something a little less grandiose than Presence. Think about being in love.

Suppose it were possible to give a complete neuro-physiological description of being in love. Would such a description make the power or the importance of being in love disappear? Would we want to say that being in love is "nothing but" being in that neuro-physiological state and that therefore being in love is "explained away?" Would we even want to say that the phrase "to fall in love" means "getting into that neuro-physical state?" I certainly wouldn't. Would knowing that neuro-physiological description lessen the beauty or the meaning or the power of the world's great love poetry or evaporate the impulse of poets to write about love? Surely not. Why, then, would an understanding of the neural and chemical pattern of a brain in a mystical, religious vision empty that vision of its power, meaning or importance?

The agnostic/atheist appeal to neurophysiology won't work. Rather than dismiss the vision, what might happen if the agnostic/atheist were to embrace it? Could that be done without invoking Presence? Is there a religious or at least mystical agnosticism?

Surely there is. Rather than trying to contradict theism, the agnostic/atheist can simply embrace the experience and rest content with that. There is nothing that I can see inconsistent with either agnosticism or atheism in acknowledging a profundity within our experience of life, and a deep and moving beauty, even an inviolable core of integrity within each human being that engenders an inherent worth and dignity to each. And having experienced and acknowledged this profundity, beauty and integrity, the agnostic can build a religious mythology on this foundation. This mythology need not invoke Presence or any other way of referring to God.[19]

## A RECONCILIATION OF THEISM AND ATHEISM

The mistake is to assume that one and only one of theism, agnosticism, or atheism must be correct and that the others are therefore false. That assumption rests on an epistemology that insists that in all of human knowledge the Law of the Excluded Middle[20] reigns supreme. My rather radical suggestion is that this

---

[19] The 20th century Unitarian Universalist, Kenneth Patton, is an example of a Humanist who has actually done this.

[20] The Law of the Excluded Middle is the assertion that all propositions are either true or else false; there is no middle ground between them.

# Chapter 3: Theology

Law grounds only science and mathematics[21]. It certainly does not apply in religion. Religion is based, not on intersubjective empiricism, but on the ultimately private regions of the human heart and soul, where one encounters Presence. Thus, the truths of religion are not empirical but existential, truths not so much of assertion but of commitment. If that is true, then there is no reason to suppose that any two religious stances, such as theism and atheism, are exclusive in the sense that the truth of one implies the intersubjective falsehood of the other. At most an existential commitment to one precludes an existential commitment to the other.

I choose to invoke Presence because that is how I experience the healing vision, as a Presence moving in and through my heart and soul. The agnostic and the atheist experience that vision in other ways. To suppose that there is one and only one correct way to experience the healing vision is to fall into the error of placing understanding prior to experience and theology prior to vision. It is mistaking the finger for the moon to which it points. Theology is a species of understanding, an understanding and recounting of the religious experience. In religion, though, experience is always prior to understanding, and vision is always prior to thought.

I use the word *Presence* to refer to my experience of profundity and beauty; the agnostic and atheist refer to it in other ways. This disagreement strikes me as a verbal one and not worth getting very excited about. What does strike me as profound, important, and well worth getting excited about is our agreement that the core of human experience is profound, beautiful, and healing. This agreement points to a common beginning from which we all derive our

---

[21] It may not even apply there. There are, after all, many-valued logics and quantum logics.

religious stands, our mythology, and in which we take our refuge, our faith. The difference lies more in how each chooses to follow the religious journey than in how each begins that journey.

**The Black Cat**

We try to find a silent black cat
In an empty, dark room. We blindfold ourselves—
Maybe blindness will help us to see in the dark.
We grope madly this way and that and finally
Declare with conviction there is no cat.

Then we sit, still and silent,
And the black cat crawls into our lap and purrs.[22]

---

[22] Collier, *How To See Deer*, p. 17.

**CHAPTER 4:**

# Missiology

*What are we called to do?*

*Missiology* is a word that is rarely if ever heard in day-to-day conversation. Think of it as *missionology*, an understanding of our mission in life. Since the word *mission* comes from a Latin word meaning "to be sent forth," a more accurate meaning of missiology is that it is an understanding of that to which we are called. But that's not very helpful, because the question of being called does not often come up often in ordinary conversation either. More typically, being called is used in a strictly religious context. It is also sometimes argued that being called implies a caller and thus, since this caller must be God, a theistically neutral Theology—or even meta-Theological framework such as I am developing—is impossible. This argument is a red herring. To paraphrase the famous remark of The Buddha quoted above: "Whether or not there is a caller, there is still the question of your enlightenment."

The real point is the call itself, from whatever source it may have come. So, I put this aside, thinking of being called as a bit of religious jargon and get on with the business of understanding the jargon. This will require that I get a clear understanding of what it means for someone to be called and what one is called to do—even those of us who do not recognize any caller.

## Rabbi Zusya

There is wonderful Hassidic story about what it means to be called. Rabbi Zusya was on his death bed. His sorrowing Hassidim gathered around and begged him for one final lesson, something that would sum up his teachings. He turned to them as said, "Very soon I shall stand before the Most High, and He will ask me the most terrible question of all. He will not ask me why I was not Abraham or Moses or Elijah. He will ask me why I was not Zusya."[1]

That is the answer to our question, in a nutshell. To what are we called? We are called to be ourselves—or perhaps the point is better put this way: we are called to become ourselves. What could be more obvious than that? What could be more difficult than that?

So far so good, but in life in general and in Theology in particular, nothing is ever straightforward. What is this "self" to which we are called to become? Obviously, this self is not our body, our biological self. If it were, our calling would be virtually fulfilled and our humanity completed, at the moment of our conception since our biology is, to a large extent, determined by our genetics. There must be more to this self business than meets the eye, and indeed there is.[2]

The self I have in mind here is created at the intersection of our biology (genetics) with our experience of the cosmos in the light of the integrity of our hearts and souls. Since that intersection never stops until our death, the creation of our self is never complete until our death. This self is utterly unique inasmuch as the combination

---

[1] Martin Buber, Tales of the Hassidim: Early Masters, p. 251.

[2] Consider, for example, Dōgen's famous remark, "In order to achieve the Self, you must lose the self."

of genes and experience each individual represents has never occurred before in the entire history of the universe and will never occur again. On the other hand, we should not be overly impressed with our uniqueness, since the same thing is true of every other living thing that has ever existed or that ever will exist.

Another way of putting all this is that we are called to become human, not in the biological sense but in the moral and spiritual sense. We are called to engage the Human Project of realizing—in the primary sense of making real—the promise of an individual specimen of Homo sapiens as a human being, and this process is unending. There are at least two dimensions of this self, and I want to explore both. The first dimension is the self as an individual, separate and distinctly human. This self becomes human as it incarnates its integrity. The second dimension is the self as a participant in humanity, a member of the whole. This self becomes human as it fits its integrity into the ever-widening circle of humanity, as it embodies Presence as *ubuntu*.[3]

## THE SELF AS AN INDIVIDUAL

To begin at the beginning, then, what does it mean to be called to our individual humanity? This calling is not about how one makes one's living. Some of us are indeed fortunate enough to

---

[3] The word *integrity* derives from the Latin word *integritās* meaning *whole* or *complete*. Thus, it is equivalent to the words *holy* and *to heal*, and all three of these words point to the goal of a fully realized person. For the most part I use *integrity* in the context of the person as an individual and *holy* in the context of the person as participating in *ubuntu*.

be able to make our living while practicing what I will term their "calling," but many more of us, perhaps most of us, are not. Our calling is not the same thing as our work, except, perhaps, in that metaphoric sense in which The Buddha said:

> Your work is to find your work,
> And then, with your whole heart,
> To give your self to it.[4]

To put the point rather starkly, our job is not our calling. Our calling is something else. We are called to become ourselves, to listen deeply within our minds, our hearts, and our souls to the voice of the Presence-as-Immanent and, having heard, to follow. Our calling is that to which we give ourselves with deep and existential integrity—faith-fully. Indeed, it is our calling that gives us existential integrity. It is that which becomes us, that which, were we to forgo it, we would die the slow, living death of existential stagnation, leading to what Thoreau called "lives of quiet desperation."[5] Our calling is the driving necessity of our selves needing to become visible. It is Presence demanding that we give the flesh of our lives to the profundity of our lives, a demand that we ignore at the cost of our wholeness.

All of this poetry and generalization is well and good, but I learned, after years of writing sermons, that generalizations without specific examples are not very helpful. It's too easy to think that they do not apply to us or that they are nothing but so much hot air.

---

[4] Thomas Byrom, *The Dhammapada*, p. 62. Other translations, e.g., Eknath Easwaran's translation, use the word *duty* rather than *work*. I do not know the Pali word, but I prefer *work*.

[5] Henry David Thoreau, *Walden*.

After all, how could we be anyone other than ourselves? We can't, of course, but that's never stopped anyone from trying. Becoming ourselves is about our integrity and our taking responsibility for our lives, recognizing that we do not have to become what we are not. We do not have to become someone or something else. All we have to do is to become as deeply and profoundly ourselves as possible. In this sense, we are enough. It was enough for Zusya simply to be Zusya.

## The Tenth Commandment

The Tenth Commandment is "You shall not covet your neighbor's wife, you shall not set your heart on his house, his field, his servant—man or woman—his ox, his donkey or anything that is his."[6] Covetousness, jealousy, envy, and the like are sins not only because they can lead to the violation of another—which, of course, they certainly can. In a deeper sense, they are sins because, by their very nature, they turn us away from our own lives, instilling in us the most intimate alienation of all—self-alienation. This is a point that is all too often overlooked. Covetousness, jealousy, and envy are sins because they are acts of violence that we commit not only against our neighbors but also—and first—*against ourselves.* They lead us to ignore our own integrity in favor of gifts that are not ours, talents we do not possess, and lives that we cannot live. There is surely nothing more futile than this, and little that is more alluring.

For example, how often have you wished you had this person's

---

[6] Exodus 20:17. This translation is that of the Jerusalem Bible.

eloquence, or that person's singing voice, or another person's aesthetic sense or athleticism? How often have you thought to yourself, "I wish I could be like…!" How often have you been discontented with your lot in life, envying those who have what you do not have?

Again, we are called to become human, and that is all. Because perfection is beyond human possibility, we are not called to perfection. To be human is to fail on occasion. It is to fall short on occasion. It is to be limited and of finite possibility, even out of control on occasion. To rise to and accept our calling is to recognize that our limitations, failures, and finitude neither condemn nor define us. What condemns us is being stuck in our failures, beating our breasts and berating ourselves for not being better than we are capable of being or as "good" as others. To be human is to do as well as we can and not as well as someone else can. For this, too, is the sin of covetousness. "You shall not covet your neighbor's goodness."

This is another important point that I have found people often lose sight of. The vast majority of us are not world-class anything, even though some few of us are. Some few are called to enormous greatness, but most of us are called to nothing more than ordinary greatness. Yet all of us are called to whatever we, ourselves, are actually able to achieve and nothing else. Some few are called to lead the effort to "save the world," but the rest of us are not. Yet without the work of those who are not called to lead, the world will never be saved. After all, what is a leader with no followers? What would Martin Luther King, Jr. have been able to accomplish without the courage of those young men and women who marched in the streets of Birmingham in the face of fire hoses and police dogs? And how many of their names do you know?

Some few are called to major artistic achievement, but most of us are not. Yet to reject one's ability to create because those creations will not achieve great artistic renown is to do violence to oneself. I cannot write as well as Dylan Thomas or sing as well as Bryn Terfel, but I am nevertheless called to write and sing as well as I can, not wringing my hands and beating my breast when I see clearly that I will never measure up to Thomas' or Terfel's standards. To be human is to rest content with whatever achievement is actually within my grasp, for to be human is to recognize that I am enough.

This is what Rabbi Zusya meant. He was not supposed to be Abraham, Moses, or Elijah. He was supposed to be just Zusya and no one else. Being Zusya was enough because Zusya was enough. If God had needed another Moses, he would have created another Moses. What He created instead was Zusya—because what He needed was Zusya, not Moses.

## RABBI BUNAM

On the other hand, this is not an excuse to stop, to give up saying, "There is no more I can do. This is the end." To realize that I will never write like to Thomas or sing like Terfel is not the same thing as saying that I cannot improve my writing or my singing. Another Hassidic story is to the point, this time about Rabbi Bunam. He once said, "I should not like to change places with Abraham! What good would it do God if Abraham became like me, and I became like Abraham? That's not what God needs. God needs Bunam to be

Bunam, and so I think I shall try to grow a little beyond myself."[7]

So how do we know what it is that we, as individual human beings, must do in order to become ourselves? How was Zusya supposed to know what it would be to be Zusya? And how is each of us supposed to know what it would be to be—or to become—us? We look within our hearts and souls, for that is where the answer lies. Far too often, though, we go out of our way to ignore what we know in our hearts, or we deny that we know it, or we forget it. I think that at our most profound levels we know perfectly well what we are called to do, but to face what we know at this level is, for so many, to realize that they have spent so much energy and wasted so much time avoiding the truth of their lives. As a result, many of us refuse to go to that next level and join Rabbi Bunam in growing a little beyond ourselves. We stumble on, living an "as if" life.

I remember the adolescent cry of "Who am I?" When I was young, we called it "needing to find ourselves," and we used that phrase to explain—and excuse—all sorts of things from changing majors in college to changing professions later in life, from dropping out of college to dropping out of families, marriages and even life as we then knew it. Sometimes "finding myself" was little more than an excuse for ducking an unwanted responsibility or was an opportunistic moment of self-indulgence. But sometimes it was—and is—something far more significant.

I think that many people—probably most people, maybe even all people—from time to time come to a point at which we feel lost. We feel as if we are trapped going down a road we have not chosen toward a destination to which we do not want to arrive. It feels as

---

[7] Martin Buber, Tales of the Hassidim: Later Masters, p. 256.

if there are no options and no exits on this freeway to nowhere we want to be. This is existential alienation, and this is when life becomes absurd.

This feeling may be especially intense during adolescence, but it is certainly not limited to youth. Suppose you have worked at achieving some goal, worked hard, maybe for years, and then finally achieved it. Surely, we all know the nagging voice in the back of the mind that says, after accomplishing something on which we have worked long and hard, "Is that all there is? And now what? Where do I go from there? What do I do next? What can give me back the feeling of bringing my best self forward into the world?"

For some this "is that all there is?" feeling happens when the children have grown up and left home for their own lives. For some it's when they have gone as far as they are able in their chosen line of work and know that this is where they will stay until they retire. For others, it's when the book finally gets published or the house built, or the invention patented and in production. There are thousands of different ways we run up against the feeling of "now what?" or even "so what?"

This is the contemporary version of a problem as old as humanity—or at least as old as civilized humanity. The Desert Fathers recognized it and named it *acedia*, from a Greek word meaning "indifference." They listed *acedia* among the spiritual ills that eventually became codified as The Seven Deadly Sins. It is more or less the spiritual equivalence of depression. When one falls into *acedia*, one's life and goals and achievements are no longer worth bothering with. One looks at it all and says, "Who cares? Why bother? It's just too much trouble. And besides, I probably can't do it anyhow."[8]

I offer myself as a case study.[9] When I was in high school, I decided to become a scientist, specifically a physicist. That decision tore at my heart. I knew that it was wrong, even though my parents, my friends, my teachers, even the culture I grew up in supported it. I even knew what I was really called to do, what being me really meant. I was called to ministry, and as I look back on my early life, that was as obvious to me as any truth could be. To embrace that truth, though, meant giving up an image of myself that, though false and inadequate, I had embraced with all the fervor of youth and that had been reinforced by nearly everyone important to me. So, I started college spending a lot of energy repressing a feeling of dread.

After a year as a physics major, I could no longer stand it. I was going down the wrong road and knew it. Instead of embracing my own truth, though, I took another detour. I thought my destination was academia, and if I could not get there as a physicist, I decided to get there as a philosopher. That worked. Sort of. I did get to academia, but I quickly discovered that I was no closer to my calling than I had been back in high school.

I was a very troubled young academic. In spite of the fact that I had earned all the right credentials and seemed to be at the promising beginning of a career, I still knew in my bones that something was just wrong. I had no business in academia. How did I know that? That's a little like asking how you know you're happy—or, as in this case, unhappy. I have found that when I am completely honest

---

[8] See Kathleen Norris, *Acedia and Me.*

[9] See the Prologue for more about this.

with myself, I know when my life is out of kilter. It is as if there is a voice—Elijah called it a "still small voice"—within the heart that tells me that I am doing something wrong. It is as if the music of my living is out of tune with the music of my heart. Eventually the out of tune jangle becomes so obvious that it is difficult, though not impossible, to overlook it.

When this happens to me, I have found only two options. On the one hand, I can ignore what I know in my bones, closing my ears to the out of tune discord, and hoping that it will resolve of itself. On the other hand, I can act on what I know, even if it requires that I change my life. The first option, ignoring the out of tune jangle, never really works. What I know in my bones is that it will not just disappear. The jangle will not resolve itself by itself any more than a leaky faucet will fix itself. Olga Grushin's 2005 novel, *The Dream Life of Sukhanov*, tells the story of a man's life falling apart because he chose the first option, trying to repress what he knew in his bones. It destroys him. This is a disturbing novel; I recommend it.

When one lets go of trying to dance, however awkwardly, to the music of one's life while ignoring the music of one's heart; the only possibility left is to choose the music of one's heart and adjust the music of one's life accordingly. This is a choice that each of us faces every day, and the choice is always and only ours alone. And so, I chose the music of my heart. I began to think about the course of my life and the current that seemed to have been sweeping through it, carrying me along. The music in my heart demanded ministry.

And so, I resigned my tenured position and entered seminary to become a minister. People told me variously that I was being foolish to give up a tenured teaching position and that I was being courageous to do so, but to me it felt like dawn after a nightmare.

I had been told that I should not be a minister unless I could not help it, but if I couldn't help it, I should be a good one. The same advice, of course, is given to people considering many professions.[10] The question I needed to face was whether or not I could help it. The more I thought about my life, the more I realized that being a minister is less about what one does for a living than it is about who one is and how one incarnates oneself in the world. If one *is* a minister, then however it is that one earns one's living, one will *be* a minister in one's life. One does not become a minister in seminary. If one is not already a minister before entering seminary, it will be waste of time and money. A seminary simply teaches ministers how to be professional, how to be a good minister.

Our calling may or may not lead us to a profession. Instead, what it really leads us to is ourselves. This, then, is finally what it means to be called: becoming increasingly who we are. It is to bring our life into harmony with the sweetly singing voice in our soul so that the music we live is the music we hear in our heart. In short, what we are called to is nothing less than the authenticity of our souls, the giving of our flesh to the wholeness of our hearts. We are called to the Human Project: we are called to become ourselves.

I have found that this is a never-ending process. Just as the price of liberty is eternal vigilance, the price of authenticity is eternal listening within the heart, listening and acting and then listening again. These are the questions we must constantly ask ourselves: what do I know in my bones about who I am; what I must do in order that my life is lived in harmony with my soul; and what must I do to give the flesh of my life to that harmony?

---

[10] And yet, we must not forget that our calling is not our job, even if we are privileged enough to be able to make a living practicing our calling.

## QUESTIONS

Another way of putting this is to ask oneself these questions: "What is it that haunts my dreams? What is it that comes upon me when I am quiet and alone with the beating of my heart? What is the wisdom that I hold in my heart that, while I cannot find the words to speak it with my lips, yet demands that I live it into my life? What is it that comes over me like dawn after a nightmare? And what do I have to do in order to grasp that dawn to my heart and put it on my life like I put a suit of clothes on my body?" This is exactly what we are called to do in our lives and in this world, for this is exactly how we redeem the promise, made at our birth, of our humanity. No one can say what this is except we, ourselves, and we do know what it is, though sometimes we need help in being reminded, and sometimes we choose to ignore or even forget it.

These questions do not have easy answers. It is not always immediately obvious how one discovers what I have called the music singing in one's heart. Just how does one find what The Buddha called one's work? One must listen to one's heart. One must still one's busy-ness. Lao Tzu writes,

> [The Wise are] able to sit patiently as muddy water clears.
> [The Wise are] able to be at rest in the midst of violent action.[11]

We must let the mud settle out of the waters of life. We must sit still in our aloneness, perhaps even loneliness, and listen to what we know in our bones but may have lost track of or forgotten.

---

[11] *Tao Te Ching*, Chapter 15.

It may be telling us something new that we have never heard before. It may be telling us something that we have missed in the past. It may be telling us to sing a completely new song. It may be telling us that we must go back the way we have come. The point is that it is *our* song and *we* must hear it in order that *our* life may sing it. Sometimes it is calling for a new incarnation within our lives. Sometimes it is calling for us to resume the life that we have been leading refreshed in the knowledge that however hard that life may be, it is yet our life and we must live it. But whatever the life may be to which we may be called, the message is that any other life would be even more difficult and dangerous to our humanity. This is what we must do in order to become human.

The Bible has a striking image for this. Elijah was faced with the threat of death, and he retreated to a cave in the desert to pray. In his anguish, he pleaded with God to end his life, for, as he put it, "I am not better than my fathers." God told him to go to the entrance to the cave, and He would speak. And there was a great earthquake that shook the mountain to its roots, but God was not in the earthquake. And a great wind arose that blew huge boulders around, but God was not in the wind. And fire fell from the heavens, but God was not in the fire. But then Elijah heard a still, small voice within his heart, and God spoke to Elijah in the still small voice.[12] Presence is imminent in every human heart, and we must listen to it.

Those times when we seem to have retreated into a desert cave, we have to listen to the still, small voice speaking in our heart. We must look past the earthquakes that threaten to shatter our lives, ignore the winds that toss our lives like so many feathers, and em-

---

[12] First Kings, chapter 19. As far as I know, this is the first place in the Bible where God is portrayed as immanent.

brace the fires that seem to burn the very soul, and listen to the still, small voice. How do we do that?

Sometimes it is possible to go off on retreat, to withdraw for a time from the daily world, and sometimes it is not.[13] Sometimes it is a matter of giving oneself the gift of setting aside a regular time for looking within, perhaps in meditation or prayer, perhaps through an examination of one's dreams, perhaps in some form of art. Sometimes it is a matter of working with another very trusted person like a spiritual adviser or a therapist. Sometimes it is nothing more spectacular than being honest with oneself, intentionally and scrupulously honest.

There are many ways, but there seems to be at least one thing that they have in common. All require intentionally setting oneself aside, stilling the jangle and chaos, and going within, to the heart of the heart, where *one* lives. All require that we ignore the image of ourselves that we or the world has of us and pay attention to our genuine self, the self that embraces the worth and dignity—the integrity—of our souls and is bathed in the interdependent web that laps the cosmos. There is no prescribed, one true technique to use to go there and listen to that beautiful song. It is more a matter of taste or personal preference. What works for one person need not work for another.

This going within is the essence of spiritual practice. I think that religion without spiritual practice is only a shell without substance. What is religion worth if it does not help us discover what we are called to do in the world and how we need to bring the music of

---

[13] See, for example, Jesus' 40-day silent retreat into the desert before he set out on his ministry. Most of us, though, are not able to give up 40 days of our lives for a silent retreat.

our souls to life? What is it worth if it does not help us discover our deeper selves and to hear the still, small voice, to see, even if it is only in the corners of our eyes, the stars of our souls shining in the deep blue twilight? What is religion worth if it does not offer us this treasure?

## THE SELF AS PARTICIPANT

Missiology proceeds from theology; the way we understand being called flows from the way we understand Presence and its manifestations in our lives. The dimension of missiology I have presented so far is our calling as an individual: what it means for me, a specific, living being, to become human. It is manifest when I listen to Presence as It dwells within my heart and soul and then act accordingly. This is Presence as immanent within my specific life.

Now, though, I am ready to look at the second dimension of being called to become human, being called to participate in humanity, to incarnate Presence as *ubuntu*. This is a calling that goes beyond any individual existence. Perhaps it can be thought of as a communal calling. It is what we are called to as belonging to, or being invested in, one another. And again, we are called to become human, but this time not simply as an individual acting within a separate life, but as a member of a greater whole. Not only are we called to become human individuals, but also we are called to become human within humanity, for we belong not simply to ourselves, but also to each other.[14] This is manifest when we listen

---

[14] In short, to become human, we must learn to practice *ubuntu*.

to Presence as it dwells within the hearts and souls of all, and then act accordingly. This is Presence-as-transcendent, the Love that binds the lives of all of humanity.

We are called to become human in the embrace of *ubuntu* and its manifestation in our lives, for no one can become human alone. The very idea is a contradiction. I am reminded of an old story that I first heard from the Rev. William Shultz, past president of the Unitarian Universalist Association.

> A monk had made a practice of going on a yearly silent retreat. He would be gone sometimes as long as a month, but never less than a week. Before going to the monastery's hermitage, he would present himself to the Abbot for permission, which was always granted, and when he returned, he presented himself again to the Abbot.

> This particular year, when he felt the need for his retreat, he presented himself to the Abbot as usual, and, getting permission, went to the hermitage. As was his practice, the first thing he did after settling his few things, was to pray. And then he opened the Bible that was kept there for retreatants to read. He did not open the Bible to any specific passage but opened himself to whatever it gave him as the object for his meditations during his retreat.

> As it happened, the Bible fell open to the account of Jesus washing his disciples' feet. He read the passage, sat back, fell into prayer, and returned to the Abbot.

"So. You have returned already," exclaimed the surprised Abbot.

"Yes," replied the monk, "for whose feet would the hermit wash?"[15]

Whose feet indeed? And this idea is echoed by Rabbi Hillel's famous remark: "If I am not for myself, who will be for me? But if I am only for myself, what am I? And if not now, when?" It is also contained in the third of the Buddhist Three Treasures: "I take refuge in the sangha," for while the sangha is first of all the community of Buddhists to which one happens to belong, eventually it comes to encompass all of humanity.

We incarnate ubuntu when we understand that, just as our parents give us our lives as individual beings, the community gives us our lives as human beings. It begins in the family and moves outward in ever-increasing circles. As babies and toddlers, our whole lives are centered in our parents. When we get a little older, the circle widens and encompasses first our siblings and other relatives and then other friends and their families. Then it widens again in adolescence as our families move out of the center and are replaced by our cohort. It widens again in early or middle adulthood to include all those whom we see to be like us, all the liberals, say, or all the conservatives, as the case may be. Or perhaps it is all Christians or all Muslims. Or perhaps it is all scientists or all psychologists or all educators. Then it sometimes widens still farther to include those who may not agree with us or think like us, but from whom

---

[15] I do not know the original source of this story, whether Rev. Schultz borrowed it or was the originator of it.

we can gain fresh insight or adopt good ideas that will broaden our humanity. Finally, it sometimes widens so much that one begins to understand that one's humanity is so inseparable from the humanity of all that this individual humanity is swallowed up in the whole.

I recognize that this picture is very much oversimplified, but I think that it is nevertheless an accurate conceptual picture. The concentric circles of *ubuntu* mirror James Fowler's six stages of faith, and that is no accident.[16] I think that his stages are exactly these circles of *ubuntu* translated into a more European accent, and I think that the point is the same: we grow into an ever-deepening humanity as we deepen our understanding that to be human is not to remove ourselves from the whole but to belong to the whole. This process of deepening is not a process of disappearing into a provincial tribe, but rather is a process of an expanding allegiance to something greater than oneself.

This deepening progresses as we gain an ever deepening understanding of the truth that Presence within me is exactly Presence with thee, and if that is the case, then my humanity is inseparable from thy humanity, my brokenness is inseparable from thy brokenness, and my salvation is inseparable from thy salvation (soteriology). What else could it mean when Christians speak of being one in Christ? What else could it mean when Buddhists assure us that each of us is The Buddha?

What else could the Quakers' belief that there is an Inner Light in each of us mean if not that the Presence that dwells within each of us is the very same Presence? This realization also provides another reconciliation of Presence as immanent and Presence as tran-

---

[16] James Fowler, *Stages of Faith.*

scendent. If the immanent within one is the same as the immanent within another, then immanence transcends the boundaries of my soul. This is immanence projecting itself into eternity (Transcendence). And if immanence within one is the same as immanence within all, then immanence is not conditioned by time or space, for it is the same within me as it is within Napoleon, Asoka, Tutankhamen, or President Obama.[17] This is transcendence leaving its footprints in time (Immanence).

In *Zen Mind, Beginners Mind,* Shunryu Suzuki Roshi speaks of the Self and the self, or Big Self and little self. As I read Suzuki, he is talking about the process of movement from thinking of one's individual self as the center of everything to the understanding that my self is indistinguishable from thy self. The goal is being able to function within life with an eye on the Self at both levels. It is the achievement of a kind of binocular vision, seeing that our self as a realized individual requires that we also see our self from the perspective of the greatest whole, what I have called Presence, and vice versa. We live incarnate within a material world, and that requires that we live as individual selves. But to live as a human individual in that material world means also living into that greater whole. This journey into realization is also the spiritual journey.

## SOCIAL JUSTICE

It does not take enormous insight to see the connection between this sense of being called and social justice. If we are called to invest

---

[17] Not to mention rather less admirable people, like Richard Nixon, Donald Trump, and an abusive alcoholic.

ourselves in the greater whole of humanity through the incarnation of ubuntu, then surely a large part of The Human Project is the healing of the brokenness of humanity. The work of that healing is the work of social justice. Earlier, I remarked that my healing is inseparable from thy healing, that the one is inconceivable without the other. Therefore, just as we are called to become ourselves and so to heal the brokenness of our own individual lives, we are also called to heal the brokenness we find within the world. Dostoevsky tells a fable about this in *The Brothers Karamazov*. In his fable, a wicked woman could be saved from damnation if she would share the means of her salvation, thus saving others along with her. But she refuses to share and is condemned.[18]

I often hear people exclaim, "I can't heal all of the world's brokenness. There is just too much brokenness." Of course there is! And we are not called to do what we cannot do. As Kant famously points out, "Ought implies can."[19] We are called to do what we can do. One often hears people saying that they are frozen by the enormity of the need and don't know where to begin, that working on one need precludes working on another, equally compelling, need.

My answer is Frederick Buechner's: "The place God calls you is where your deepest joy and the world's deepest hunger meet."[20] Once more, Lao Tsu is to the point. If you would learn what social justice work you are called to, you must still the muddy waters with

---

[18] *The Brothers Karamazov*, Part III, Book 7, Chapter 3.

[19] This is actually a simplified version of Kant's remark in *The Critique of Pure Reason*, "The action to which 'ought' applies must indeed be possible under natural conditions," Norman Kemp Smith translation, p. 473. We are morally obligated to do only things that we can do, never things that beyond our actual capability.

[20] Frederick Buechner, Wishful Thinking: A Theological ABC, p. 119.

the calmness of your soul and when you begin to see your passion meeting the world's needs, give your life to it in whatever ways you are able. In short, once again, spiritual practice is the answer.[21]

In my case, this means that I have given my life to the work of racial reconciliation through understanding the legacy of slavery, especially the legacy of my slaveholding ancestors.[22] I do not pretend that this is work everyone needs to do, but I do assert that it is work that our culture needs to do, for this is one major place where we are broken together. May we heal together as well.

---

[21] Compare this well-known quotation from Edward Everett Hale: "I am only one, but I am one. I can't do everything, but I can do something. The something I ought to do, I can do. And by the grace of God, I will." (quoted in *A Year of Beautiful Thoughts (1902)*, Jeanie Ashley Bates Greenaugh, ed., p. 172.

[22] See Collier *The Great Wound: Confessions of a Slaveholding Family.*

**Burned**

The sky opened. Fire fell in torrents
And burned everything. The Big House.
The shacks. Everything. Shriveled
Like forbidden graven images.

"Thou shalt have no other gods before me!"
"It was not us!" they will say.
"It was long ago! It was someone else!"

And who shall say, "Thy people shall be my people,
And those who are unloved shall be beloved"?[23]

---

[23] Collier, unpublished.

CHAPTER 5:

# Ecclesiology

*Why do we form religious communities?*

In the previous chapter, I told the story of the monk who wondered whose feet the hermit would wash. This points to another branch of Theology—namely, ecclesiology (from the Greek *ekklein*, to call out). Ecclesiology, then, asks how and why people are called out to form religious communities. In classical Christian thinking, this is sometimes called a theology of church.

My thinking about ecclesiology began when I noticed that every major religion gathers its people into communities. They are not simply scattered here and there. This observation led me to start asking myself questions. Why do they do that? What holds these religious communities together? What is the difference between a religious community and any other sort of community? What makes a religious community religious? For that matter what makes a religious community a community? It is these questions that ecclesiology addresses. At first blush, it may seem odd that these questions are set apart as one of the major subdivisions within Theology, but a closer look is quite revealing.

The classical Christian answer to the question of why Christians come together into a community is that God calls The Church together, gathers believers as a shepherd gathers a flock. It is God that holds them together, and thus The Church is sometimes referred to as the Mystical Body of Christ. A difficulty appears almost immediately, though. Given all of the schisms and divisions that have occurred through the centuries, it may appear as if God's grip isn't all that strong.

One solution to this problem is the suggestion that it is not God that is losing a grip on the Church but humanity that is losing its grip on God—turning away from Presence, if you will. It is this turning away that leads to schism and division. Another solution is that, as a bumper sticker I once saw put it, God is too big to fit in anyone's church. Thus, there are multiple Churches (denominations) because each embodies an aspect of a greater truth than any one church could possibly hold alone.

This is a good beginning, but it still leaves open the question of why *all* religions seem automatically to lead people to form communities. Even Religious Humanists form communities. Without a community, there would be nothing but a crowd of individuals who happen to agree with one another in matters religious but otherwise go their separate ways. That hardly constitutes a religion. Without an organization—an institution—there is nothing to hold people together. But not just any sort of institution will work. A religious institution is one that incarnates that which binds the adherents to one another. In short, the institution of religion is a community. There is something very profound in the idea of a religious community, something that points us directly to the heart of both religion itself and the project of becoming human.

As I often do when puzzled, I turned to etymology, and considered the words *religious* and *community*. As mentioned previously, the etymology of *religion* is not entirely clear, but one quite plausible suggestion is that it comes from the Latin *religāre*, which means *to tie fast*. *Religāre*, in turn, comes from the prefix *re-* which is used here as an intensifier, and *legāre, to bind*. Thus, the word suggests that religion is a powerful and intense binding together of people. *Community* comes from the Latin *communis*, which in turn comes from the Indo-European root *ko-moin-i*, indicating something held in common. It also has ties to *communitas*. A communitas is a group of people held together as a unity and hence indicates a whole, a unit, be it a village, a town, a nation or whatever else.

In both words, then, there is the idea of being bound together, held fast, a unity. Indeed, one might even begin to think that the term *religious community* is, in an important sense, redundant. Then I thought about what happens when the two words are put together. Communities can be held together by all sorts of things that range from the powerful (culture, class, political beliefs, etc.) to the decidedly temporary and superficial (physical proximity, hair color, etc.). When one considers the extra dimension of a community being bound religiously, it suggests that the thing that binds this sort of community together is that which creates deep and profound ties and brings together that which was separated, broken, divided. A religious community, then, is one in which one finds healing for the broken heart, and as I have said many times already, to be healed this way is to be made whole—that is to say, holy.

Recall the discussion above about existential aloneness. In summary, I noted that as one matures, one discovers that one is an individual, different from the rest of the world. This task of differentiation is one of the crucial tasks necessary if one is to become a healthy person. Yet, at the very same time, one also discovers that success in differentiation also ushers in aloneness. If I am truly and ultimately different from all that is around me, it appears that I cannot ever be at one with them again. They are not-me, and this not-me-ness creates what seems to be an irreducible barrier between me and the rest of the world, a barrier that seems so utterly impenetrable that it is impossible to breach. In particular, no mere you could ever become a Thou to me. This is the ultimate human brokenness.

If one thinks in these terms, this is the true nature of Original Sin, and it is what leads to all the other sins. Sin is those actions and states of being that lead people to believe in and accept as ultimate this separation and division between people. Hatred is sinful, because hatred is the perception and preservation of separation. To be healed from sin, to be able to see an It as a Thou once again, requires that we find a way across the barriers of separation, and this is exactly what love is. When I genuinely love another, in whatever sense, I become able see the other as Thou; I am able to see that even though we are, from one point of view separate, we are also, from another point of view, inseparably one.

This is not a new idea, as we have already noted. I have obviously borrowed Martin Buber's language from *I and Thou*[1] to talk about these ideas. This is also the insight that lies behind the feminist idea of the primacy of relationship. It is the insight that led Jesus to teach that one must love even one's enemies, the insight that led The Buddha to proclaim that only love dispels hatred; and the insight that is enshrined in The Torah as the commandment to love one's neighbor as oneself.

---

[1] Buber, op. cit.

## *UBUNTU* AND COMMUNITY

This insight is one that I have appealed to often already and named *ubuntu*, borrowing the Zulu word. When one has *ubuntu*, one understands—in the existential sense of standing under—the realization that it is only when one grasps another to one's soul that one can be truly and deeply human. Bishop Tutu has written that *ubuntu* is a difficult word to render into English, because there is no equivalent word in English. My understanding of *ubuntu* is that it is a form of love, and I have named it this way already. We cannot become human without love; we cannot become human without embracing *ubuntu*.

Thinking of *ubuntu* as a form of love, though, is still problematic because English is not very expressive of the nuances in love. As I have pointed out, it has only one word that has to cover everything from intense, if temporary, attraction ("I love that song") through sexual commitment to the profound and unconditional love of God. So which sense of love is captured by *ubuntu*? Further conversation is needed.

A good place to start, perhaps, is ancient Greek with at least three different words to talk about love, *eros*, usually thought of as sexual love; *philos*, usually thought of as the love of friends; and *agape*, usually thought of as the unconditioned, divine love of God.[2] *Ubuntu* is that form of love which emerges from both *eros* and *philos* and links them to *agape*. This is fairly easy to see in the case of *philos*. When one feels *philos* one sees in another an image of one's own humanity. It is through this recognition of common humanity

---

[2] There are actually more than these three Greek words, but I will confine myself to these three. They are sufficient to make the point.

that one is able to build a deep connection with the friend.

The same thing happens in *eros*, so long as we understand *eros* to be a deeply shared and profound commitment rather than simple titillation or shallow lust.[3] When one feels *eros* for another, one discovers such a powerful connection with one's partner that the whole sense of other loosens and a new whole is created. This may be why the second person singular, "thou," is rarely used in English and almost exclusively in the context of weddings.[4] In either form, then, love is impossible in isolation; the verb "to love" is necessarily a transitive verb.

Imagine expanding love—both *eros* and *philos*—beyond the immediate, beyond one's partner and friends. Imagine expanding love to allow the feeling of envelopment that love embodies to encompass all of humanity. Imagine this expanded love to lose any conditionality, but simply to be. One would love another simply because that other exists and not for any gain or power or advantage. This would be love that is not instrumental, for one's own ends, but simply love. This is what I call *ubuntu*, and it is the closest we human beings can come to *agape*, especially as it expands even beyond the human to all beings whatever.

The deeper levels of community building, I think, begin in *philos*. When one begins to remove the conditional aspects of friendship and loves another simply in virtue of shared humanity, then one begins to move into ubuntu. The community formed at this

---

[3] See, for example, Audre Lorde's important essay, "Uses of the Erotic: The Erotic As Power" in her collection, *Sister Outsider*.

[4] The Plain Talk of the Society of Friends is an important exception to this. The idea is that since there is that of God in all of us, in loving God we must also love one another. Thus, we must learn to see each person as Thou. While this idea evolved well before Martin Buber wrote his book, the idea is, I think, the same.

level of commitment becomes a religious community, a community bound together by the love that heals the separateness that divides humanity against itself. When seen in this light, the connection between religion and community becomes clear. Religions form communities because the impulse that leads to one also leads to the other. A truly religious community is sometimes called a Beloved Community and is a goal always calling us beyond ourselves.

We cannot become human without communities, because we cannot become human without transcending the barriers that separate us, without transforming You (object) into Thee (relationship). That transformation is the work of *ubuntu*. Simultaneously, we cannot become human without healing the brokenness that would leave us profoundly alone in an uncaring and indifferent universe. Uncaring and indifferent the universe may or may not be, and alone we certainly are, but profoundly alone we are not. The work of *ubuntu*-love is the coming to see that simultaneously with being alone, we also are tied fast to one another.

In the last chapter, I also spoke of increasing circles of *ubuntu* that mirror the concentric circles of faith outlined by James Fowler. Following that model, I began to see how the circles of community open as one's consciousness of connection through *ubuntu* expands. One's first community is oneself and one's mother. The second is one's family. The notion of family slowly expands and eventually begins to include close friends. In time those friends begin to supplant one's family, and around the time of adolescence, one begins to move away from family to form the third circle in which peer groups are paramount. Peer groups coalesce into communities in the form of teams, schools, and so forth. Eventually, one's loyalty to these larger communities is often transformed into patriotism and nationalism in which one begins to think that the only proper way of being a nation is *our* way of being a nation. ("My country... right or wrong.") A further step is the insight that other nations, other people, other civilizations are as "proper" as one's own. And finally, one begins to see that nations are but artificial barriers and that it is all of humanity that matters, not simply these small, artificial, and temporary divisions.

The same thing happens within religious communities. For example, the third of the Three Jewels of Buddhism is "I take refuge in the sangha." At first the sangha is the group of Buddhists to whom one belongs, the monastery, for example. But then it expands to all those within one's lineage; Soto, for example, or Rinzai. But this expands again to include all those within one's practice of Buddhism, all who follow the Zen way. And then it grows still further to embrace all those within the branch of the Buddhist tree that includes this practice, Mahayana. Mahayana, though, is only a single branch, and so the sangha expands again to include the entire Buddhist tree. Finally, one begins to understand the profundity of The Buddha's teaching that we are *all* Buddhas, even non-Buddhists, and so the sangha must expand again to include all sentient beings everywhere.

It is *ubuntu* that brings religious communities together, *ubuntu* that draws us out from the isolation of existential aloneness into the communal reality of our emerging humanity. The whole concept of humanity is, I maintain, a communal and religious ideal, and being an ideal, it is also something we reach for and often fall short of. This falling short (or missing the mark, as it is sometimes called) is a classic understanding of sin. I realize that many 21st century people, even religious people, tend to avoid the language of sin, but we can't avoid a concept simply by avoiding the usual words used to talk about it. We really do embrace the idea of sin, however we may choose to talk about it.

For the rest of this chapter, I want to use what I think of as the quintessential American sin, slavery and its legacy of racism, to see how ubuntu calls us back into right relationship when we fall short of its ideal. There are three aspects of the return: sin, guilt, and atonement. In its turn, atonement requires three steps: confession, forgiveness, and restitution.

## SIN

To begin, I said above that sin consists of violence, *i.e.* those acts that violate the integrity of another. They are those things that people do, be those things advertent or inadvertent, that ignore, transgress, obliterate, belittle, begrudge, tarnish, or otherwise injure or diminish the ability of another to perceive Presence within the soul. To sin is to restrict or diminish the ability of someone to become fully human.

Notice that I do not say "injure or diminish the ability of another to perceive Presence within *his or her* soul," but "within *the* soul." This is, in part, because sin is reflexive—that is, when we sin against another, the sin rebounds and becomes a sin against ourselves as well. When we diminish the ability of others to perceive Presence within themselves, we simultaneously diminish our own perception of Presence within ourselves. We also sin when we blind someone to Presence within a third person.

For example, we sin against our children—commit acts of

violence against them—when we teach them to be blind to the integrity of other people. Thus, not only is it racist to discriminate actively against people of other races, but also it is racist to teach our children, either by word or example, that other races are not as worthy of our love and respect as our own. Teaching children racism, even if it is done unconsciously though acts of unrecognized micro-aggression, is an act of violence against them. It is a sin.

In 1982, Bishop Desmond Tutu, addressing the evil of Apartheid, made this profound observation:

> The evil of apartheid is perhaps not so much the untold misery and anguish it has caused its victims (great and traumatic as these must be), no, its pernicious nature, indeed its blasphemous character is revealed in its effect on God's children when it makes them doubt that they are God's children.[5]

Let me paraphrase this into the racial history of the United States so that the point is unmistakable:

> The evil of slavery and its legacy of racism are not so much the untold misery and anguish they have caused (great and traumatic as these have been and continue to be). No, their pernicious nature, indeed their blasphemous character, is revealed in their effect on God's children when they tend to make those children doubt that they are God's children.

I say again that this is the essence of sin, that sin is those actions that turn us away from Presence, that blind us to its reality, both

---

[5] Quoted in Michael Battle's *The Ubuntu Theology of Desmond Tutu*, p. 162.

within our own lives and within the lives of those around us and thus break *ubuntu*. The black hole at the center of our acting so that others begin to doubt their own holiness is the fact that we are thereby denying our own holiness. The rock that we cast into the eye of the soul of another, rebounds and strikes our own eye.

I have used racism as my example here to make the point clear, but sin is both great and small, both obvious and subtle. Most of the sins that we commit are not spectacular, and often pass without notice. And yet they turn us inexorably away from one another, blinding us to Presence with the souls that surround us. Consider:

- We ignore the homeless, the hungry, the helpless because we think that they are somehow less important and less worthy of our love and compassion than our friends.

- We disparage, belittle, deride, and demonize others who disagree with us, insisting that those who think differently than we must either be less intelligent and insightful than we or else are being intentionally and perversely obtuse. ("Friends don't let friends vote Republican/Democrat.")

- We insist that those who are different from us must become like us in order to become acceptable.

- We isolate, ignore, and even persecute those who suffer from disease, deformity, or disability.

- We create circumstances and institutions that make it possible to hurt the less powerful and then blame the powerless for their powerlessness, thus actively perpetuating those very circumstances and institutions.

- We create a culture of deprivation and teach the children of both the privileged and the deprived to accept the deprivation on the grounds that the deprived are essentially different from the privileged and deserve their deprivation.

Surely these are sins. Surely these sins are all around us and would be obvious if we could only open the eyes of our souls to see them. Surely this list could be extended enormously. These might be considered cultural sins, sins that are committed not so much by individuals, though individuals perpetuate them and carry them forward, but sins that are committed and sanctioned by and on behalf of the culture.[6]

We also sin against one another in our ordinary lives with little actions, actions that are insidious because they live almost invisibly in the immediacy of our daily lives and add up, making it possible for us to perpetuate the cultural sins. Consider these examples:

- Our arrogant refusal to humble ourselves and apologize genuinely when we hurt each other, be that hurt physical, psychological, or spiritual,
- Our equally arrogant refusal to forgive others when they hurt us and humble themselves,
- Our fearful and destructive nursing of grudges, clinging to old wrongs and past grievances as if the wrong committed against us is more important than the healing of the breach between ourselves and others.

And to add a few specifics from my own life:

- I failed to intervene when I witnessed over acts of racism and racial hatred.

---

[6] Think, for example, about the difference between individual racism and systemic white supremacy.

- I allowed myself to use my white male privilege to overpower others.
- I have participated in the bullying of others.[7]

All of this is sin. All of this prevents us from becoming human. All of this keeps us from seeing the power and fullness of Presence in our own lives and in the lives of others. All of this is counter to *ubuntu*-love and tends to diminish our appreciation of it and its reality in our lives. All of this leads to religious ignorance.

## GUILT

The assertion that when we sin, we are guilty is quite straightforward, but the whole idea of guilt has come in for some rather harsh press over the last 150 years or so. I think that this is at least in part because of a confusion between appropriate and inappropriate guilt. Guilt is appropriate when it is the felt understanding of having fallen short, as St. Paul correctly put it, of doing that which we ought not to have done and failing to do that which we ought to have done. Appropriate guilt is the spur to atonement and drives us to correct our behavior. In short, appropriate guilt is the awareness of *ubuntu* calling us to deepen our humaneness through corrective action.

---

[7] One might hope that these sins could always be healed, but that is not the case. Suppose I cannot or refuse to change my behavior. Or suppose that the trauma of the sin so infects the sinned against that it poisons relationships with other, even across generations. Or suppose either the sinner or the sinned against has died. In such situations, healing from the sin is extremely difficult, not impossible, but very difficult.

On the other hand, guilt is not always appropriate. Inappropriate guilt has at least two forms. In one form, it freezes us rather than motivates us. It prevents the restoration of right relationships, even when the injured party has forgiven the perpetrator, because the guilty party remains stuck in former actions. For example, suppose a drunk driver hits and seriously injures someone. And suppose further, this driver is so ashamed of themselves that they cannot face the person they injured. Try as they might they cannot bring themselves to speak to or allow themselves to be open to the forgiveness the injured person offers. They are stuck in their guilt. This state of being stuck remains a barrier between sinner and sinned against. This form of guilt is often the result of an inability of the sinner to forgive him/herself rather than the inability of the injured to forgive, and I suspect that it is best dealt with in a psychological context rather than a religious one.

The other form of inappropriate guilt is guilt felt over acts that one did not actually commit. For example, I discussed at some length in my book, *The Great Wound*, the question of whether or not the descendants of slaveholders inherit the guilt of their ancestors. My point was that this guilt is not appropriate because no one is ever responsible for the actions, the sins, of another.

Yet there is more to responsibility than this. We are not only responsible *for* our actions, but we are also responsible *to* other people. We descendants of slaveholding families are not responsible for the actions of their racist forbears, but we *are* responsible to the future world we help to create and hand on to future generations. And that responsibility includes working for the healing of the lingering and festering wounds created by American slavery.

## Atonement

Appropriate guilt arises from *ubuntu*, from feeling that because of our actions, we have fallen short and have erected barriers between our selves and others. This guilt drives us to act to transcend those barriers and restore a right relationship. In short, guilt arising from *ubuntu* is the motivation for atonement. Following Bishop Tutu, I think that genuine atonement requires three things: confession, forgiveness, and recompense. Each of these has both an outward and an inward component.

*Confession.* To begin with confession, then, when one confesses, one must speak words such as these: "These are the things that I (or we) have done to you and your people. These things are sins I (or we) have committed against you and before God." Without seeking out those whom we have driven from our hearts and confessing what we have done, there is little—if any—chance of breaching the barriers we have erected. The responsibility for pulling down these barriers always lies with the sinner and never with the sinned against. Thus, the responsibility for the confession of the sin of American racism and beginning its healing lies with Euro-America.

It is not enough for these words of confession to be just words of the mouth. One must first speak them with the words of the heart. Unless one feels the shame of denied and broken *ubuntu*, the words of the mouth remain hollow and meaningless. It is easy for anyone to *say* that they have sinned, but to *confess*, one must also *understand existentially* that one has sinned. One must stand under the reality of the sin and feel the barriers that bar *ubuntu* from flowing freely between oneself and another. One of the most difficult tasks of the Truth and Reconciliation Commission[8] was that of discerning when the heart was speaking as well as the mouth. The members had to distinguish between those whose confession was made simply in order to gain amnesty, on the one hand, and those whose confession was made in order to be forgiven and to transcend the barriers Apartheid had erected between peoples' souls on the other hand.[9]

Perhaps Apartheid and slavery are extreme examples, but they illustrate the depth of genuine confession. This depth of commitment is necessary for any genuine confession, even though the stakes are usually not that high. This, I believe, is why Yom Kippur is the most sacred day on the Jewish calendar. It is the Day of Atonement, the day on which the sins of the previous year are confessed, forgiven, and recompense made. It all begins with confession.

*Forgiveness.* Let us suppose that one has made a genuine confession. It is now up to the sinned against to forgive. Forgiveness is often misunderstood. It is certainly not forgetting the sin. "To forgive and forget" is not only an impossible task. It is also destructive because the impossibility of forgetting far too often makes genuine forgiveness impossible. Everything that has happened to us is part of our history. It is written in our memory, and even in our bodies. The sins that are committed against us will never be truly forgotten

---

[8] The Truth and Reconciliation Commission (TRC) was set up by Nelson Mandela's government to work toward discovering the truth about Apartheid and reconciling the Black and White communities in South Africa.

[9] See for example, Pumla Gobodo-Madikizela's book, A Human Being Died That Night: A South African Woman Confronts the Legacy of Apartheid.

any more than the sins we commit will ever be forgotten. Forgiveness is not pretending that the sin never happened. It *did* happen and pretending otherwise is fraudulent. Typically, all it does is to seal the resentment within the heart and poison our souls from within.

Forgiveness is something else entirely. Genuine forgiveness is setting aside the power of the sin to hurt us. As long as the sin holds power over our heart, the barrier between people will remain. Once again, some form of outward acknowledgement is necessary: "Thank you for coming to me and confessing. You are forgiven." And again, it is not enough simply to say this with the words of the mouth; the words of the heart are also necessary.

The deeper the sin, the more difficult this is. Sometimes it even happens that people are held in such thrall that they are unwilling or unable to let go of that power. It is sometimes more frightening to forgive than to hold a grudge and allow the sin to eat away at the soul. On the other hand, it sometimes happens that however much we may want to forgive, the hurt is so deep that we just cannot. It is not that we are afraid of forgiving but that we simply cannot. It is like having a deep wound in the flesh. We want it to stop hurting, but the pain will not go away, no matter what we do. Sometimes it takes years for forgiveness to happen, and sometimes it never happens. But until we are able to forgive, able to allow the power of the sin against us to evaporate, the barriers still remain, and atonement will not have happened.

***Restitution.*** Even confession and forgiveness are not enough by themselves to achieve atonement. An essential part of the restoration of a right relationship is restitution. In many cases, the very act of confession is also an act of restitution. That I admit my guilt to another person and that person accepts my confession can be sufficient if it is understood by both of us that my confession contains an implicit avowal that I will not repeat the act, that I have "learned my lesson." But notice that even in this case, in which confession and restitution are contained in the same action, they are still conceptually distinct.

Sometimes, though, an implicit avowal to change my behavior is not enough, and I need to make that avowal explicit. I need to make it very clear that I understand the gravity of what I have done and the necessity of my reformation. This is what happens in 12-Step Programs. Not only is one required to go to those whom one has injured, but also one must explicitly dedicate oneself to major changes in behavior. Until both happen, atonement for the sins committed while drinking uncontrollably remains but a goal.

Sometimes restitution takes the form of reparation. The word "reparation" really means "the act of repairing," but it has come to imply financial restitution. This is often the case, but not always. For example, consider this story that I read years ago about an act of restitution after sexual abuse.

A woman had been abused by her father's brother for years while she was growing up. Her father had never attempted to intervene, largely because he had not noticed what was happening. Years later, she told him about the abuse, and he reflected on clues that he had missed or failed to follow and so to understand. When he learned the truth, he was overwhelmed at his failure as a father. He immediately flew from his home in New York to Seattle, where she was living, and confessed his failure to her. She needed extensive therapy, and he insisted on paying for it, saying that since he should have known and intervened to stop the abuse, it was his responsibility to pay for the damage his failure had caused.[10]

These three aspects of atonement constitute conceptually different acts that are sometimes collapsed into the same thing that is actually done, but all are necessary for full atonement. As I have laid them out, it may seem as if they are straightforward, but far too often they are not. What is one to do, for example, when one is able to confess but the person sinned against is not available to receive one's confession? Sometimes the sinned against cannot be found; sometimes the sinned against is even dead. What then? What is one to do when one is ready to forgive but similarly the sinner cannot be found or has died? Or what is one to do when the sinner will not or cannot admit guilt or the sinned against cannot forgive? What is one to do when both the sinner and the sinned against have long since died and yet the effects of the sin continue to haunt their descendants? How are we to atone for the sin of slavery?

## A Case Study

To see how this works in the real world, consider my family.[11] The earliest any of my family arrived in the New World was 1609.

---

[10] I cannot document this story. It is, though, one of those stories that is true whether or not it actually happened. See also the film "Monsoon Wedding." The father's benefactor has sexually abused his niece. In the dramatic climax of the film, the father confronts the benefactor and refuses to allow him to take part in or even attend the wedding, saying, "This is my family! I would protect them from myself if necessary." One of the most powerful lines in all cinema.

[11] This history is explored in much greater depth in my *The Great Wound: Confessions of a Slave-Holding Family.*

My mother's distant ancestor, young ship's carpenter's apprentice named John Powell, arrived in Jamestown that year aboard the *Swallowe*. The first Collier, Isaac Collier, arrived in York County, Virginia about 1655, and just about the first thing he did was to establish a plantation. His grandson, Charles Collier, purchased 350 acres nearby in what is now part of NASA/Langley Airbase and established his own plantation. I am directly descended from this Charles Collier.

The Colliers enslaved Africans and African Americans from the very beginning until Emancipation in 1865, and my grandfather's cousin, Barron Gift Collier, Sr., was actively involved in Jim Crow activity in the 1920s. As far as I can tell for sure, the Powells did not hold anyone in slavery until the late 18$^{th}$ or early 19$^{th}$ century. Benjamin Powell, my 4$^{th}$ great grandfather, willed four enslaved people to his son, George Cader Powell, in 1833. And somewhere along this line, some sub-Saharan genes entered my gene pool.

The legacy of this slaveholding is a line of racism running through my family. The most virulent post-Emancipation racists that I have actually encountered were my paternal grandmother and an uncle by marriage, but I have no reason to believe that the others, all of whom benefitted from both slavery and Jim Crow laws and practices, did not share some degree of this racism. The first people of whom I am sure fought against it were my parents. Yet, of course, they had an enormous uphill battle and never completely overcame the racism they grew up with.

The question I wrestle with is how to atone for the sins of these ancestors. These people were not honorable people. How do I honor these dishonorable ancestors whom I see as undeserving of honor? How does one honor the dishonorable without leaving open the very wounds that need to be healed? How is atonement possible?

I found a solution in the film "Amistad." The climax of the film is a hearing before the U.S, Supreme Court to determine whether or not these enslaved people are protected by the laws of the U.S. The leader of the enslaved, Cinque, speaks with John Quincy Adams, his lawyer, about what is going to happen. In the course of that conversation, he speaks eloquently about his ancestors, and says that the line of his ancestors all the way back will stand with him and help as they can because he is the culmination of their line. They act in history through him, and they are honored by his honorable actions and life.

And there is my answer. My ancestors' crimes against humanity (and what else is slavery but a crime against humanity?) cry out for redress, for atonement, for being set to rest. When I was very young and she was very old, I met that last living person to have been enslaved by my family. She died in 1961 "about 100 years old." And so, neither my ancestors nor the people they enslaved are still living. So how can these crimes be atoned for? And by whom?

By me. The task falls to me, and this why I am called so powerfully to work for racial reconciliation. My ancestors call out from beyond the grave for me to atone for their crimes, and I honor them by confessing my family's sins and working to repair the damage they inflicted on so many people. I think again of my racist grandmother whose hatred was so deep that she did not even acknowledge the humanity of people of color. How can I forgive her for the racism she worked to plant in my heart? I forgive her by working to erase the very racism she embraced.

It's a matter of the responsibility for/responsibility to distinction discussed above. To suggest that I am responsible for my ancestors' actions is to miss the point entirely. That would be an example of inappropriate guilt. Of course, I am not responsible for what my ancestors did. But I *am* responsible to my descendants and to my culture to extinguish the legacy of despair and racist hatred that my ancestors handed on to me. And now I realize that I am also responsible to my ancestors to expiate the guilt and shame their actions created.

I know that I will not be able to erase the hatred of racism entirely, and that realization can be a temptation to freeze and do nothing. But if I give in to that temptation, then I dishonor my own ancestors; I dishonor those they enslaved and their descendants; and I dishonor my own children and grandchildren and their children and grandchildren. I dare not do that, for then I take on my own guilt. I cannot do it all, but I commit myself to do whatever it is that I can do. For to do nothing would be a crime before God and against humanity.

The healing of the wounds of slavery requires a profound level of confession, forgiveness, and restitution. Pumla Gobodo-Madikizela has thought deeply about these same issues and their implications for South Africa in the wake of Apartheid. She is a clinical psychologist who served on the Human Rights Violations Committee of the Truth and Reconciliation Commission. As part of her work, she conducted a series of in-depth interviews with Eugene de Kock, who was the commanding officer of the death squads during Apartheid. *A Human Being Died that Night* is her account of those interviews. In this book, she describes forgiveness this way:

> Forgiving may appear to condone the offense, thus further disempowering the victim. But forgiveness does not over-

look the deed: it rises above it. "This is what it means to be human," it says. "I cannot and will not return the evil you inflicted on me." And that is the victim's triumph.[12]

She also remarks:

On the one hand, to dismiss perpetrators simply as evil-doers and monsters shuts the door to the kind of dialogue that leads to enduring peace. Daring, on the other hand, to look the enemy in the eye and allow oneself to read signs of pain and cues to contrition or regret where one might almost have preferred to continue seeing only hatred is the one possibility we have for steering individuals and societies toward replacing longstanding stalemates out of a nation's past with genuine engagement. Hope is where transformation begins; without it a society cannot take its first steps toward reconstructing its self-identity as a society of tolerance and coexistence.[13]

And she closes her book with these words:

Mercy should be granted cautiously. And yet society must embrace those who, like Eugene de Kock, see and even lead on the road of shared humanity ahead. Our capacity for such empathy is a profound gift in this brutal world we have created for one another as people of different races, creeds, and political persuasion.[14]

---

[12] Op cit., p. 117.

[13] Ibid, p. 125.

[14] Ibid, p, 139.

This is a powerful and very important book.

The complexity of atonement is enormous, and its enormity is a testament to the fact that it arises only in a communal context, only in the context in which our humanity flourishes within the relationships we form with one another. Atonement is an expression of *ubuntu* and is a manifestation of Presence, a manifestation that we, by our actions, are able to realize. That realization is a measure of the maturity of our journey to become human.

**Distance Disappeared**

Sometimes, when I am as helpless as a tree in a forest fire,
I lean my heart against the hearts of those
Who love me. Their love fills me, water
Flowing into a mountain pool,
Clean and cool. I rest my heart
In their hearts, in the stillness of water,
In the silence of distance disappeared.[15]

---

[15] Collier, unpublished.

CHAPTER 6:

# Pneumatology
### *What Is Spirit?*

Pneumatology, the study of spirit and spirituality, is another of those technical terms that tend to put people off. The reality is, though, that most people have spent a fair amount of time thinking about it. It is difficult to define spirituality or even write comprehensibly and sensitively about spirituality. Even the attempt to find language that is both understandable and adequate to talk about it is fraught. The language of spirituality is ambiguous and ranges from the intellectually offensive through the incomprehensible to the deeply moving and profound.

By the very nature of spirituality, its language has to be metaphoric, poetic, and suggestive rather than explicit and indicative. But in spite of these difficulties, it is an essential aspect of Theology and of religion.

## THE SPIRITUAL EXPERIENCE

How we talk about spirituality, though, is far less important than our ability to experience it. Before there is language, there is experience. Before there is talk about spirituality, there is the experience of the spiritual. Most people have experienced the spiritual, even if they did not recognize it as such. A few examples are to the point.

- Have you ever stood by the ocean watching the waves coming into shore and felt as if you were melting into a vastness, as if there is an unbroken continuity between yourself and the sand and the rocks and the sea anemones and everything else?
- Have you ever gone out into a cloudless summer night, looked up at the stars, and felt a sudden warm embrace from all that vastness around you and, far from feeling small and insignificant, realized that you were an essential part of the whole, as essential as every one of those stars?
- Have you ever looked into the eyes of someone you love very deeply and realized that, because of your love, there is a sense in which the two of you, though obviously separate people, are nevertheless joined as a single being?
- Have you ever been so deeply captured by a work of art that you could not move and knew that, somehow, in the deepest places of your heart, you were elevated and changed and overcome by it?[1]

If you can answer yes to any such question, you have experienced the spiritual.

The result of each of these experiences is a kind of knowledge, a knowledge that is not mediated by empirical verification. Rather, this knowledge is mediated by one's being opened to a wholeness

---

[1] This is actually an aesthetic experience, but it illustrates how deeply connected the religious and aesthetic experiences are.

that lies just beneath our normal consciousness.[2] This knowledge sustains and shows us the difference between being trapped in existential aloneness and transcending the limitations of self as ego into self as spirit. Wordsworth, reflecting on these experiences, said that in them "we see into the life of things." In his great poem "Lines Composed a Few Miles Above Tintern Abbey" he says this about his experiences:

> ...I have felt
> A presence that disturbs me with the joy
> Of elevated thoughts; a sense sublime
> Of something far more deeply interfused,
> Whose dwelling is the light of setting suns,
> And the round ocean, and the living air,
> And the blue sky, and in the mind of man [sic].

There are myriads of these experiences, some more vivid than others, and I think that we all have them from time to time, even though we often do not realize how profound they actually are. In them we understand, even if it is only for a moment, how much more there is, both to our wonderful universe and to ourselves, than we ever comprehended before. But just what is it that we see in them? What is this joy that disturbs and yet reveals the core of who and what and even why we are at all? What is this "life of things" Wordsworth speaks of?

People sometimes say of these experiences that they take the breath away, but I prefer to say that they give us our breath back again. They reveal to us the source of our spirit. This is what opens

---

[2] For a more detailed discussion of this sense of knowledge, see the discussion above in Chapter 5 of Part I.

us to the possibility of understanding the truth that even though we are indeed separate individuals we are yet, also and equally, bound together with all that is. This is the beginning of *ubuntu* made manifest and palpably real. It is Presence within us, and it sustains us as human beings.

Think again about these lines from T. S. Eliot's poem "Burnt Norton," the opening poem in his *Four Quartets*:

> At the still point of the turning world. Neither flesh nor
> fleshless;
> Neither from nor towards. At the still point, there the dance
> is,
> But neither arrest nor movement. And do not call it fixity,
> Where past and future are gathered. Neither movement
> from nor towards,
> Neither ascent nor decline. Except for the point, the still
> point,
> There would be no dance, and there is only the dance.

It is these moments, when we rest at the still point, that sustain our humanity and make the dance possible. And what is the dance? It is the dance of the loves that we share, the friendships, the moments of touching hearts, the warmth of living, the light of joy, and the illumination of human contact.

My experience is of a profound intimacy that reveals to me a wholeness and a continuity that is holy. I choose, then, to call this wholeness and continuity *Spirit* and the cultivation and the living of my life in the light of Spirit I call my spirituality. Spirit's image in my soul—or, if one prefers, my heart—is what creates my integrity. Therefore, when called to become myself, I am called to align myself with Spirit, to align my spirit with Spirit.[3] What is important, though, is not the language but the experience the language points to. Ignore the Buddha's finger and pay attention to the moon. What is important is being open to the experience, reveling in it and finding rest in this "still point of the turning world," in this "life of things."

## THE LANGUAGE OF SPIRITUALITY

But human beings are ultimately linguistic creatures, and so we are driven to talk to each other, especially about those experiences that touch us the most deeply. It is in these conversations about spirituality that the difficulties arise. Somehow the words we use seem inadequate to capture the power and importance of what we experience.

There is something fascinating, though, about the language of spirituality, fraught with difficulty as it is. When one looks carefully at the word's cultures use to talk about spirituality, one discovers some surprising similarities. And this happens even in cultures and languages that until fairly recently have had little or no contact with each other.

For example, it is written in the Hebrew scriptures that human beings do not become alive—*ensouled* is the technical term—until God breathes the breath of life into them. The Hebrew word for *breath* here is *ruach*, which also means *spirit*. As it turns out, there are other words in other languages that share this breath/spirit con-

---

[3] Think again of Dōgen's famous admonition that in order to find the Self one must lose the self.

nection. The Greek word *pneuma* (from which we get such English words as *pneumatic* and *pneumonia*) also means both *breath* and *spirit*, as does the Latin word *spiritus*. Yet none of these words share an etymology. These disparate cultures developed the same meta-phorical way of talking about spirituality and did so independently of one another.[4]

One finds the same idea in many other cultures with little or no contact with the ancient Hebrews, Greeks, or Romans. For example, the Sanskrit word *atman* also means both *breath* and *spirit* and is used to indicate the presence of God within the soul—Presence-as-immanent—a usage that goes back at least to the Vedas, oldest of the Hindu scriptures. As a final example, the Zulu word for *spirit* is *umoya*, which is also the word for *wind*. To be sure, wind is different from breath, but it strikes me that the idea is similar, the wind being thought of as the breath of the earth.

As different as all these cultures are, they share the idea that somehow the breath or the wind gives us a way of talking and thinking about what we call the spiritual. Each of these cultures is telling us that there is something about our breath that suggests to the human mind a connection to that which is greater than we, a connection to a more profound level of reality than we experience day-to-day. Jung called this kind of cross-cultural sharing an archetype, and he believed that archetypes are hardwired into our brains and are given content by one's culture and experience.

The archetype of breath, then, provides many cultures with a way of thinking and speaking about the spirit. This is why the branch of Euro-American systematic theology that deals with

---

[4] To be sure, this is not universal. Not all languages work in this way, but I find it fascinating and suggestive how many do.

the spiritual in general and the Holy Spirit in particular is called *pneumatology.*

## THE HOLY TRINITY

One might have thought that my having left Christianity had relieved me of needing to address The Trinity. But the more I thought about it, the more I realized that literally billions of people have found great comfort and healing in the idea of the Trinity. I must have missed something important, and so I began to ask myself what I had failed to understand. It haunted me. I needed to make my peace with The Trinity. Here is what I have come to think.

A common criticism of Christianity is that the notion of the Trinity is inherently contradictory, that God must be either one or triune but cannot be both. I think that this criticism misses the point entirely. In fact, the Trinity is an ingenious way of solving a difficult problem: the relationship between Presence-as-transcendent and Presence-as-immanent.

I discussed transcendence and immanence above, but to recap briefly (and reverting temporarily to more conventional religious language), assume for a moment some notion of Divinity and consider. Is the Divine external to the world, approachable only through an extraordinary act of crossing over an otherwise un-bridgeable boundary (the Divine as transcendent), or is the Divine within all existence, as intimately within us as our very breath (the Divine as immanent)? These conceptions of Divinity seem to be equally plausible, and indeed, all theistic religions contain both. Yet, on the surface at least, they also seem to be incompatible.

# Chapter 6: Pneumatology

The idea of the Trinity is an attempt to reconcile these two conceptions of the Divine. If we think of God the Father as the transcendent God, and God the Holy Spirit as the immanent God, then we can think of transcendence and immanence as being joined in the divine figure of Jesus, God the Son. A common—even orthodox—way of understanding this idea is that Jesus, the only Son of God, is therefore unique among humans.

The problem I have with this is that the orthodox understanding makes Jesus to be a divine figure, human and God at the same time. But if Jesus is divine then he is different from ordinary people. We are not divine in the way that Jesus is believed to be. And yet we also experience both the transcendent and the immanent in our own lives. This makes of Jesus yet another transcendent figure and thus fails to reconcile the transcendent and the immanent as we ordinary human beings actually experience them.

I would argue that there is no necessity for a special person—be that person mythic or historical—in order to reconcile the transcendence and the immanence of Presence. The ideas of transcendence and immanence are, after all, human ideas, created to understand and articulate our various experiences of Divinity. They are rational articulations, but Divinity is a reality that far surpasses the ability of human rational language to express. It is therefore inevitable that any articulation will fall short of the whole. Paradox is unavoidable when we restrict ourselves to rational articulation of the extra-rational. This is also why people so often turn to story and poetry to convey these experiences and why these rational discussions fail to carry the power and importance of the experience.[5]

---

[5] For example, most rituals appear absurd from the outside but are filled with potency and power from the inside.

As I have said before, the immanent is the transcendent leaving footprints in time; the transcendent is the immanent projecting itself into eternity. Both are reconstructions of an experience of Divinity, and therefore neither is the whole of Divinity. (The map is not the landscape.) Thus, it is not necessary to posit the Christ in order to reconcile these aspects of Presence. Both are a reality in every human life. Indeed, both are a reality in every being. If either were to withdraw from our world, we and everything else would vanish into dust.

On the other hand, if one thinks of the Trinity as a mythic expression of this truth, then I have no quarrel with it. God the Son (Christ) becomes a metaphor for all of us. What the doctrine is telling us is that the immanent and the transcendent are reconciled in each of us. This would mean that the Second Coming is upon us in the birth of every child. Indeed, just as we are all The Buddha, we are all The Christ, a distinctly unorthodox, perhaps even heretical, conclusion.

It follows from this that Jesus, The Christ, is now among us, within the being of every person we meet. As is written, "The Kingdom of God is within you."[6] I believe that this is the real Gospel message: each of us is already holy. What we have lost is the vision, the ability to stand under (to be existentially committed to) that holiness; we have not lost holiness itself. As the old Universalists insisted, the religious task is not to become saved. On the contrary, the religious task is to realize (in the sense of making it real in our daily lives) the salvation that is already ours. It is ours by virtue of the fact that the essence of our existence is the reality of Divinity

---

[6] Luke, Ch. 17, verse 21. This is sometimes translated as "The Kingdom of God is among you."

expressing itself, now as immanent, now as transcendent, within our lives in experiences such as those noted at the beginning of this discussion. Once again, *ubuntu* becomes holy love, the love that heals the brokenness of our lived lives, for *ubuntu* is the apprehension of Presence in every life.

This alternative understanding of the Trinity makes complete sense to me. It is compatible with the original Unitarian doctrine of the unity of God because it folds these two aspects of Divinity back into a unity that far surpasses any human attempt to entrap it within language. It is also compatible with the Buddhist notion that we are all The Buddha. The Universalist idea of universal salvation is the same as the Buddhist idea that all are already enlightened and that the religious task is to realize the enlightenment that we already have (that is, the task is to awaken to our Buddhahood). We do not have to become The Buddha; we have to incarnate the Buddha that we already are. We do not have to become saved; we have to incarnate the salvation that is already ours. To paraphrase the famous comic strip, *Pogo*, we have met The Buddha To Come (Maitreya Buddha) and he is us.

However, this understanding of the Trinity also puts me well outside of the orthodox Christian understanding of the Trinity, and that is why I am unwilling to call myself a Christian. This is where pneumatology intersects with theology. Still using traditional religious language, the God I believe in is not a God that stands away from humanity, a God from whom we are walled away by sin, original or otherwise. The God I believe in is a God who is involved by love in every moment of time, a God whose being is enshrined in every life in ways so vast that our awareness of it is dim, apprehended in moments of intense insight that inform and direct our living. The God I believe in is not contained in language, but is reflected, darkly and tangentially, through the mirror of language, pointed to, but not captured.

## WHAT SUSTAINS US

I want now to shift to somewhat different language, the language of sustenance. In this language, the leading question of pneumatology is "What sustains us?" In one sense, sustenance means that which nourishes us and gives us the ability to grow, as food sustains us. In another, related sense, it means that which is the substrate or foundation of something, that which makes something possible, as air and water sustain life. It is in this latter sense that pneumatology asks what sustain us. "What sustains our existence?" An even more general version is "What sustains existence itself?" As the 20th century philosopher, Martin Heidegger, famously asked, "Why is there anything at all rather than simply nothing?"[7]

Notice that this is not a scientific question. Pointing to the Big Bang isn't the answer. It just puts the question off for a bit. The question is not why there are human beings or any of the other things that happen to exist. The question is why there is—or ever has been—anything, including the singularity that exploded and became the universe. This kind of thinking opens the window between Theology and philosophy, specifically the branch of philosophy called ontology.

Another version of the same question is, "what is it that allows

---

[7] "Warum gibt es etwas mehr als nichts?" Martin Heidegger, Being and Time (Sein und Zeit) Max Niemeyer Verlag, Tübingen, 1953.

the universe to continue from one moment to the next?" When the ancient Greek philosopher Heraclitus said that one cannot step in the same river twice, he was puzzled by just this question: How is it that identity persists over time? How could I be the same me that I was an hour ago or a year ago or thirty years ago? In fact, *am* I the same me? If the river is not the same from one moment to the next, then why am I—or anyone else—the same person from one moment to the next?

Heraclitus' answer was that neither we nor the river nor anything else are the same from moment to moment. He taught that all is in flux, changing every moment, now this and now that. (Interestingly enough, this is also the Buddhist answer: nothing is permanent.) The problem with this answer is that it makes memory (and therefore also time) to be a real puzzle. I certainly *seem* to be the same man I was at breakfast this morning. The river certainly *seems* to be the same river I remember from my childhood. Time certainly *seems* to require a certain continuity, or all would be chaos. How can I account for the fact that I remember myself at breakfast and can remember a continuity from that moment to this? What is it that sustains not only us but also every thing that is, even time itself? What sustains us?

Reverting now back to my preferred language, that which sustains us and makes our existence and the existence of anything possible is Presence. I and thee and the universe are Presence unfolding into Love. What sustains me, what gives me the nurture that allows me to grow into my humanity? Presence sustains me, Presence that I do not feel but experience and within which I "live and move and have my being."[8] Presence, as the Love that empowers us to love, sustains me. Presence as revealed in these profound experiences:

- those moments of insight and elevated experience
- those relationships and loves and moments of learning about ourselves and others
- those intense realizations that we are not alone, as isolated and separate as we may appear to be
- those instants when we feel the deep, flowing ocean of holiness in our hearts and souls and we know that there is more to our living than we can ever imagine.

Presence, within us, around us, above and below, in front and behind. If we have eyes to see and hearts to feel.

## Spirituality and Spiritual Practice

With all of this in mind, let us return for a moment to our breath. I think that the reason that we human beings so often use the image of our breath for our spirit is that there is an intimacy about these moments and the insights into our deepest reality that they bring us. These experiences are perhaps the most intimate moments of our lives, moments in which we stand, as it were, naked in the presence of Presence.

William James said of these experiences that they are, among other things, inexplicable and ultimately indescribable. (The tech-

---

[8] Acts, 17:28.

nical word is *ineffable*.) Yet in spite of that, we human beings are social creatures and are driven to communicate, and so we search around for a suitable metaphor to express the ineffable experience of profound intimacy. There is little as intimate and yet as absolutely vital to our lives as our breath, our *spiritus*, our *pneuma*, our *ruach*, our *atman*.

What all of this means is that my concept of spirit is also somewhat unconventional, if not downright unorthodox. I do not think of spirit as a nonphysical entity that is trapped in a physical body waiting to be released by death. Our spirit is something else. It is our ability to experience the most profound level of our existence, the level of our being at which we are indelibly whole and linked together with one another. It is our ability to experience our worth and dignity directly and to dwell within the light of a mutually embracing love—*ubuntu*. When I speak of our spirit and our spirituality, I am talking about a growing and existential ability to stand under a truth that human language cannot capture, but only point to. This truth is Presence becoming manifest. Therefore, we do not and cannot speak this truth; we give it our lives as it expresses itself.

Our spirit, then, is the expression of Presence dwelling within us as profound intimacy, as intimate as our breath moving in and out of our lungs. It is this profound intimacy that sustains us and creates our integrity. Our spirituality is our experience of that spirit and the discipline to live our daily lives within its light. Spiritual practice is the intentional cultivation of our experience of our spirit. It is this practice that enables us to guide our lives by the light of that which is greater than we and yet gives us our deep integrity—Presence.

It is certainly true that not everyone has, or even cares to have, a spiritual practice. Yet without it, religion remains stunted and arrogant, just as without the insights of rational religion, spiritual practice remains nothing but an insipid and vapid quietism. Mature religion needs both and forgoes either at its great peril.

Dōgen Eihei was one of the greatest Japanese Zen masters. He lived in the 13th century and founded one of the major branches of Japanese Zen, called Soto. A remark attributed to him that I find deeply profound is "If you are ready, anything can bring Enlightenment." Like much of Zen, this sounds simplistic, yet when you begin to go more deeply into it, you begin to see the power behind its succinctness, also like so much of Zen.

Spiritual practice is not Enlightenment; it is preparation for Enlightenment. The question that spiritual practice addresses is how one prepares to awaken to the enlightenment that one already has. Spiritual practice is simply practicing being awake. It is when one takes waking up seriously and opens to awakening that one begins true spiritual practice. The point, then, of spiritual practice is to prepare oneself for whatever it is that moves one into awareness of the profoundly intimate within the heart, into a vision of the deep integrity that I have called spirit. It must be cultivated, grown intentionally. One must open oneself. It is a discipline, and like any discipline, it must be learned and practiced.

Even a cursory study of comparative religion reveals that there are many, many ways of opening oneself, and they all work, or they would not have persisted for thousands of years. There are, however, some things that they have in common. Perhaps one of the most striking things they have in common is that the majority involve stillness. Consider Zen as an example. One often hears people saying that in Zen meditation—which is called zazen—you must empty your mind. I have found that this is not exactly true, even though it is a common way of putting things. After all, emptiness leads only to emptiness. The truth is that zazen, when done properly, requires that one still one's mind, and in that stillness to pay attention to what is found there.[9]

Stillness does not lead to emptiness; stillness invites hearing the small voice within.[10] The busy, buzzing mind cannot see through the fog of confusion that typically surrounds our daily lives. The *Tao Te Ching* abounds in images of stillness and the necessity of achieving it. To reconsider just one of these images:

[The Wise are] able to sit patiently as muddy water clears.

[The Wise are] able to be at rest in the midst of violent action.[11]

This is what spiritual practice does for us. Spiritual practice quiets us and stills the mind; stillness leads to openness; openness prepares the heart for Enlightenment—profound intimacy.

The only practices that can be genuinely spiritual, then, are those that can still life sufficiently that the practitioner can pay attention to and dwell with and within an open heart. It is only when the heart is profoundly open that we can grasp the truth that is expressed in Buddhism as "we are all The Buddha." Another way of saying the same thing is that it is only when the heart is profoundly open that one can live more fully in the light of ubuntu. Being guided by the light of *ubuntu* is what truly sustains us, however it

---

[9] The difference is like the difference between jumping into an empty swimming pool and diving into the calm water of a still pond.

[10] I believe that prayer is not about speaking but about listening.

[11] *Tao Te Ching*, Chapter 15.

may be that one is comfortable talking about it.

When one is open in this way and finds *ubuntu* flowing though one's heart, then the world is no longer the same. To be sure, trees are still trees and mountains are still mountains, but when one has seen Presence within the world and understood that Presence pervades not only one's own heart but also the heart of those very trees and mountains, then one's life has changed. The walls that once divided self from other are suddenly not quite so absolute and impenetrable, and we begin to understand that our broken heart can be healed only together with the broken hearts of all. This is realization that the Spirit is the meeting ground of our greatest joy and the world's greatest hunger.[12]

---

[12] See Frederick Buchner, op. cit.

**Untitled verses in the Japanese style**

Raven in cedars;
Hoarse laughter;
Old bullfrog croaks.

Into my own pond:
Old Bashō's frog—
Plop![13]

---

[13] Collier, *How To See Deer*, p. 37.

CHAPTER 7:

# Eschatology
*What happens after death?*

I turn now to the remaining branch of Theology, eschatology (from the Greek *eskhatos*, meaning *last* or *end* plus our old friend, *logos*), an understanding of the end. Many people think this is the essence of religion. For these people, the primary concern of religion is not this life but the life to come. This life is thought of as but a preliminary, a chance to prepare us for the life to come, either after death or when everything comes to a crashing end. The central question of this understanding of religion is "What will happen to us and to the world when it is all over?"

There are two versions of this, depending on what one thinks "when it is all over" means. In the first version, it means "when I die" (the life after death version), and in the second, it means "when time and space and everything within it come to an end" (the Cosmic Judgment version). Either way, the central questions are not "What are we doing now and how will that heal us?" but "Where are we going, and what will happen when we get there—wherever 'there' is?" In this understanding of religion, it is the next life that is of central importance. This life and how we are living it is secondary, important only inasmuch as it prepares us for living well in the next life. I think of this question as the classical eschatological question.

I realized that this is way of thinking is not an artifact of Christianity, or even the Religions of The Book. Both classical Hinduism and many versions of Buddhism, with their doctrines of reincarnation, also emphasize the next life and see this life as preparation for the life to come. The goal is not life now but eventual liberation from *samsara*, the cycle of birth and death.

It will hardly come as a surprise that I beg to differ with this view of religion. Far from leading to healing, it suggests an essential division between the saved and the unsaved. That is why I put this chapter off until the end. I think that this way of thinking about religion is more often than not simply a red herring. It diverts our attention from what I believe to be the genuine and central question of religion—what do I need to do to bring healing to myself and to the world? For me, soteriology, not eschatology is the beginning of Theology. The question of healing (or salvation or Enlightenment or whatever else) is found at the core of all of the major religions. For example, one of the key passages of the Gospels occurs when Jesus is asked point-blank "What must I do to inherit eternal life?"[1] (the life after death question). Jesus' answer does not even hint at a future life. He says that one must live this life, now, at this very moment, in the love of God, and that love is expressed most exquisitely in the love of one another. As I read The Gospels, Jesus taught that it is this life that is critical, and if this life is lived well and properly, then the next life will take care of itself.

In a similar vein, The Buddha was once asked whether he thought that God exists. His answer? The by now familiar "Whether there is a God or there is not a God, there is still the question of your enlightenment." In short, forget about God and learn to live now, in this very moment, awake and cheerfully. This also corrects

---

[1] The Gospel According to Luke, Chapter 10, verse 25.

a common misconception. Enlightenment is not the Buddhist heaven, achieved after living a good life. Enlightenment is in this life, at this very moment. There is no nirvana-to-come, only nirvana now.[2]

Notice that both versions of the classical eschatological question (life after death and the end of all time) assume that there is, in some sense, a self that survives the destruction of the body, whether in death or at the end of time. Let us look a moment at that assumption. There are really only two possibilities: either there is a self that survives death or there is not. Suppose there is not. Then does it not follow that the only rational course is so to live that one's life is rich and fulfilling rather than broken and filled with sorrow, pain, and hatred? Suppose there is a death-surviving self. Then, again, there are only two possibilities: either we face some form of reward and punishment after death or we do not. Suppose we do not. Then does it not follow that the only rational course is so to live that one's life is rich and fulfilling rather than broken and filled with sorrow, pain, and hatred? Suppose we do face reward and punishment. Then is it not inconceivable that anyone would be punished for living a life that is rich and fulfilling rather than broken and filled with sorrow, pain, and hatred?

It would seem that, in any event and in spite of appearances, both versions of the eschatological question collapse into the question of how to live a healed and holy life in this very moment. This understanding is the basis of Jesus' concern for living this life well and properly. Jesus also remarked that the kingdom of God *is* within, not off at some future time. The Kingdom of God is to be

---

[2] For a Christian version of this, see Brock and Parker, *Saving Paradise.*

found neither at the time of our own earthly death nor at the time of the end of time (if such there be), but now, within us, at this very moment. I believe that even though one must prepare for the future, the key to any future life lies in the present, for if we do not bring healing into the world here and now, when and where will we bring it? Here, then, is my eschatology of the present.

## THE SECOND COMING

I want to begin, though, with an aspect of the more conventional treatment of these issues that I find important: The Christian concept of The Second Coming of Christ. The idea of the Second Coming has been given rather unfortunately short shrift in recent years, especially among the more liberal and more secular thinkers. I have actually heard it referred to as "nothing but the prattling of a primitive religious myth." Religious myth it is, but it is, in no way, primitive, even though some versions of it are decidedly simplistic.

In spite of what one sometimes reads or hears, there is nothing unique about the Christian myth of the Second Coming. In fact, it is so common in religious mythology that Jungians would call it a religious archetype, the Savior-to-Come. Like all archetypes, it is built into the structure of human consciousness. We inevitably cast our own religious thinking into the molds of religious archetypes, filling their forms with our specific content. Most of the world's religions have their own ways of filling the archetype.

- The Jewish version, of course, is that there is a Messiah to come, who will redeem Israel.
- The Christian version is that this Messiah has come and

will return at the end of time.

- In Hinduism, it is said that Lord Krishna is born into every age just at the time when the people have strayed too far from understanding the true nature of Brahman/Atman. The point of his return is to teach the people, so that they can return to the true path of escape from samsara (rebirth). The most recent visit of Lord Krishna is recorded in the Bhagavad Gita.[3]

- In Buddhism, Gautama Siddhartha is said to be only the most recent in a whole series of Buddhas. Another Buddha, referred to as Maitreya Buddha, will come at an unknown time in the future.

- Shi'ite Muslims talk about the Hidden Imam, The Mahdi, who is in hiding but will return when he is needed, decisively defeating the enemies of the True Faith and establishing a reign of peace, justice, and righteousness.

- In the Aztec religion Quetzalcoatl brought civilization to the people and then sailed away on the Western Sea after promising to return and re-establish his sacred kingdom. Essentially the same myth is also told in the Mayan religion, where he was called Kukulcan.

- And on the frontier between sacred and secular mythology, we find, for example, King Arthur, hidden away on the mystical island of Avalon until he is needed to save Britain from its enemies.

It seems that these myths of the Savior-To-Come are all over

---

[3] Bhagavad Gita, Swami Prabhavananda and Christopher Isherwood, trans.

the religious landscape, as thick as bees on honey. Even Religious Humanism has a version of it: The Golden Age of the Future, when justice, mercy, and compassion, guided by Reason, rule human affairs. One rough-and-ready way to distinguish conservative from liberal religion is that conservative religion tends to look back to a Golden Age of the Past and seeks to re-establish it while liberal religion tends to look forward to a Golden Age of the Future and seeks to create it.

This is not to say, of course, that conservative Christianity does not have a Golden Age of the Future of its own. Of course, it does. It is the Kingdom of God established when Christ comes again in His glory. I am suggesting only that if one looks carefully at the conservative version of this myth, one will see that the images of this Golden Age are essentially a return to Eden rather than a new age of justice, peace, compassion and good will, never before seen on Earth. It is this new age that liberal religion embraces, and, of course, it is as much a religious mythology as the return of Christ in Glory.

The question that I think is important is how we are to understand this archetype. What are we telling ourselves when we fill it with our own content? Just exactly who is this Savior-To-Come? I found a key to understanding it in a point that The Buddha made over and over: Siddhartha Gautama is not very important. As a matter of fact, dependence on him is nothing more than yet another form of attachment and thus inevitably prevents genuine Enlightenment.

A few examples will illustrate his point. When asked whether or not he was a god, he replied that of course he wasn't. Pressed to tell the people what he was, he responded that he was awake and that anybody can wake up. Or again, he once likened himself to a raft that one uses simply to cross the river, but once across the river, only a fool would carry the raft around with him. And finally, one of the more startling and thus effective sayings in Zen is "If you meet The Buddha on the road, kill him!" The point being that you cannot depend on that Buddha out there in the world external to you, but only on this Buddha in here, in your own heart and soul. After all, as he says over and over, we are all the Buddha.

If the Buddha told us not to rely on him, then on whom did he say we should reply? He was quite clear about this in *The Dhammapada*:

> Who shall conquer this world
> And the world of death with all its gods?
> Who shall discover
> The shining way of the law?
>
> You shall, even as the man
> Who seeks flowers
> Finds the most beautiful,
> The rarest.[4]

We must rely on only one person: We must rely on ourselves. True Enlightenment is the realization that each and every one of us is The Buddha. Who, then, is Maitreya Buddha? Each one of us is Maitreya Buddha. Who is the Messiah? Maitreya Buddha is the Messiah. Each of us is the Messiah. When will Maitreya Buddha come? When will the Messiah come? They come with every baby

---

[4] Thomas Byron, *The Dhammapada*, p. 17.

that is born. Enlightenment is not something to be achieved off in the future; enlightenment is right now within our grasp, at this very moment. All we have to do is to wake up and realize our own Buddha-nature, our own essential nature: Presence within us.

## TIME

There is an understanding of time embedded within all this. There is no Golden Age lying just out of our reach, ahead of us in the future, because there *is* no future. The future is not real since it hasn't happened yet. It is nothing more than an expectation, a plan, a hope, a fantasy. Similarly, there is no Golden Age lying lost behind us in the past, because there *is* no past. The past is not real because it is over, finished, done with. It is nothing but a more-or-less vaguely understood memory.

The only time that is real is this very moment, this instant in which we live and move and have our being. And how long does this moment last, how long is now? No matter how long or short one may say now is, that span, having duration, has a beginning, a middle, and an end. At the beginning, the end has not happened; at the end, the beginning is over. Neither is now. Now has no duration. Now is eternal.[5]

Therefore, to be enlightened is to be alive, fully and completely, now, in this very moment. To be enlightened is to be eternally alive. Eternal life is not living for a very long time. Eternal life is being alive *outside of time*. When do you propose to achieve enlighten-

---

[5] For a good fictional discussion of this, see Ruth Ozeki's novel, *A Tale for the Time Being*.

ment if not at this very moment? There is no other "time." When I realized this, I suddenly understood some passages of sacred texts that had long puzzled me. For example, in a crucial conversation, a rich young man asks Jesus what he must do to attain eternal life, and Jesus tells him that he must sell all that he has, give it to the poor, and follow him. Or consider this passage from the *Tao Te Ching*:

> Those who truly know how to live
> Walk without fear of buffalo or tiger.
> They encounter battle without armor or weapons.
>
> The buffalo will find no place to gore,
> The tiger no place for its claws,
> And the sword no place to pierce or slash.
>
> What is the reason for this?
> It is because death has no reality.[6]

Both passages had seemed to me to be pointing to a way to escape physical death, but I also realized that this has to be a misunderstanding. If eternal life is being alive outside of time, both passages are actually teaching us how to live whatever life we may have outside of the shadow of our inevitable physical death. They are not about denying death; they are about disarming death.

Time inevitably brings death. It is inescapable. Therefore, Jesus was not offering the rich young man a way to live forever, to be biologically alive until the earth passes away. Instead, Jesus is telling

---

[6] *Tao Te Ching*, Chapter 50.

the man that his teachings will free him from the encumbrances of attachment to wealth. It is those attachments that prevent the man from stepping outside of time. "Follow me and I will teach you to let go of the very attachments that prevent your seeing the deeper truth that lies outside of time. And when you see this, you will no longer fear death."

Lao Tsu makes essentially the same point, though in a different cultural context. It is not that those who truly know how to live are immune to death. Of course not. Rather those who know how to live realize that death, inevitable though it is, is real only within time. To live outside of time is to deny death its power to terrify.

Of course, both Jesus and Lao Tsu are speaking of ideals. In the lives that we actually live, we have bodies (some would say that we do not have bodies but that we *are* bodies), and those bodies grow old, sicken, and die. This cannot be escaped. No one can actually live entirely outside of time, but we can step into that eternal now. And when we step back out again, as we must, we have the ability to let go of such an attachment to our bodies that the death of those bodies holds no fear.

When we think in these terms about Jesus' answer to the question about eternal life, we can see that he was saying that salvation (the achievement of eternal life) is not about life *after* death at all. He was saying that it is life outside of time, something that is achieved through loving God so deeply and profoundly that you see God as clearly within your neighbor as within yourself, and love God as fiercely in your neighbor as in yourself. This is life eternal; this is salvation; this is Enlightenment.

When you are truly alive in this eternal now, the question of your own death becomes unimportant. At what other moment do you propose to be alive than at this very moment? And when else do you propose to die than at this very moment? For that matter, when else were you born than at this very moment?

To live eternally, to live in this very moment, is to realize—to make real—the truth that each of us is the Savior-To-Come, whether one's local mythology happens to name that savior Maitreya Buddha, The Christ, the Messiah, The Mahdi, King Arthur, or The Golden Age of the Future. The poet, June Jordan, was right: "We are the ones we've been waiting for."[7]

Notice something else important. If everyone one of us is The Buddha, then what happens to the distinction between me and thee? Does it not disappear? If you are The Buddha and I am The Buddha, then we are not as distinct as we may have thought we are. In *The Dhammapada*, The Buddha says, "See yourself in others, then whom can you hurt? What harm can you do?"[8] The point is not to see oneself in others as if in a mirror. The point is to see that the edges that separate us are irrelevant to a deeply religious and enlightened life.[9] What matters is the fact that we are both The Buddha. The edges that separate us do not make us human. What makes us human is the shared Buddhahood that joins us. To be human is, if you will, to perceive our shared Buddhahood, and this stands at the heart of everything religious. And once again, we come face to face with ubuntu.

---

[7] June Jordan, "Poem for South African Women."

[8] Thomas Byrom, op cit., p. 49.

[9] As Joshu said in the context of a very important Zen koan, "Mu!"

## A Christian Version

So far, I've depended pretty heavily on Buddhist images and metaphors, and I realize that these images and metaphors may not be as familiar as other images. Since this discussion should not depend on a specific set of religious images, let me recast these ideas in other words that may be more familiar.

Consider Jesus. He was once asked what the most important law in all of the Torah might be. It was kind of a trick question, because any answer ran the risk of suggesting that the others are bendable or at least secondary. Typically, enough, though, Jesus rose to the occasion. He said that there are actually two: Love God and love your neighbor as yourself. Very subtle! He was asked what *the* most important law is, and he specified *two* laws. Did he fail to answer the question? No. He answered it quite well. These "two" laws are the really the same law looked at in two different ways. To love God is exactly to love our neighbor and vice versa. One cannot separate them, saying, "I do love God with my whole being, but those folks down the street I could just as easily do without." The latter belies the former. To be sure, God is real in my own life. But God is also, and equally, real in the lives of those folks down the street I really don't much care for. In fact, God is as real in the lives of every person living as God is in my life, however I may judge those other people.

At this point in Luke, Jesus is challenged to say just who our neighbor is, and he responded with the story of the Good Samaritan.[10] We often miss the point of this story, because we forget (or

---

[10] Luke, Chapter 10 verses 29 through 37.

don't know) who the Samaritans were in Jesus' time. They were a sect of Jews living north of Judea who were considered the worst sort of heretics by the Judean Jews. The Romans were hated, to be sure, but they were, after all, Gentiles. (And what can you expect of a Gentile?) The Samaritans, though, were renegade Jews, and they were despised as Jews who had turned from the true understanding of God's Torah. To Jesus' Judean audience they were unclean, heretical, and blaspheming Jews, and here, Jesus was saying not only that they are to be loved, but also that this Samaritan was the only person who correctly loved the injured man lying on the road.

It was the Samaritan who showed the kind of love Jesus had in mind: *ubuntu*. I love my neighbor when I show enough compassion to understand that the pain and suffering of one—the injustice visited upon one—is visited upon all, and genuine *ubuntu* is expressed when I work for the healing of the suffering of all, right now, beginning with this person right in front of me, at this very minute.

Jesus tells us that we must love not only those who are easy to love, but also those who are difficult to love. We must love not only those who love us and practice compassion to us, but also those who hate us and seek our hurt, the abusive husband, the hate-filled neo-Nazi, the drunkard father, the Ku Kluxer with his burning cross. To love God as we ought, we must embrace *ubuntu* and open our hearts to all those in whom God's Presence is indwelling. And, of course, God's Presence dwells within all.

This, I believe, is the essence of Jesus' teaching. For example, his admonition to love our enemies follows from this, as does his insistence that we must not judge others but help them. It is the core of Martin Luther King, Jr.'s call to non-violent resistance to Jim

Crow, and the essence of the Hindu notion of ahimsa, which is the foundation of Gandhi's program of Satyagraha.[11]

## BACK TO DEATH AND THE END OF TIME

"But," one may well ask, "What has any of this to do with eschatology ? What does it tell us about death and the end of time?" As noted above, later in Matthew, Jesus says to his disciples that the Kingdom of God is not lying off in some far-off future, or even in the near future. He says that the Kingdom of God *is within us*.[12] Right now. At this very moment.

Putting this together with Jesus' admonition to love one another in this radical way, I understood that to live in God's Kingdom is to practice ubuntu-love and to stand under the banner of the compassionate embrace of every human being. Since the very same God who dwells within me also dwells within thee, thy most profound reality is my most profound reality. To love you, then, is to love the God within you, and therefore I cannot simultaneously love God and hate you. How can I love in this way while worrying about some illusive vision of a life to come? To paraphrase Jesus slightly, sufficient unto the day is the suffering it brings.[13] The task is to bring healing into the world now, today, and let whatever may happen after we die take care of itself—as it inevitably will.

---

[11] *Satyagraha* is what Gandhi called his non-violent liberation movement. It means *Struggle for Truth*.

[12] Luke, Chapter 17, verse 21.

[13] See Matthew Chapter 6, verse 34.

It has been argued[14] that this or at least something very like this is at least consistent with the understanding of salvation and paradise that held sway over the first millennium of Christianity. Brock and Parker argue that it was not until about 1000 CE or so that the idea of a paradise beyond death became the dominant paradigm. Until then, paradise was seen as something one could achieve here and now on earth through the acceptance of salvation.

## A Personal View

So, here is my eschatology in a nutshell. Where are we going? We aren't going anywhere, because there is only here, where we are right now. And where is that? It is as if we are moving along a river. Sometimes the river flows in freshet over rapids and sometimes it flows slowly and quietly beside wide meadows and shaded glades. We can struggle against its flow all we want. We can fret and fuss and try to control where the river takes us. We can even try to dam it and stop its flow. But none of this is a skillful means, as the Buddhists say, because the reality is that no matter what we do, the river carries us downstream.

Is it not better the notice our place in the river than to try to be someplace where we are not? (You shall not covet your neighbor's place in the river.) Is it not better to trust the river than to worry ourselves about where it is taking us, something that we cannot know and cannot change? Please do not misunderstand me. I am not talking about passivity here. I am not suggesting for a minute

---

[14] See, for example, Rita Nakashima Brock and Rebecca Ann Parker's *Saving Paradise.*

that we simply sit still and let happen what will, be it good or evil. Even Lao Tzu says:

Therefore, do what needs to be done
But do not be arrogant.
Do what needs to be done
Without showing off.
Do what needs to be done
Without hubris.
Do what needs to be done
Without thought of reward.
Do what needs to be done
Without violence.[15]

Especially, I would add, do what needs to be done without violence to ourselves, the essential form of which is to try to be something or someone we are not. The real work of life is simply to understand our place in life—that to which we are called (eschatology intersects missiology)—and embrace it. How can anyone be faulted for standing under Presence as it is manifested in his or her life and living within the light of that Presence? If we do this, if we embrace our call, why should we worry about where the river takes us or what others may or may not do? If we embrace our call, how shall we despise Presence as it is manifested in others? How shall we fail to show compassion and ubuntu for all?

Where does this metaphorical river take us? To the sea, of course, the same place every river takes things. Death is what we typically call the sea's drinking deeply of the river and swallowing

---

[15] *Tao Te Ching*, Chapter 30.

us. It is yet another form of self-violence to pretend that we will not die, that we will somehow avoid the sea's swallowing us, and to struggle incessantly against that inevitable moment when we disappear into the sea. I can't think of a surer prescription for failure than that. Of course I will die; of course I will disappear into that sea. As will everyone I love. And in that moment of death, time will stop for me. Of course it will.

And what will happen after that? I don't understand the question. If time has stopped for me, how can I experience any "next" event, any "after"? And what difference could it possibly make? I cannot imagine any untoward result of living my life in this very moment, as well, joyfully, and lovingly as I am able, letting the non-existent future take care of itself.

I am content to let myself die when the time comes. I am not at all worried about any next life, be it as a reincarnated me or in heaven or hell, or even total oblivion. Another image of death that I have always liked is this. Think of our lives as the flame of a candle. The candle tilts and tilts ever closer to another candle, and at the moment of our death the flame moves from the first to the second as the first goes out. Is the flame on the second candle the same as the flame on the first? Or is it a different flame? Does it matter?[16]

One of the reasons why I like this image is that it leads one to let go of any notion of reincarnation. Reincarnation? Maybe. Maybe not. Does it matter? And if there is nothing that is permanent, what is this "self" that reincarnates? To be perfectly honest, I don't care, because this is not a useful question, not a skillful means. Why should we waste our energy pondering questions we cannot an-

---

[16] I believe this to be a Buddhist image, though I have not found a citation for it.

swer? It is enough to embrace the life that we have at this moment.

When the time for death comes, I hope that I can embrace it with the same warmth, joy, and love with which I have embraced my life. After living as long as is given to me, I am not interested in a long struggle in order to put off the inevitable for a few months, a struggle filled with machines and nausea, pain and disfigurement, and other indignities. Let me rather rise to meet the lips of the sea with a kiss and disappear into its waves, listening to the mermaids singing their song, whether or not they sing to me.[17] And then be gone. That is enough for me.

It has been suggested to me that this eschatology leaves the living with no comfort in the face of death, especially the death of a loved one. I have two responses. First, we all find our metaphors for thinking about questions that can have no answers. Among these questions and the metaphors people use to wrestle with them are those that lead to an eschatology. These metaphors and the eschatology based on them are the ones that help me. I find great comfort in the idea of dying into the embrace of Presence, even though others may not. And I find no comfort in the idea that there is an ego that transcends the threshold of death.

Second, remember my epistemology of religion. When someone says, "I know that Grandma in in heaven looking down on us," this is a religious knowledge claim. Therefore, it means that they find comfort and healing in a mythology that grounds such an eschatology. It helps them in the Human Project. That I do not find comfort in such an eschatology does not contradict their claim nor does my eschatology contradict theirs. Asking which of these

---

[17] See T. S. Eliot, "The Love Song of J. Alfred Prufrock."

eschatologies is the correct one is not a meaningful question. The real question is what gives *you* comfort, what brings healing to *your* heart and soul. This is a question that cannot be answered by one person for another. I have tried to express my answer in this chapter.

Finally, what about the end of everything? What will happen when even time itself closes its eyes and slides into the sea and is gone? What then? Once again, there is no point in pursuing questions which we cannot possibly answer and worrying about events over which we can have absolutely no control. To wring my hands over the far distant future is at best a distraction from the genuine business of living, which is to embrace Presence within my heart and soul, giving it the flesh of my life in the form of *ubuntu*. Anything more than that, I believe, is simply none of my business.

**What I Know**

I do not know where we go when we die;
And I do not know what the soul is
Or what death is or when or why.

What I know is that
The song once sung cannot be unsung,
And the life once lived cannot be unlived,
And the love once loved cannot be unloved.[18]

---

[18] Collier, *How To See Deer*, p. 14.

# Embracing Presence

# PART III:
# Credo:
# I Believe

"Credo: Indo-European root:
kerd-, heart."

## CREDOS ARE IMPORTANT

They articulate profound beliefs that mediate Theology and life. As we know, the word *credo* is a Latin word meaning *I believe*. To reiterate, this level of belief is not about the words used to express the belief, but about the heart- and soul-felt commitment that lies behind the words. It is important not to forget that the word itself comes from the same root that gives us the English word *heart*. A credo is not about the mind; it is about the heart. It is not about what one thinks; it is about that in which one places one's deepest and most profound trust. It is not about one's ideas; it is about one's faith, where one takes one's refuge. Therefore, a credo is a statement made from the depths of the heart of one's faith.

All such faith statements are necessarily provisional, reflecting how one expresses this depth at a given moment. Like any living thing, a living faith is one that grows and deepens as one lives one's life. The deeper my understanding of my humanity grows, the deeper my faith becomes, and therefore my credo evolves. No genuine credo, then, is or could be the end of a living faith. Rather, it is the beginning of a deepening faith, for as the Jewish proverb has it, "Those who think that they are finished—usually are."

It is also true that no genuine credo is easy to live up to. It must be a statement originating in the heart and soul that constantly calls us to become deeper in our humanity than we thought we could be. It is the way we express our call to grow constantly into our humanity, a task that forces us, from time to time, to change our lives as we realize how far we have fallen short. The constancy of this call means that all of us will sometimes fall short of our

credo. Our falling short does not mean that we are necessarily hyp-
ocrites. It simply means that we are constantly called to move on,
to deepen, to do better than we have, and to understand that there
is more to us than we are at a given moment. In short, it means that
we are always simply becoming human.

For example, consider the first assertion of the Nicene Creed: "I
believe in one God." When this is part of someone's genuine credo,
it is an assertion that one places profound trust in the unitary God,
a trust that is prior to all other trust and is constantly expressed
in the living of one's life. Not even the saints were able to do that
without lapse. As St. Paul famously put it, "...though the will to do
what is good is in me, the power to do it is not: the good thing I
want to do, I never do; the evil thing which I do not want—that is
what I do."[1]

Furthermore faith—profound trust—is not static. It deepens
as one's life unfolds, and that deepening is never simple.[2] Thus it
happens that what is necessary in order to live one's life in harmony
with the deep words of one's heart changes as one's life unfolds.
Indeed, the very words one uses to express one's credo sometimes
change—or at least one's understanding of what those words mean
and what that profound commitment requires change. Credos,
then, spoken or unspoken, are important.

The metatheology that I have developed so far is interesting
enough, but until it informs my life with meaning and understanding, it is empty, like having a mold with nothing to pour into it. To
pour one's life into the mold is to articulate one's credo, using the

---

[1] Romans, 7:18-19.

[2] See, for example, James Fowler's *Stages of Faith*.

insights of a developed theology. Now, it is certainly true that not everyone who writes a credo does so with a specific Theology in mind—or is even aware of Theology as a discipline. And yet, I do suggest that behind every credo there lies at least an implicit Theology. For some people, the credo is enough, and they are content to leave the Theology alone and silent. I have found that is not enough for me. I need to allow the Theology to speak as well as my Credo. And so now, having articulated at least a metatheology it is the time to turn my attention to my Credo.

A model is helpful. Because I am more deeply influenced by Buddhism than any of the other of the world's religions[3], the model that I will use for this is the shared Buddhist statement of faith, The Three Jewels, which contains the Four Noble truths and the Noble Eight-fold Way:

I. I take refuge in the Buddha.

II. I take refuge in the Dharma:

The Four Noble Truths:

1. Life is filled with dukkha.
2. Dukkha is the result of attachment to the impermanent.
3. There is escape from attachment.
4. Escape is found in following the Eight-fold Way:
    1. Right meditation
    2. Right action
    3. Right attitude
    4. Right Mindfulness

---

[3] I sometimes refer to myself as Buddhish.

5. Right livelihood
6. Right speech
7. Right effort
8. Right thought[4]

III. I take refuge in the Sangha.[5]

Here, then, is my credo as an annotated version of the Buddhist Three Jewels.

### I. I put my deepest trust in a Presence that grounds all existence.

I look into the world, and I experience a mysterious Presence that thrills me and fills my heart with awe. It is not just something that breaks through the surface now and again, on rare and totally unexpected occasions, though it may do that, too. It is something that is always there. It is not something the perception of which is reserved for a few very special people. It is something that anyone can see, anyone at all. All one need do is open the eyes of the heart, and it is there. I stand out under the stars. I stare out to sea. I climb the high mountains and gaze in wonder at the sparkling light. To be sure, I can see it in these exalted places. But I look also into the absolutely ordinary. Presence is there too, always ready to be seen. Consider....

- If Presence sparkles in the light flooding the high mountains, it also streams out of the dark storm clouds, out of the

---

[4] "Right" should be understood as "effective" rather than "correct."

[5] For a fuller discussion of how I understand The Three Jewels, I refer the reader to my book, *Finger-Pointing Essays*. Much of the discussion in this chapter also appears in that book in a somewhat different form.

fog flowing across the shore, out of the evening, out of the morning. It is also in the dirty yellow smog our cities wear like a soiled cap. It is in the light that rests in the darkness of night; it is in the darkness hiding in the glaring noonday sun. Look to the ordinary light of every day, for Presence is there.

- If Presence moves in the waves, stumbling their way ashore, it is also in the stumbling child learning to walk. It is in the grace of the athlete, the power of the dancer, the weakness of the ill and the dying. It is in the wind blowing through the light green leaves of spring and the confetti leaves of fall. It is in the smell of cooking food, in the fumbling sounds of anger, and in the infectious roar of laughter. It is in the lioness stalking her prey and in the gazelle falling to her death. Look to the ordinary motions of life, for Presence is there.

- If Presence transfixes the eye staring at the scattered stars on a clear night, it is also in the tangle of grass in your own front lawn. It is in the apple growing on the tree, in the rose, in the iris, in the tomato, the zucchini, and the cabbage. It is in the laundry waiting to be washed; it is in the mud from which the roses grow. It is in the festive meal, and it is in the dirty dishes piled in the sink. It clutters the floor with the morning newspaper and the toys left behind by children. Look to the ordinary, to every moment and encounter of life, for Presence is there.

There is a story told of a holy man and one of his disciples.

The disciple came to him in despair, saying, "Master, let me leave this place and go to the Holy Mountain, for I have lost my hold on God. Perhaps I can find Him again on the Holy Mountain."

His Master looked at him in compassion and sent him home, saying, "If you cannot find God in your own back yard, what makes you think you can find him on the Holy Mountain?"[6]

For that is the way it is. Every moment, every action, every instant of this life contains mystery, wonder, and beauty—if I would but open my eyes and see it.[7] There is no such thing as a God-forsaken place, for every place is filled with the same holiness. It is only my unwillingness to see that blinds me. Presence is not the skin-deep surface loveliness that withers with time and familiarity. It is a profundity so powerful that when I see it, I know that I am whole and that it is the brokenness that is the illusion; I know that the deeper truth is that a healthy love pervades all, a love that is the perception of Presence. It is everlasting because it is not in time, not in space, not in becoming, not in passing. It is eternal. It is mysterious. It is beyond real. It is as familiar as the beating of my own heart, as common as a drop of rain or a grain of sand. Perhaps its very commonness hides it from me. But it is there. I have no need to go to the Holy Mountain, for the Holy Mountain is here.

*II. I put my deepest trust in the Way of Life that reveals to me Presence in life. This way of life is expressed in Four Fundamental*

---

[6] This may be a Hassidic story, though I have not found a reference for it.

[7] See William Blake's poem, "Auguries of Innocence."

*Truths:*
1. *Life cannot be lived without aloneness and dread.*
2. *The terror caused by the aloneness and dread is the result of being stuck in thinking that the separation between me and thee is the ultimate truth.*
3. *If this terror is caused by being stuck, then it is possible to disarm the terror by getting unstuck.*
4. *The way to disarm the terror is to practice a spirituality that allows me to become unstuck and reveals the depth of Presence in all that I do. This spiritual practice consists of effective and intentional*
   > *Meditation*
   > *Action*
   > *Attitude*
   > *Mindfulness*
   > *Livelihood*
   > *Speech*
   > *Effort*
   > *Thought*

*1. Life cannot be lived without aloneness and dread.* The great task of childhood is to become a separate person, filled with the autonomy and integrity that makes us individuals. One way or another we all do that, some with great health and happiness and some kicking and screaming, filled with denial and agony. But all of us discover eventually that we are who we are. And while that is a wonderful discovery, it is also a terrible discovery, because it inevitably fills us with a certain existential dread. We also discover that, in our autonomy and integrity, we are alone. We are one, separate from all those others out there. No one can think our thoughts, or feel our feelings, or, most terrible of all, die our death with us. I am truly and ultimately alone.

The reaction to this discovery of what I call existential aloneness is inevitably surrender, though there are two very different kinds of surrender, and each has millions of variations. The first is the surrender of giving in to aloneness. I can surrender—give in—by hunkering down in its face and living a cowering life of fear or quiet desperation.[8] And I can give in to aloneness by denying it and going my way pretending that it is not so. But once I know this dread and aloneness, I can't just unknow it. Once I have felt that freezing finger of existential dread, it lingers somewhere in my memory and I know it. Denial is nothing but the pretense that I don't know something that I do know.

Sometimes I try to wall that memory off and avoid it with every ounce of my strength. But then it occasionally breaks through and the despairing loneliness wells up like contaminating oil, and I flee in terror. Sometimes I unthinkingly hoard it and use it as a weapon to dominate others, thinking that if I have enough power over enough people, I will be able to escape. But hoarding power only leaves me scrambling forever after the illusion of more and more power. And then, eventually the dread returns, and the illusion evaporates into smoke, leaving me again alone and despairing. This surrender—be it quiet desperation or denial—doesn't work. It leaves the dread alive and gives it the power to dominate my life.

The second form of surrender is the religious sense, in which I do not give up in the face of aloneness, but embrace aloneness, and

---

[8] Donald Trump exemplifies such a life.

in that embrace paradoxically discover the possibility of transcending it. The truth is that there is an important sense in which despair really is part of everyone's life. It is part of the price I pay for being an individual, separate, and autonomous. The idea that I can live a life without the aloneness and the despair that it brings is simply foolishness. Everyone, I believe, has experienced that aloneness; we all experience that despair.

It is better, I believe, to embrace it, recognizing that while I feel my aloneness, I am not my aloneness; while I feel despair, I am not my despair. Is it not better to open myself to the possibility of transcendence and transformation than to offer myself as a victim to despair and surrender my life over to it? Is it not better to accept the truth that great joy brings great sorrow? As is written in *The Tao Te Ching*, "The Tao is not static; it circles back on itself." Is it not better, then, to embrace both the joy and the sorrow of life, and so to transcend the illusion that they are two? And this leads it the Second Step.

**2. Terror caused by the aloneness and dread is the result of being stuck in thinking that the separation between me and thee is the ultimate truth.** Why does the realization of individuation bring such terrible aloneness and dread in its wake? We usually think that these bodies we live within are the end of the matter. We usually think that we stop at our skin, that our consciousness is somehow trapped inside our skulls. It is true that no one can feel exactly what I feel, or think exactly how I think, or dream my dreams. It is true that no one can die my death. It is true that I am within my body and that no one is—or could be—in my body with me, that I really am alone in here.

Yet though all this is true, it is true only from one point of view. Suppose there is another way of thinking about these things. If joy and sorrow are two yet not two in the sense that lovers are two yet one within the love that joins them, then maybe I can think of the separation between me and thee in the same way. We are two in the sense that we are individuals, but if Presence is within my heart and also within your heart, then surely it is the same Presence. And if it is the same Presence, then just as surely it is true that we are also not two. It is also true that we are, seen from this perspective, really one. Is not the aloneness and dread caused by being stuck in only one way of thinking about life? If I could but embrace thee in *ubuntu*, we could both overcome aloneness.

In fact, many people find that it is threatening even to contemplate the idea that we are not two. It is as if they think that in order to realize that we are not two, we have to give up the idea that we are individuals, and therefore we have to give up our very existence.[9]

**3. If this terror is caused by being stuck, then it is possible to disarm the terror by getting unstuck.** The essence of a stuck life is falling into the mistake of thinking that we have to conceive of the world in one and only one way. But I do not have to conceive of the world in that one and only one way. I can think of the world in many different ways, simultaneously, and if I can do that, then I can embrace *both* my individual, separate being *and* my being part of a whole, together with others, joined in ubuntu. Both are essential ways of being real. The only way to avoid the dilemma is to embrace both horns by realizing that we can be both individual

---

[9] This is the error of dualist thinking. To disarm terror, I must give up dualism.

and collective simultaneously. If I can do that, then I can break the hold of dread without disappearing. I really can unstick my life.

*4. The way to disarm the terror is to practice a spirituality that allows me to become unstuck and reveals the depth of Presence in all that I do. This spiritual practice consists of effective and intentional*

> *Meditation*
> *Action*
> *Attitude*
> *Mindfulness*
> *Livelihood*
> *Speech*
> *Effort*
> *Thought*

This Fourth Step is the step of Spiritual Practice. Spiritual Practice has come up often in this discussion, both because it is a difficult and complex business, and because it is critically important. Among the complexities is the fact that because of the nature of language, one appears to be saying that one first does this and then one does that and then one does the other, each practice leading to the next one. But that's not the way it seems to work, at least that's not the way it works in my life. All of these apparently different practices are of a piece and need to be engaged simultaneously. Indeed, it is even a mistake to think of them as different practices, just as playing the cello consists of many different actions, but they are all done at once and must be thought of a single whole action, the making of music.

Think about a finely faceted diamond. It is not that light first goes through this facet and then goes through that one and then goes through another. Light goes through all of them simultaneously and so the diamond sparkles in the sunlight, filled with fire. This is what the spiritual life is like; Presence within my soul passes through the many facets of my life simultaneously, and so I sparkle. The practice consists of the cleaning of the facets of my life so that the light of Presence can shine through them all.

Or again, think about moving around on a two-dimensional space. I am not first at an x-coordinate and then at a y-coordinate. I am at both coordinates simultaneously. I think of life as the movement through a many-dimensional space in which I exist with many coordinates at once, each dimension a different part of my life. The spiritual practice consists of learning to move through all of them together so that life becomes a dance expressing The Presence within my heart.

Or yet again, think about a written word. It does not consist of separate letters so that I read the first letter and then the second letter and then the third. The various letters come together to make a whole word; and the words come together to make a whole sentence; and these sentences come together to make a whole paragraph. I do not read letters; I read whole words and sentences and paragraphs. Just so, I do not engage in this practice and then that one and then the other one. I engage in all of them together, simultaneously, reading the poetry of Presence from the pages of my life.

With this understanding, then, that I am not listing things to be done, one after the other, but rather several things that are really one thing, these are the eight letters of the poetry of spiritual practice that I have discovered to be useful for me to break the hold of dread and loneliness, a practice that is an adaptation of the Buddhist Noble Eightfold Way. I see no reason not to name these with the Buddhist names:

When I practice these eight diligently and intentionally, with humility, I find the dread beginning to evaporate and the profoundly beautiful light of Presence beginning to fill my heart. When I fail to practice them, or when I do so but carelessly and without humility, perfunctorily and without attention, the fog returns, the light dims, and dread fills my heart all over again.

*III. I put my deepest trust in the lace woven of Presence that fills the universe and moves through every heart, creating a whole of the bits and pieces of existence.*

It begins when I discover that I am not just bits and pieces. I am connected, whole, entire. There may be parts to me, but they are in order. They work together, creating the person, the human being that is me. I am not talking about human anatomy and physiology here. I am talking about those things that make me human, spiritually and morally alive, and more than simply a biological specimen. I am talking about the discovery that not only am I *Homo sapiens*, but I am also human. This is the Human Project and putting my trust in Presence is the religious aspect of carrying that project out.[10]

This is the discovery that spiritual health is not something to be gained, but rather something to be remembered. Holiness is not something that only very few and very special people find on some far-off Holy Mountain, but rather it is something that is right

---

[10] For a more detailed discussion of The Human Project, see Part I, chapter 1, above.

here, right now, in this very moment, within this very heart. I have only to find it, to embrace it, and to live it into the fleshiness of my time on earth. This is Presence that some choose to call God while others choose to use different language. The language is not what is important. What is important is the realization that it is, at every moment, right here in my own heart, and I have only to look to find it. The spiritual practice is the looking.

When I look within this way something amazing happens. When I find Presence in my own heart, I find it everywhere. I find it in my family. I find it in my friends. I find it in my church. I find it my colleagues. I find it in my community. I find it in total strangers, walking down the street. I find it in flowers and trees and grass, in rocks and rain and rivers, in dirt and stars and wind. I find it everywhere. At the risk if repeating myself, it is not so much that the discovery takes my breath away, as it is that the discovery gives me my breath back again. Everywhere I look, everything I see, at every moment, in every place there is nothing that is not tied delicately and exquisitely into Presence. It astonishes, amazes, and transforms life. This is nothing new. Among many other places, this is expressed beautifully in the ancient Hindu myth of Indra's web of gold that pervades the universe and holds it together.

Presence weaves a lace so fine that it is almost invisible, so beautiful that it sparkles and shines and glistens with a light that escapes the merely mortal eye and can be seen only by the eye of the heart. It is so powerful that there is nothing that can break it. And when I see this astounding thing, I begin to understand what *ubuntu* actually is. For those moments, when I surrender my heart to Presence that fills the universe, there is nothing that is not deserving of my compassion and my care.

I speak, obviously, of some extraordinary moments, those moments of being lifted and rung as a bell (remember Annie Dillard), but there is more. When those moments pass, they do not pass utterly. They have changed me. When I return to the routine, ordinary, busy and blustery days of my living, the echo of that bell, or as e. e. cummings might put it, the echo of the echo of the bell remains. They have transformed my living and made me aware of something that cannot be lost but only hidden. It is tucked away in my heart and soul, nurturing me and making my life different than it was.

Those moments reveal a richness and texture to life that I had not known was there but now cannot forget. And in the remembering, I discover *ubuntu*, a love that engulfs me and creates a compassion for this incredible world. I begin to understand that not only is the joy of all my joy, but also the pain of all is my pain; not only is the healing of all my healing, but also the brokenness of all is my brokenness; and not only is the enlightenment of all my enlightenment, but also the illusion of all is my illusion.

In short, I begin to understand how it is that I must live in the world, giving and accepting, speaking and listening, loving and being loved. I begin to see how it is that since none are saved unless all saved, my work is to bring salvation into the world as fully as I can, and Bodhisattva-hood becomes obvious. It is not a thing to be achieved; it is a thing to be discovered and then lived, not for incarnation upon incarnation—for who knows what happens after death. Rather, it is to be lived right here in this very moment. It is when I can hold this in my heart, when I act and move from this heartedness, that I begin to become genuinely human. Sometimes I actually achieve this state, even in the busy-ness of life. The goal is to achieve it and keep it. I'm working on that.

In summary, then, here is what I believe. I do not expect or even suggest that anyone else believe as I do. You must find your own credo.

*I. I put my deepest trust in Presence that flows within all existence.*

*II. I put my deepest trust in the Way of Life that reveals to me Presence in life. This Way of Life is expressed on Four Fundamental Truths:*

1. *Life cannot be lived without aloneness and dread.*

2. *The terror caused by the aloneness and dread is the result of being stuck in thinking that the separation between me and thee is the ultimate truth.*

3. *If this terror is caused by being stuck, then it is possible to disarm the terror by getting unstuck.*

4. *The way to disarm the terror is to practice a spirituality that allows me to become unstuck and reveals the depth of Presence in all that I do. This spiritual practice consists of effective and intentional*
   > *Meditation*
   > *Action*
   > *Attitude*
   > *Mindfulness*
   > *Livelihood*
   > *Speech*
   > *Effort*
   > *Thought.*

*III. I put my deepest trust in the lace woven of Presence that fills the universe and moves through every heart, creating a whole of the bits and pieces of existence.*

Thus, Credo: I believe.

# CODA: Grace

The moon gives way to dawn; the sun
Slides upward in the sky so carefully
That we scarcely note its motion, only to fall,
And, with infinite care, snuggle itself
Back to the horizon.

The gentle night flows across the world
As irresistibly as rain falling on a river.
And then? Morning follows behind.
On they flow, time and stillness
And the slowly rocking eternality of life.

Here we stand, watching as it repeats itself,
A vast mantra patiently calling us. And we?
We strain to hear the echo of that mantra,
The faintly ticking sound of our hearts
Beating in unison, like two drums
In perfect rhythm. Is this love
That we hear rising from the eternal rocking
Of day into night into day?

We walk along the beach; we stroll through a forest;

# Embracing Presence

We wander carelessly into evening and dawn.
We gather and drink and laugh on manicured lawns,
And sing of love as if we understand.

Behind what seems an easy grace,
A shudder slides undaunted.
Our lives move onward; our days are haunted.

   Our minds touch like starlight on still water.
   I know you the way the moon silvers darkness,
   Or tides rise into shore and fill the marshes.
   I know what you do with your infinite life
   And the days that fill it like a deeply singing cello.

   The music of time surrounds us, my friend,
   A mist that drenches the cobweb of our hearts.
   We reflect each other the way drops of dew
   Reflect sunlight. The tide slips
   Its way out and the marshes empty.

   Fog rises and eats the stars like oysters,
   Leaving only flat, cold water.
   And you, my friend, are a memory slipping away
   Like the dying notes of an out of tune cello.

Never still, never full.
Our lives move across time
And space. And are gone?
Echoes sounding down the canyon.

## CODA: Grace

Starlight reflected on still water.
Moonlight casting shadows across the meadow.
Music resting in the corners of the heart,
Waiting to be called into sound.

The touch of one soul on another
Is never lost or forgotten or stilled.
It is like a single bead of crystal
Holding the whole world and giving
It back again, but only when we look
Deeply into the hard, cold glass.

A half-drunk cup of lukewarm coffee
Leaving circles on the table.
A wasp, hitting itself on the window.
Over and over. It cannot understand
Why it cannot fly through the clear air.

I stare at the cloudy morning light
As hazy as smoke from last night's cigars,
Hovering and acrid, stale and rancid.
A melancholy, out of tune song
Ricochets across the room.
A single seagull flies through the morning
And barks its long, lonely cry.

In the garden a hummingbird flies
From flower to bright flower. It hovers;
Springs like a dancer leaping across the stage,

Stops, drinks deeply, and moves on.
Orange nasturtium, red sage,
Cream flowers of the lime tree,
And deep blue agapanthus.
Suddenly, like a dream barely remembered,
It is gone as if called by the gods into the sky.

I am left alone to wander.
Confused and angry like the trapped wasp?
Darting and purposeful, like the hummingbird?

It's about that hummingbird,
Darting from flower to flower
Like an inconstant lover
Scattering kisses as wantonly as stars
Tossed across the night sky.

We suppose that life is an easy grace,
A grace unbroken that flows onward
Across a placid meadow, smooth and beautiful.

An easy grace is like a hummingbird
That hovers forever before a single flower.
Grace is a mountain that rises in the distance.
Grace is a dance that creates joy
And lives within stillness. Grace is
A music that weaves itself across silence.
Without silence there is no music;
Without stillness there is no dance;

## CODA: Grace

Without distance there is no grace.

I do not love you only to let you go.
I love you like the mountain holds its lake.
I love you like night holds its darkness
And morning holds its light and caressing breeze.
I love you like my heart holds music.
I love you to let you go
Even as I hold you in my soul.

Love moves across the heart
Like rain in the mountain meadow
Or snow falling, silently and cold,
In the winter night, piling up on the mountain.
Love begins like a distant melody,
Barely heard, slipping into the soul
Like sunlight slipping into leaves
Of roses or like starlight scattered across
The darkened summer sky, vast and beautiful.

It grew, slowly, and filled my heart
Until one morning I awakened and it was there,
As undeniable as thunder. And who knows
How I knew. But I knew.

Grace is the ground between
Loving and letting go.[1]

---

[1] Collier, *How To See Deer*, p. 7.

# Bibliography

This bibliography contains not only all those works that are cited in the text but also all those that I consulted in my research that are not cited in the text. Most, but not all are books that I have read over the years. Of course, there is more to be read. I do not pretend that this is anything like exhaustive. It is only what I have read.

Aitken, Robert. *A Zen Wave: Basho's Haiku & Zen*. New York: Weatherhill, 1978.

Aitken, Robert and David Steindl-Rast. *The Ground We Share: Everyday Practice, Buddhist and Christian*. Boston: Shambala Publications, Inc., 1994.

*American Heritage Dictionary of the English Language*. fourth edition, Boston: Houghton Mifflin, 2000.

Anderson, Alan Ross and Nuel D. Belnap, Jr. *Entailment*. Princeton, New Jersey: Princeton University Press, 1975.

Armstrong, Karen. *The Battle for God*. New York: Alfred A. Knopf, 2000.

Armstrong, Karen. *The Great Transformation: The Beginning of Our Religious Traditions*. New York: Alfred A. Knopf, 2006.

Barad, Karen Michele. *Meeting the Universe Halfway*. 2007.

Battle, Michael. *Reconciliation: The Ubuntu Theology of Desmond Tutu*. Cleveland, Ohio: The Pilgrim Press, 1997.

# Bibliography

Battle, Michael. *Ubuntu: I in You and You in Me.* New York: Seabury Books, 2009

Brock, Rita Nakashima and Rebecca Ann Parker. *Proverbs of Ashes.* Boston: Beacon Press, 2001.

Brock, Rita Nakashima and Rebecca Ann Parker. *Saving Paradise: How Christianity Traded Love of This World for Crucifixion and Empire.* Boston: Beacon Press, 2008.

Bryom, Thomas, trans. *The Dhammapada.* New York: Vintage Books, 1976.

Buber, Martin. *The Way of Man According to the Teaching of Hasidism.* New York: The Citadel Press, 1994.

Buber, Martin. *I and Thou.* New York: Touchstone, 1970.

Buber, Martin. *Tales of the Hassidim: Early Masters.* New York: Schoken Books, 1947.

Buber, Martin. *Tales of the Hassidim: Later Masters.* New York: Schoken Books, 1948

Collier, Kenneth W. *Finger-Pointing Essays.* Santa Barbara, California: Bandanna Books, 2007.

Collier, Kenneth W. *Full Circle,* Self-published, 2015.

Collier, Kenneth W. *How To See Deer,* Self-published, 2016.

Collier, Kenneth W. *The Great Wound: Confessions of a Slaveholding Family,* Self-published, 2018.

cummings, e.e. *i six non-lectures.* Cambridge, Massachusetts: Harvard University Press, 1978.

Dewey, John. *Logic: The Theory of Inquiry.* New York: Henry Holt & Company 1938.

Dillard, Annie. *Pilgrim at Tinker Creek.* New York: Bantam Books, 1975.

Dostoevsky, Fyodor. *The Brothers Karamazov*, Richard Pevear and Larissa Volokhonsky, trans. New York, Farrar, Straus and Giroux, 1990.

Eliot, T. S. "Four Quartets" in *Collected Poems 1909-1962*. New York: Harcourt Brace & Company, 1963.

Fowler, James. *The Stages of Faith*. New York: HarperCollins, 1981.

Gettier, Edmund. "Is Justified True Belief Knowledge?" *Analysis*, 23 (1963), pp 121-123.

Gobodo-Madikizela, Pumla. *A Human Being Died That Night: A South African Woman Confronts the Legacy of Apartheid.* Boston: Houghton Mifflin, 2003.

Greenaugh, Jeanie Ashley Bates. *A Year of Beautiful Thoughts*. Originally published 1902, reprinted by Ulan Press, San Bernadino, CA, 2012.

Grushin, Olga. *The Dream Life of Sukhanov*. New York: G. P. Putnam's Sons, 2005.

Hick, John. *Faith and Knowledge*, second edition. Ithaca, New York: Cornell University Press, 1966.

Hick, John. An *Interpretation of Religion: Human Responses to the Transcendent*. New Haven, Connecticut: Yale University Press, 2004.

*The Jerusalem Bible: The Reader's Edition*. New York: Doubleday and Company, 1968.

Jordan, June. *Directed Desire: The Collected Poems of June Jordan*. June M. Jordan Literary Estate Fund, 2005.

Jung, Carl Gustav. *Memories, Dreams, Reflections*. New York: Vintage Books, 1965.

Kafka, Franz. "Letter to a Friend," found on the Internet, translator unknown.

Bibliography

Kant, Immanuel. Norman Kemp Smith, trans. *Critique of Pure Reason*. New York: St. Martin's Press, 1965.

Keene, Donald. *An Anthology of Japanese Literature*. New York: Grove Press, 1955.

Keene, Donald. *Modern Japanese Literature*. New York: Grove Press, 1956.

Kuhn, Thomas. "The Structure of Scientific Revolutions" in *Foundations of the Unity of Science, Vol 2*, Otto Neurath, Rudolph Carnap, and Charles Morris, eds. Chicago: The University of Chicago Press, 1970.

Lao Tsu. *Tao Te Ching*, Kenneth W. Collier, trans. Unpublished.

Lao Tsu. *The Tao Te Ching*, Jonathan Star, trans. New York: Jeremy, P. Tarcher/Putnam, 2001.

Lorde, Audrey. *Sister Outsider: Essays and Speeches by Audre Lorde*. Freedom, California: The Crossing Press, 1984.

Maezumi, Taizan and Bernie Glassman. *The Hazy Moon of Enlightenment*. Boston: Shambala, 2001.

Norris, Kathleen. *Acedia and Me*. New York: Riverhead Books, 2008.

Ozeki, Ruth. *A Tale for the Time Being*. New York: Penguin Books, 2013.

Paul, Samuel A. *The Ubuntu God: Deconstructing a South African Narrative of Oppression*. Eugene, Oregon: Pickwick Publications, 2009.

Plato. *The Republic*, Francis MacDonald Cornford, trans. Oxford, UK: Oxford University Press, 1968.

Popper, Karl. *Conjectures and Refutations: The Growth of Scientific Knowledge*. London: Routledge and Kegan Paul, 1963.

Popper, Karl. *The Logic of Scientific Discovery*. London: Routledge Classics, 2002.

Rahula, Walpola. *What the Buddha Taught*. New York: Grove Press, 1974.

Rich, Adrienne. *What Is Found There: Notebooks on Poetry and Politics*. New York: W. W. Norton, 1993.

Schilpp, Paul Arthur, ed. *The Philosophy of John Dewey*. LaSalle, Illinois: Open Court, 1957.

Suzuki, Shunryu. *Zen Mind, Beginners Mind*. Boston: Weatherhill, 1970.

Swami Prabhavananda and Frederick Manchester. *The Upanishads: Breath of the Eternal*. New York: The Penguin Group, 1957.

Thich Nhat Hanh. *The Miracle of Mindfulness*. Boston: Beacon Press, 1975.

Thich Nhat Hanh. *Living Buddha, Living Christ*. New York: Riverhead Books, 1995.

Tutu, Desmond. *No Future Without Forgiveness*. New York: Image, 1999.

Tutu, Desmond and Mpho Tutu. *The Book of Forgiveness*. New York: HarperOne, 2014.

Whitehead, Alfred North and Bertrand Russell. *Principia Mathematica*. Cambridge, UK: Cambridge University Press, 1910.

Wiesel, Elie. *Souls on Fire: Portraits and Legends of Hasidic Masters*. New York: Random House, 1972.

Wilkins, Roy with Tom Mathews. *Standing Fast: The Autobiography of Roy Wilkins*. New York: Da Capo Press, 1982.

Wittgenstein, Ludwig. *Tractatus. Logico-Philosophicus*, C. K. Ogden, trans. Oxford, UK: Routledge & Kegan Paul, 1961.

# About the Author

Kenneth Collier was born in Tulsa, Oklahoma, on March 26, 1945, and was raised in Wilmington, Delaware. He earned a PhD in philosophy in 1971 and taught philosophy for several years at Southern Illinois University at Edwardsville, specializing in epistemology, philosophy of science, and logic. In 1976, Collier left teaching to enroll in seminary and earned a Master of Divinity at Starr King School for the Ministry. He was ordained to the Unitarian Universalist ministry in 1979. After serving several churches in five states and both coasts, he retired in 2007.

The major influences in his religious thinking are Buddhism, Christianity, and Taoism. Collier describes himself as a "Buddhish Unitarian Universalist."

He is the author of two previous books, *Finger-Pointing Essays* and *The Great Wound: Confessions of a Slaveholding Family* and is currently working on a rendering of the *Dao De Ching*. He and his wife, Anne Anderson, live in Santa Barbara, California. He has 4 children and 9 grandchildren.

Made in the USA
Monee, IL
20 January 2022

89390148R00194